Building Knowledge Systems

Developing and Managing
Rule-Based Applications

Building Knowledge Systems

Developing and Managing Rule-Based Applications

Michael A. Carrico
John E. Girard
Jennifer P. Jones

Intertext Publications
McGraw-Hill Book Company

New York St. Louis San Francisco Auckland Bogotá
Hamburg London Madrid Mexico Milan Montreal
New Delhi Panama Paris São Paulo
Singapore Sidney Tokyo Toronto

To
Julie Carrico
Jan Girard
and Michael Jones

Developmental Editor: Carol Lehn

Library of Congress Catalog Card Number 88-83064

10 9 8 7 6 5 4 3 2 1

ISBN 0-07-023437-X

Intertext Publications/Multiscience Press, Inc.
One Lincoln Plaza
New York, NY 10023

McGraw-Hill Book Company
1221 Avenue of the Americas
New York, NY 10020

Composed in Ventura Publisher by Context, Inc.

Contents

Preface

The management information system (MIS) community is faced with many challenges and opportunities posed by rapidly changing computer technology. Although relatively new to most professionals, artificial intelligence (AI) has taken root as a decision support technology because it offers a productive opportunity to automate some types of reasoning. All information professionals and those who aspire to work in the computer industry must educate themselves and capitalize on AI technology in order to remain competitive.

AI is providing profitable and strategic solutions in many application areas. One field in particular, knowledge systems, offers great advantage for commercial use and is easily integrated into conventional business data processing environments. Knowledge systems tackle the traditionally elusive problem of decision support by, for example, automating some of the thinking that drives your business, not just the paperwork.

This book arose from the frustrating realization that AI tools, literature, and courses tend to be theoretical and miss the concerns of the business community. Many years of publicity and effort have resulted in only a few production applications which can lay claim to being profitable knowledge-based systems. This book explains knowledge systems in detail and provides practical examples and instruction for optimizing system development and gaining positive results from the technology. Emphasis is placed on rule-based knowledge systems because they best complement existing architectures. Written from the perspective of data processing professionals, *Building Knowledge Systems* is a radical departure from the pack. This book shows you how to build knowledge systems by showing you how knowledge systems work.

WHO THIS BOOK IS FOR

This is the first practical book on rule-based knowledge systems written by data processing professionals for data processing professionals and students. If you are a manager, it is essential that you have some background in the facts of the artificial intelligence business in order to invest wisely in this technology. If you are a systems professional, you will gain an understanding of what is *new* and what is *hype* about knowledge systems technology, and you will learn that you are certainly capable of working with the technology. Students will get a candid look at the way MIS professionals assess the *business value* of knowledge systems.

This book is for the intermediate-level computer science professional who is at the introductory level in artifical intelligence. It can be read cover to cover or used as a reference book. The book assumes a familiarity with computer science terminology in providing the definitions and introductory material needed to understand the more complex AI material. Hands-on experience is not necessary, but comfort with common AI concepts and vocabulary would be a useful background to have.

WHAT YOU NEED TO KNOW

This book concentrates on the development of knowledge systems. Therefore, introductory or overview material is kept to a minimum by recommending sources where the information can be found. You are, nevertheless, encouraged to be familiar with certain topics in order to obtain the maximum value from this book. As a computer science-related book, many of the explanations are related to programming, software and hardware. It is important that you be familiar with these areas. There will also be discussions using relational database terminology. Book stores and libraries carry a wide variety of introductory material and computer terminology dictionaries.

You should be familiar with the fundamentals of structured design methodology in order to understand the development approach we recommend. Structured design methodologies are proven successful tools for systems development. The book supports this premise and expands on some structured design concepts. There are a variety of different methodologies in use — you only need to be familiar with one. A structured design approach supports well-written code and documentation, making optimal use of quality assurance features.

Experience with rule-based shells is optional. The examples and guidelines in the book make it possible to follow step by step. However, some previous experience with expert system building shells is beneficial. Many vendors have demonstration disks available for their products. You are encouraged to make use of them and of trade publications and the bibliography to assist in getting some additional demos to experiment with. Periodicals are a valuable source of information. There is a listing in Appendix B.

WHAT IS INCLUDED

This book treats the business of building knowledge systems as a professional software engineering activity and integrates the best of professional techniques with the special requirements of knowledge systems. We focus on the use of shells; tools that deliver knowledge system performance with a minimum of exotic coding. The mystique of knowledge systems project management and programming is gently demystified, and its bottom line values for business uses are explained in detail. The techniques of artificial intelligence are explained in common industry terms with frequent reference to professional project management and software engineering techniques.

Each chapter begins with some introductory material that lays the groundwork for the concepts covered in the chapter. A summary at the end of each chapter provides highlights of the information that was discussed. There is a strong emphasis on examples throughout the book, so that the reader can see how various techniques work. The examples are general enough to allow the reader to code them in virtually any, commercially available, rule-based expert system shell.

Part A provides some basic definitions and concepts. It outlines why rule-based shells are recommended and presents some myths and facts about knowledge systems. Finally, the examples used throughout the book are presented and how they are used explained.

Part B presents design and development techniques in a detailed usable format. It covers the necessary information for developing a knowledge system including knowledge acquisition, representation and coding techniques, tips for selecting hardware and software, and some pointers about human factors that are important if you decide to develop your own system.

Part C provides extensive advice on the key issues of knowledge systems project management. It defines the project life cycle and details strategies for identifying potential applications, feasibility studies, administration and staffing of projects, quality assurance, and maintenance of the system.

ACKNOWLEDGMENTS

The authors wish to thank their families for their patience and assistance, without which this book would not have been possible.

Thanks also go to Jack Repcheck for enthusiastic support and optimism when the going was rough.

Introduction and Concepts

1

Artificial Intelligence

The field of *artificial intelligence* (AI) has blossomed over the last decade from a purely academic pursuit to a practical technology. The academic definition of AI states that it is the subfield of computer science that focuses on the computer's ability to manipulate nonnumerical symbols and infer new facts from sets of known facts. A more practical definition is "Artificial Intelligence is the study of ideas that enable computers to be intelligent."[1] The goal of these ideas is to utilize hardware, software, and theories to make computers more useful. In other words, AI can be considered a group of problem-solving techniques or tools that emulate human thought to help in increasing knowledge, processing productivity, or making decisions. The term artificial intelligence covers a broad range of areas (see Figure 1-1).

Cognitive science is the field of study that seeks to understand and mimic human mental processes. This is the science that fuels the fields of AI. For more information, see Joseph Weizenbaum's Computer Power and Human Reasoning.[2]

---

1 Winston, Patrick Henry, *Artificial Intelligence*, 2nd ed. Addison-Wesley Publishing Co., 1984.

2 Weizenbaum, Joseph, *Computer Power and Human Reasoning*. W. H. Freeman and Co., 1976.

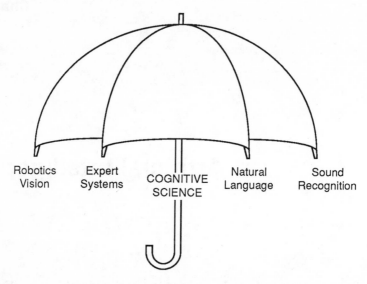

Robotics Vision   Expert Systems   COGNITIVE SCIENCE   Natural Language   Sound Recognition

Figure 1-1 Fields included under the umbrella term "artificial intelligence."

Robotics is the study of machines that perform mechanical manipulation and how to make them function with some "intelligence" and autonomy. This almost always involves some vision technology. Most of the existing systems are still reasonably unsophisticated; they are repetitive instead of intelligent. This is due to the limited capability of the software, hardware, and sensors. Although most applications are military, robotics is proving to be very valuable to the manufacturing industry. There are robotic automobile painters and assembly line workers.

Vision systems are those that successfully interpret a two- and three-dimensional pictures from a two-dimensional image obtained through manmade sensors. This involves processing the image, classifying it and then interpreting the scene.

Natural language understanding is the ability to communicate with a computer by inputting conventional language text, such as English, Russian, etc., instead of a highly structured language such as SQL. Natural language understanding enables an unsophisticated user to issue commands to a system, thus broadening the usability of powerful computer technology. There are currently a few applications for narrowly defined problems (this is a subset of truly natural language).

Sound recognition is the field in which processing and reasoning about acoustic sensors such as alarms, spoken words, or automobile engines takes place. Readable language is an output of sound recognition. Sound recognition systems take an audible sound and make it readable. Note that a readable language still has to be interpreted by a machine or person. In terms of AI goals, a voice print would be used for sound recognition to output the equivalent of natural language.

Knowledge systems are software systems that have structured knowledge about a field of expertise. They are able to solve some problems within their domain by using knowledge derived from experts in the field. Knowledge systems use symbols to represent concepts, which are manipulated using different techniques. This approach emphasizes data interpretation. They consist of a collection of utilities and programs for the development environment and the delivery environment. This is illustrated in Figure 1-2. You may want to make special note of the components in the system. All of them will be referred to later in the book.

Current AI technology supports the recognition of simple objects with machine vision and has a limited understanding of speech and natural language. Robots can perform complex tasks that have been programmed by experiential learning. Artificial intelligence tools have the ability to solve problems and make judgments based on human knowledge that has been encoded in the tools and can type queries to a user in limited language.

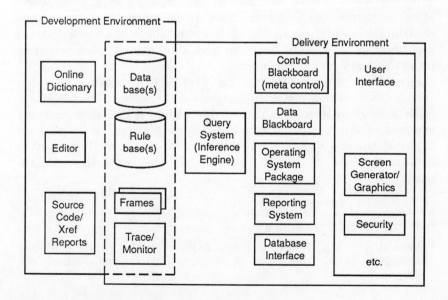

Figure 1-2 Anatomy of a knowledge-based system.

ARTIFICIAL INTELLIGENCE AND COMPUTER SCIENCE

"Software engineering and Artificial Intelligence are either going to have to join hands or software engineering people are going to have to reinvent Artificial Intelligence."[3]

The converse of this quote is also true. For some reason artificial intelligence has been defined with few connections to conventional programming. This is probably because AI's goal is to emulate people, and the idea of having computers "think" was uncomfortable to many. The controversy stemmed from the fact that AI went off in its own direction and ignored the business side of computer science.

The only difference between some of the other fields of computer science and AI is the way in which they process data. Traditional computing activities focused on **manipulating** data, primarily in the form of "number crunching" machines. In contrast, AI systems concentrate on **interpreting** the data and their symbolic relationships as a means for emulating human thought. This fascination with the thinking process meant incorporating many of the studies and theories of cognitive science along with the computer sciences. The shift in computer science from manipulation of data to interpretation is summarized in a time line beginning with the 1940s (Figure 1-3).

Each new generation of tool pushes at the boundaries of the last. Some applications have been pushing the capabilities of third-generation languages like Cobol and Fortran for years. For applications requiring data interpretation and reasoning there is a point where it just becomes too difficult to build and maintain complex programs using third-generation languages.

Fourth-generation tools were the first step in providing a labor saving device which made third-generation systems easier to build. Fifth-generation tools capitalize on the utility of the "shell" concept explored in the fourth-generation tools and are specifically good for building systems that are difficult in third- and fourth-generation tools. Figure 1-4 depicts the evolution of the generations of languages.

---

3   Simon, Herbert A., *Whether Software Engineering Needs to Be Artificially Intelligent.* IEEE Transactions of Software Engineering, v. SE-12, n.7, July 1986.

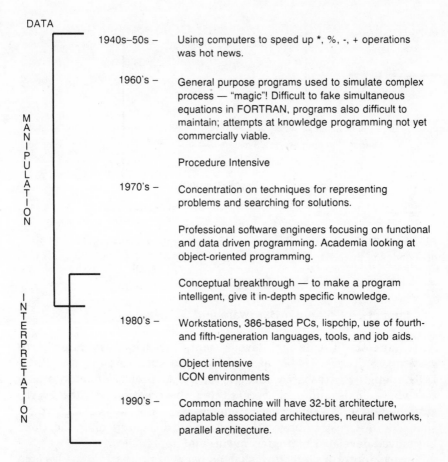

DATA

1940s–50s –	Using computers to speed up *, %, -, + operations was hot news.
1960's –	General purpose programs used to simulate complex process — "magic"! Difficult to fake simultaneous equations in FORTRAN, programs also difficult to maintain; attempts at knowledge programming not yet commercially viable. Procedure Intensive
1970's –	Concentration on techniques for representing problems and searching for solutions. Professional software engineers focusing on functional and data driven programming. Academia looking at object-oriented programming. Conceptual breakthrough — to make a program intelligent, give it in-depth specific knowledge.
1980's –	Workstations, 386-based PCs, lispchip, use of fourth- and fifth-generation languages, tools, and job aids. Object intensive ICON environments
1990's –	Common machine will have 32-bit architecture, adaptable associated architectures, neural networks, parallel architecture.

MANIPULATION

INTERPRETATION

Figure 1-3 Shift in computer science from data manipulation to interpretation.

Research Versus Commercial Applications

Academia has been building AI applications on powerful work-stations with symbolic languages such as LISP to prove theories. This has led to several sample systems but few that are usable in the real world. Industry is now working on applying the theories to benefit corporate bottom lines by using existing hardware and conventional third-generation languages such as Cobol, "C," etc. This transfer of the technology has left the business world with many learning pains and questions about how to develop, maintain, and use artificial intelligence systems. This book answers the questions for one of the fields of AI: knowledge systems.

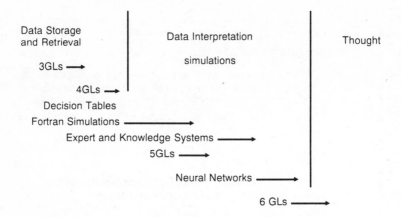

Figure 1-4 The evolution of languages: each generation pushes at the boundaries of the next.

AI's Impact on Computer Hardware and Software

AI is impacting the design, development, and use of computer hardware and software. Use of exotic languages such as LISP and PROLOG, along with research budgets, locked AI professionals into narrow views. This approach necessitated the creation of LISP workstations and saw a divergence from the software engineering profession. The "interesting projects" provided good theoretical applications but moved developers into unconventional approaches.

New computer architecture such as parallel processing has become important, but more clever software is needed to optimize computing power. Communication interfaces continue to be an issue because of the AI workstation integration bottleneck. Existing environments' operating systems are evolving to take on a more global view of the machine. Resources are being redefined within the operating system as procedural attributes. For example, multiuser systems have many message passing and activator capabilities.

KNOWLEDGE SYSTEMS

The mystique of AI has left many confused. Now the mystique is disappearing, causing a stampede of entrepreneurs, charlatans, medicine men, and legitimate resources. This book will help sort it all out by speaking professional common sense.

Applying knowledge systems technology is an important step in the automation of tasks that are difficult to automate with third- and fourth-generation languages. Among the many areas in which the knowledge systems field of AI can assist the MIS manager are training, online monitoring, planning, software engineering, diagnostics, leveraging of human resources, etc. Knowledge systems can improve productivity and quality in your computer-assisted operations by freeing human experts from strategic tasks where your human expert is the only expert, wants to retire/change jobs, is frustrated because the task has become routine has too much to do with too few resources, or is needed 24 hours a day, 7 days week.

The major advantages to using knowledge systems include:

1. They are always available, not affected by distraction, sickness, etc.
2. For many expert tasks, they will perform as well as or better than the human expert who contributed the knowledge.
3. A more flexible use of knowledge is possible when compared to a similar program built using conventional techniques.

The major disadvantage is that knowledge systems tend to be singleminded and lack common sense. The current set of tools perform best when they are limited to a narrow view of knowledge about a particular task. The following example shows how even a narrowly scoped knowledge area can require a significant amount of common sense.

Narrow knowledge area	Common sense we assume
Troubleshooting a faulty televison set	Knowing the difference between an antenna cable and a power cord, a brightness knob and a power switch.

A simpler example would be troubleshooting a television set with a particular problem — the screen is dead. The expert called in to investigate the problem assumes that the person who has identified the problem has turned the television on and has checked to make sure that it is plugged into a working electrical outlet. You might laugh at these examples of common sense. Yet, time and again, we all make assumptions about everything we do and sometimes it gets us into big trouble. Perhaps the greatest challenge in designing a knowledge system is defining the "givens" that must be assumed.

USING RULE-BASED SHELLS

Throughout this book and in practice we recommend using rule-based shells for your knowledge systems development. They are a valuable productivity tool and increase the ease of development and maintainability of systems. Shells are a form of reusable code. They provide preconstructed, essential utilities such as user interfaces, report generators, and the part of the program that scans, selects and applies rules and data. This allows the developer to concentrate on the programming of the knowledge. Why start from scratch when 80% of your application may already be built? Rule-based shells are equivalent to database generators and other similar tools, which have become extremely popular in software engineering organizations. The shell handles the data dictionary, operating stack, concurrent calculations, I/O functions, audit and recovery functions, etc. automatically and in the background. All you really supply to the system are carefully constructed statements of knowledge about a subject area.

Advantages and Disadvantages

The key benefits of using shells include improved productivity, ease of developing and maintaining a system, ease of portability between shells and environments, and the vendor support and training that is available. The use of a shell can greatly decrease the cost and development time of your project. It may take several years to become productive in any low level language, such as LISP. The low level languages involve coding primitive routines for performing functions which already exist in a shell. Shells provide a structure for developing systems which encourages consistent use of concepts and terminology. This is especially valuable when more than one person is involved in developing the system, as with a development team. It also makes the system easier to maintain because it is modular. *Note*: There are no standards yet between tools.

We recommend starting with rule-based shells instead of a highly object-oriented language such as SMALLTALK for several reasons. The if-then cause and effect nature of rules is more intuitive for people with traditional software engineering backgrounds. This makes it easier to learn and trainees can become productive in a few months. Shells exist now in many environments, and are written in common languages, such as "C." The performance of "C"-based tools is good enough for real-time use and need not require a special delivery environment or extraordinary programming skills. This makes portability between shells more straightforward. Shells have become sophisticated enough that significant and profitable AI problems can be solved using rule-based techniques.

If you have the resources to build your own shell there are several factors that you should consider. Take a look at your staff's ability to develop a shell and make sure that you have the time to do it properly. Remember that the time and cost to develop your own shell may not be justified if a tool already exists that will accomplish the same functions.

If you are considering selecting a shell from the many existing shells, there are other factors that must be considered. Match the tool to the application needs. This includes ensuring that the shell provides all of the functionality that will be required, and that it provides a representation scheme(s) that is appropriate for the application. The shell you select should have an adequate developer interface and utilities. Your staff's ability to use an existing shell will be directly affected by the type of interface it provides. Do not assume that, because the "demos" look great, that the tool will be easy to use. Technically, the shell should fit the needs of the development and delivery environments and should integrate well with the environments. Consider the portability of the shell and the type of maintenance that will be required to support it. Look closely at the inferencing techniques that are used, they will affect the efficiency of the shell. Finally, weigh the user interface provided and make sure that user control of the system is appropriate for the sophistication level of the user.

There are disadvantages to using a shell instead of one of the AI languages. You lose some flexibility using a shell and possibly increase execution time due to the overhead of a higher level language. If your application is truly unique and not even a small part of its requirements can be developed using a shell, then a low-level language may be your only alternative. For example, use of LISP, an object-oriented language, or a simulation language might be more desirable when developing simulations. There are several shells that have been designed to perform simulations, but so far, the ones worth mentioning are very expensive ($36,000+) and many require a LISP workstation.

MYTHS AND FACTS ABOUT DEVELOPING AND WORKING WITH KNOWLEDGE SYSTEMS

Myths (really misunderstandings about knowledge systems) continue to circulate throughout the computing community, even as the practice of knowledge systems construction matures toward a system engineering discipline. The facts presented here help dispel some of the more common myths. These myths and facts are not necessarily mutually exclusive. However, the explanations should serve to give you a better understanding of common misconceptions about working with knowledge systems.

MYTH — Knowledge systems or expert systems are "artificial intelligence"

FACT — Knowledge systems will not be called "artificial intelligence" for very long. Instead, they will be considered conventional programs which use new representation techniques.

Most new, unknown, and mysterious things maintain an aura of intelligence until they are understood. When the first computers were discovered to be very fast numeric calculators, people thought they were intelligent. For many years, when an error was discovered on a computer-generated document, it was always "the computer's fault." The introduction of the personal computer changed the public's perception of where to focus when finding fault, from the computer to the source of the programming and information used by the computer.

The pursuit of artificial intelligence follows two separate and distinct paths: one to make the computer appear to act intelligently, the other to create computers that are capable of teaching themselves. So far, whenever a program has been described in enough detail to explain its results, the aura of self-intelligence, teaching, or awareness has disappeared.

Knowledge systems are built from design and construction techniques that are very similar to conventional program engineering techniques. They can be developed only when sufficient information has been gathered from experts to make the system appear to know as much as the expert. Thus, the association of knowledge or expert systems with the term artificial intelligence will seem misleading and inappropriate.

MYTH — Conventional programming languages provide the flexibility necessary to be used in the development of knowledge systems.

FACT — Knowledge system shells are far superior for this purpose. While it is true that it is possible to code knowledge systems in conventional languages, it is much more difficult, and the resulting code is not easily maintainable. The knowledge relationships tend to get "lost" in the representation because of the extensive coding required. Knowledge system shells represent the knowledge relationships in an overt fashion which is easier to comprehend and maintain. Their use in day-to-day business operations can improve development productivity dramatically.

MYTH — The only problems worth doing require very large knowledge systems. "Toy" systems are not worthwhile.

FACT — The *only* criteria for this **business decision** should be whether or not the system (whatever its size) makes business sense and is cost-effective.

Some (not all) knowledge systems can be developed very quickly and economically. A "toy" system may be small in terms of development effort and the scope of its functionality but could still have a significant effect on business operations and costs. The size of the system is irrelevant in determining whether or not it's worth tackling the problem.

MYTH — All PC systems are "toy" systems.

FACT — When programmed properly, PC-based tools can create systems which are very large.

Reference to PC systems as "toy" systems is usually made with regard to the size and speed of the delivered system. A PC is capable of delivering systems which have many thousands of rules.

MYTH — LISP or PROLOG are necessary for the delivery of complex knowledge systems.

FACT — Business systems are generally built using a "shell" which has been written for the express purpose of coding knowledge. Both languages are well suited to representing new ideas and can be used in a raw development environment. You, however, would probably not write a new database language or fourth-generation tool from scratch, and in the same fashion, you need not write a new knowledge system shell if you can find a ready made tool on the market that meets your needs. Business topics tend to be more straightforward than research topics and do not require the extreme flexibility of the low-level AI languages. Therefore, why code at the primitive level when a shell will achieve the same result more easily and productively?

MYTH — Domain experts (subject matter experts) can code and maintain knowledge systems.

FACT — Small systems can be built by almost anyone who knows how to use knowledge systems tools. However, knowledge systems programming is just as much a programming discipline as any other type of systems programming. Issues to be addressed during the development of larger systems **must** include data modeling, quality assurance, quality control, testing, modular design, maintenance, etc.

In addition to a deep rooted understanding of computer science, the expert must have the time to develop and maintain the system. It is rare, indeed, to find an expert in a specialized field with both the time to spend programming and a computer science background. The easy way to determine if you want your domain expert to program a knowledge system is to ask yourself whether you would have that same person program a similarly sized program in a conventional language.

EXAMPLES IN THIS BOOK

In order to demonstrate *how to build* knowledge systems, the authors chose several examples of "domains," or subject areas. The major examples include automobile repair, plant identification, phone service, loan applications, and employee evaluations. Other minor examples that appear from time to time are not mentioned here. Use of several domains was found necessary because no one domain is appropriate to use for all sections of the book. By analogy, a chair could not be used as an example for all techniques in a comprehensive book on carpentry.

The auto repair example is used because most readers will have some knowledge, as a user, maintainer or both, of automobiles. Books about auto repair present knowledge in a similar, straightforward, methodical fashion with a standardized vocabulary, which makes it easier to convert them into knowledge systems. Auto repair appears frequently in the practical discussions in Part II of this book. For example, auto repair is used in the explanations of classification and diagnostic paradigms, to show backward chaining, to show how knowledge may be extracted from books, and as the feature example of coding complex knowledge systems. A complete source listing for the example is presented in Appendix A.

The identification of fruits is used to show decision table and decision tree knowledge structures, backward chaining, and simple examples for generating rules.

The Uneeda Phone Company is used to show how to use conflict identification (collisions) to configure a phone service order.

The EZ2 Geta Loan Company is used as an example of a domain that might be structured by an induction rule tool.

The employee evaluation is used to show an example of an application which could be either a knowledge system or a spreadsheet, and in a discussion about frames.

SUMMARY

Artificial intelligence is the discipline of creating machines that mimic human behavior or intelligence; machines that can sense and think. It is an umbrella term for a variety of fields of study that include robotics, cognitive science, vision systems, natural language understanding, sound recognition, and knowledge systems.

Knowledge systems capture the expertise and reasoning abilities of experts in a field or domain. They reproduce the problem-solving abilities of the experts based on the knowledge that has been coded into the system. Knowledge systems consist of a series of programs and utilities that handle both the development and delivery environments.

Rule-based shells are recommended for the development of knowledge systems because they provide the essential utilities that free the knowledge coder from having to develop user interfaces, mechanics for implementing the knowledge collected, reports, etc. Instead, the programmer can concentrate on gathering information from the experts involved in the system and coding it for use within the shell. Shells provide improved productivity, ease of developing and maintaining a system, and they help to reduce the costs of development.

How Do Rule Based Knowledge Systems "Think"?

Knowledge systems are systems that use expert knowledge in a subject area *and* information about objects and relationships to reason about a situation. The term "knowledge system" is used throughout the book. This may be confusing to some because of the widespread use of the term "expert system." Expert systems are knowledge systems which have limited expertise in a given domain or subject area. For example, an expert system might be able to diagnose a carburetor problem based on symptoms, whereas a knowledge system would understand maintenance and repair of the car as a whole, including detailed knowledge of how the component parts interrelate. Expert systems are a subset of knowledge systems. This book will take the broad view and address knowledge systems, which includes expert systems.

An interesting point relating to the term "expert" system is that its name presupposes how the system will perform. Whether an expert system is behaving expertly or not depends on the view of the user. This ambiguity has led to varying ideas of what expert systems are able to do, the most popular being that "expert" implies a narrow focus and limited breadth of scope and flexibility.[1] In any case, this has become a popular term to describe systems that utilize knowledge of a particular area for problem solving. Can you imagine "novice" systems being useful?

In order to compare the simple actions of a rule-based system to the human reasoning process, we offer a humorous analogy to animal behavior. Rule-based systems "reason" at a simple level with much less sophistication than the average human. They resemble a *simple creature with good hunting instincts*. The creature's mission in life is to grab a piece of food, a *goal or goals*, which thereby gives its existence meaning (A goal is the end result desired). To get to the food, it employs patterns of **stimulus and response**, i.e., previously built-in experiences (*rules*) and all available senses and mobility (*sensor interfaces* to the outside world). The creature is incubated by programming in the goal, rules, and interfaces. "Life" is then breathed into the husk by invoking the **inference engine**. This is the part of the knowledge program that does the reasoning (scans, selects, and applies rules and data that apply to the particular goal).

Since it is the *inference engine* rather than any **procedures you coded** that animates the creature, its behavior is a direct manifestation of the knowledge and experience you have provided to your creature in the rules. Your creature will use the rules you provide in every way it can (it may surprise you) in the effort to reach the goal. Inference engines employ two fundamental strategies while manipulating information to locate a path to a goal: backward chaining and forward chaining. These strategies can be further modified by the concepts of "depth-first" or "breadth-first" search preferences.

BACKWARD CHAINING: START WITH A GOAL, FIND THE FACTS TO SUPPORT IT

Backward chaining is the classic pursuit of goals and objectives by relying on experience (rules). Backward chaining is the most common inferencing method found in rule-based tools. An inference engine backchains by determining the highest priority goal from your

---

1 Bobrow, Daniel G., Sanjay Mittal, and Mark J. Stefik, *Expert Systems: Perils and Promise*. Communications of the ACM, v.29, n.9, September 1986.

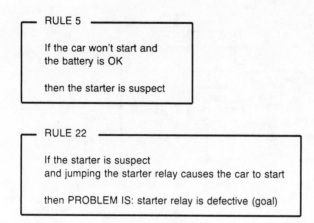

RULE 5

If the car won't start and
the battery is OK

then the starter is suspect

RULE 22

If the starter is suspect
and jumping the starter relay causes the car to start

then PROBLEM IS: starter relay is defective (goal)

Figure 2-1 Rules that lead to a goal.

specifications, then asking questions (collecting facts) about the rules in order to find a rule or rules that lead to the goal.

As shown in Figure 2-1, the inference engine would see that rule 22 can supply the goal (determining the problem), but in order to reason about rule 22, it needs to know if the starter is suspect. **Note that the order of the rules is unimportant in a knowledge system. The inference engine determines when and where to look.** The inference engine searches all other rules in the system and finds that rule 5 can reason that the starter is suspect. Rule 5 becomes part of the chain, so to speak, that will be used to prove the goal. Figure 2.2 is a picture of the "image" of the situation that the inference engine would assemble in its "mind": "Starter relays are a common cause of problems. I was told to always check there first. Let's see now . . . what are the things I need to check?"

If the starter really is at fault, then a "trace" of the system strategy would reveal a series of steps that resemble the following:

1. Searching for goal to pursue
2. Found goal in rule 22: "starter relay is defective"
3. Starter suspect — not known yet
4. Searching for answer to **starter suspect**
5. Found **starter suspect** as potential conclusion to rule 5
6. Invoking rule 5
7. Battery test — not known yet
8. No source for **battery test** — asking user
9. User says battery is OK
10. Car starts — not known yet

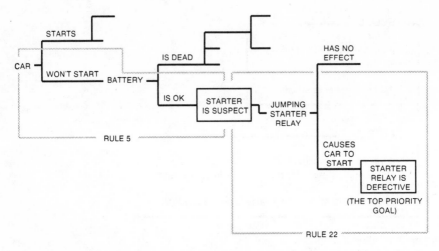

Figure 2-2 Logic the inference engine would go through in processing rules 5 and 22.

11. No source for car starts — asking user
12. User says car won't start
13. Rule 5 is true: **starter is suspect**
14. Returning to rule 22
15. No source for **jumping starter relay test** — asking user
16. User says jumping relay causes car to start
17. Rule 22 found to be true: Goal completed: **starter relay is defective**

You will notice from the trace that the system worked backwards to the most remote question that had to be considered to "chain together" the facts after finding a candidate **goal**. If the facts had failed to support rule 5, the inference engine would seek other rules and information in the knowledge base to obtain a judgment that the starter either was or was not suspect. If no other internal source is available, the inference engine will step up and ask the user directly.

So is that all there is to it? No! You still need to read the rest of the book. Backward chain systems are not always concerned with diagnostics; the next part of the book contains examples of many kinds of reasoning. Backward chaining systems are not limited to conversational interviews, either. Most of the questions you saw above in rules 5 and 22 could have been answered by having the computer call automated test instruments.

Two of the early and famous backward chaining systems you should know about are the medical diagnostic systems, PUFF and

MYCIN. *Expert Systems: AI in Business* by Harmon and King contains a good review of these and other backward chaining systems.[2]

FORWARD CHAINING: START BY COLLECTING FACTS, SEE IF ANY GOALS APPLY ALONG THE WAY

True forward chaining is less widely available in commercial rule-based tools than backward chaining. Many tools that claim to offer forward chaining simply scan the rule base from front to back. In practice, we have found that **true** forward chaining really is not necessary, because the effect can be emulated by using combinations of paradigms supported by backward chaining tools.

Forward chaining systems do not operate from the concept that the THEN portions of rules contain goals to be achieved. Let's take a look at OPS-5, a well-known forward chaining system, as an example. The OPS-5 inference engine forward chains by taking all available data in one initial unit and placing it in working storage. Next, OPS-5 steps forward through the rule base looking for rules that might be satisfied by the information in working storage. A list is made of rules that are potentially satisfied and, based on priority, which of the candidate rules should be invoked is determined. Conclusions from the candidate rules that are allowed to pass are added to the knowledge in working storage. The inference engine then cycles through the rules again to see if any new candidate rules appear as a result of the additional information. The cycle continues until the inference engine determines that additional scanning will not improve the state of the system's knowledge.

The most famous forward chaining application is XCON (also known as R.1). XCON takes unedited sales orders for DEC equipment worldwide and produces correctly configured and discounted orders. See Harmon and King[5] for discussions of OPS-5 and XCON.

DEPTH AND BREADTH SEARCH STRATEGIES

Depth and breadth search strategies are additional aspects of the behavior of the inference engine. They significantly affect the man-

---

2 Harmon, Paul, and David King, *Expert Systems: AI in Business*. Wiley, 1985.

ner by which an inference engine will pursue goals and manage the information it gathers. The extent to which these behaviors are manifested in a given application depends to a large extent on how the knowledge engineer represents knowledge in the rules.

Depth-First Search

Depth-first search is the default behavior of most backward chaining inference engines. Depth first refers to the fact that the inference engine is preoccupied with finding a path from opening questions down to a goal. In a depth-first situation, the inference engine gathers as little information as is necessary to find a path to a goal. The example above, where rules 5 and 22 form a chain to reach the conclusion that the starter relay is defective, is a typical example. If the rules provided by the knowledge engineer offer a series of simplistic paths to the goal, depth first is the behavior that will be evidenced by the inference engine.

Breadth-First Search

Breadth-first search is a behavior in which a knowledge system considers all information and alternatives at a given level of abstraction before selecting a "deeper" path toward a goal. In a breadth-first situation, the inference engine gathers considerable information in intermediate steps. This can be useful in a design activity where one might have to backtrack and reassess a former position. If the rules provided by the knowledge engineer contain a lot of intermediate hypotheses which must be examined in order to find secondary paths to the goal, then breadth first is the behavior that will be evidenced by the inference engine. The fruit identification decision tree example in Chapter 6 provides a good illustration. In that example, the inference engine must first determine an intermediate concept — whether or not a fruit is citrus — before it can complete the investigation and determine a type of fruit.

Depth Versus Breadth

An example of breadth-first versus depth-first search can be made by comparing the mythical strategies of two biologists trying to classify a new life form found on a trip to Mars:

The depth-first biologist would compare the life form to known life forms and try to establish a pattern match at the detail level. He would then work back up the known taxonomy of life forms and ultimately classify the new life form as animal, plant, or fungus.

The breadth-first biologist would first attempt to determine by gross characteristics whether the new life form was animal, plant, or fungus. If it were animal, he would next determine if it has an exoskeleton or an endoskeleton in order to group the new life form with vertebrates or invertebrates. He would continue to navigate his way down through the species until he reached a point where he could say with confidence, "This life form is like."

CAN RULE-BASED SYSTEMS LEARN?

Can a rule-based system grow and learn on its own? The answer is **yes, but** you will probably want to keep a human in the circuit most of the time. Everyone knows how children, in the absence of broad experience and common sense, come to some outrageous conclusions, such as "The pineapple is the chief product of the pine tree."

The child who said this has not gained the experience that humans often name objects by metaphors or analogies that have nothing to do with reality. However, he did have the common sense to realize that objects are often named by their inheritance (a *pine* apple must be related to a *pine tree*).

How about an example closer to MIS? Let's consider MMMS, a *Mythical Mainframe Monitoring System,* as an example. MMMS monitors mainframes, interprets their condition, and takes action. MMMS takes two kinds of actions: 1) It sends reports to the operators, and 2) it takes some direct actions by sending commands to the mainframe. If MMMS is capable of learning, it might notice someday that an inexperienced operator reset the mainframe (in desperation) because a routine problem could not be identified. MMMS would "learn" that resetting the *entire* system caused the problem to go away. It would create new rules to describe this line of reasoning. When MMMS sees this routine problem again, probably without warning and perhaps at prime time, it would bring the entire system to a halt. The solution worked, but MMMS did not have the common sense or experience to realize that another solution might have been preferable under the circumstances.

The bottom line is you can't expect your knowledge systems to exercise common sense or sophistication if you empower them to learn new rules independently. Set limits on the initiative you allow your system and keep an eye on it from time to time, as you would a child.

SUMMARY

Knowledge is coded into a rule-based system by transforming the expert's knowledge into a series of if-then rules. Rule based systems "think" by tracing a path through the rules to reach the goal of the system. Knowledge systems employ an inference engine that scans, selects, and applies the rules and data. The inference engine employs two basic strategies in locating its path through the rules to the goal: backward chaining and forward chaining.

Backward chaining starts with a goal and then tries to find the facts to support it. It determines the highest priority goal from the user's specifications, then uses the rules to generate questions to gather additional information. Based on responses to the questions, the inference engine traces and retraces paths backwards from the goal until all of the if conditions of the rule that declares the goal have been fulfilled.

Forward chaining works from the opposite direction. It begins by gathering as much information as it can, then steps through the rule base looking for rules that may be satisfied by the information already gathered. Information from rules that are fully satisfied is added to the knowledge, and the inference engine cycles through again. When it determines that additional scanning will not improve the state of the system's knowledge, it stops.

The performance of the inference engine is also influenced by the search strategy that is employed to scan the rule base. The search can be carried out depth first or breadth first.

You might imagine that all of the registers, flags, and recursive programming code it's going to take to enable a computer to parse your knowledge base and explore multiple hypotheses in *your* knowledge expressions is going to drive you and your computer insane. But remember, the purpose of a shell is to provide all of the procedural functions built in. You only have to supply the knowledge base and the goals, the tool determines how to use the knowledge to achieve the goal. That is why we recommend that you use a shell.

B

Road Maps

The road maps will be your master guide for Chapters 3-7. The purpose of the road map is to remind you of the sequential procedure to follow when building your knowledge systems. In using the road map, it is assumed that you have already determined that the project is feasible and worthwhile. You may wish to refer to the Chapters 10 and 11 on identifying potential applications, feasibility, and sizing. The map is the same whether you are delivering a prototype, a production system, or a section of a larger system.

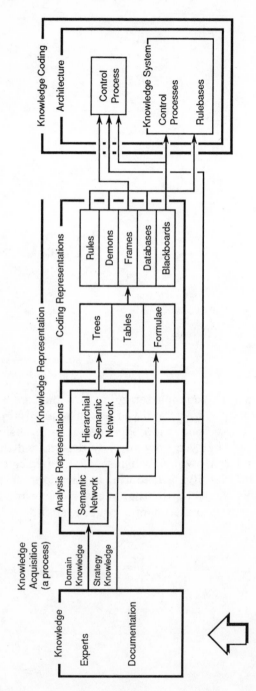

3

Paradigms

A[1]**paradigm** (pattern or model[2]) is a representation for the internal model that humans use to *think* about something. Poorly defined in most books, it is essentially the style of the train of thought that an expert uses to reason about a problem. It is a simple concept that has become overly complex in the AI community. It is important for you to be aware of some typical paradigms and to recognize the paradigm used by your expert. Knowing the expert's paradigm helps you to focus your thoughts during interviews and will make it easier to structure the expert's knowledge.

Many authors in this field talk about paradigms in an informal, after-the-fact manner. They assume that the reader already knows all the paradigms and agrees with the author's unspoken definitions. In contrast, our chapter on paradigms should make the essential mechanics of "thinking" clear without venturing into classical cognitive psychology. Many people tend to use the term freely without defining it. Due to the lack of definition and experimental/academic influence, a large number of paradigm types have been suggested which often

---

1 A Road Map will appear at the beginning of each chapter in Part B to pinpont your position on the Detailed Road Map, already given.

2 *Scribner–Bantam English Dictionary*, 4th printing. Bantam Books, Inc., 1980.

seem to confuse the issue. Examples of some of these paradigm types include:

• Classification
• Diagnosis
• Hypothesize and Test
• Collisions
• Design and Configuration
• Planning and Scheduling

This list is by no means complete, and there will no doubt be disagreement by some people as to whether it is correct. Don't worry about completeness and correctness, just use these descriptions as *guidelines* to help you identify how an expert thinks.

When interviewing experts and structuring knowledge, it is useful to think in terms of a paradigm. Knowing the expert's paradigm helps you to focus your thoughts during interviews and will make it easier to structure the expert's knowledge (the difference between directed research and nondirected research). It will also help you to draw associations in the expert's commentary and will help you to ask leading questions. Knowing the paradigms you use in structuring the expert's knowledge will help you to devise test cases and validate the system.

It takes experience to recognize a paradigm. Think about paradigms as you go about your business and you will start to see them. *Hint:* Watch how you explain someone else's actions by using analogy to describe the other person's patterns.

You will often see the term *domain paradigm* used. It implies that the realm of knowledge on a particular area, the domain, has a specific paradigm applicable to it. In the next sections, we will explore a variety of paradigms. It will be obvious to you that each one can be applied to an unlimited number of bodies of knowledge, though not all paradigms are appropriate in every domain. Each paradigm provides a different perspective of the knowledge under examination, mirroring the range of human approaches. Never assume that any two experts will use the same paradigm when working on the same domain.

CLASSIFICATION

The classification paradigm is the process of sifting out the correct or best alternative from among several choices. This is a one-to-many-to-one selection exercise; you start at a given position and select from several alternative paths to move forward. Classification is an easy paradigm to pursue because your goal is to identify a general pattern or trend, not to delve into details. Classification with certainty considerations becomes another paradigm, hypothesize and test, as discussed below.

Some examples of classification are:

1. Family relationship validation. Validation of family ties is important to many legal, social, and religious activities. A knowledge system which understands all the intricacies of family relationships can efficiently sort out a person's place in a family tree and completely explain its reasoning in the case of difficult to trace relationships. In case you think that family relationships is an easy subject, consider the recursive impact when an immediate family member marries the child of a stepparent. The best published example of why this is an "expert" subject is the song "I'm my own Grandpa," by Guy Lombardo.[3]

2. The auto repair demonstration system (Appendix A) contains a special front-end rule base (the SYMPTOMS rule base) which attempts to classify which general auto subsystems are at fault in a malfunctioning car.

In Figure 3-1 you can see that the SYMPTOMS rule base oversees the calling of the other rule bases. Think of it as the chief mechanic who looks the situation over and then calls in his "specialists." The engine expert has a little more clout than the other staff mechanics because he can also do some delegation.

DIAGNOSIS

The diagnosis paradigm is more challenging than the classification paradigm because your goal is to identify a detailed cause and effect pattern relationship in a sea of possibilities. This is a one-to-many-

---

3 Lombardo, Guy, "I'm My Own Grandpa", Enjoy Yourself. DECCA Records DL-8136, New York, 1953.

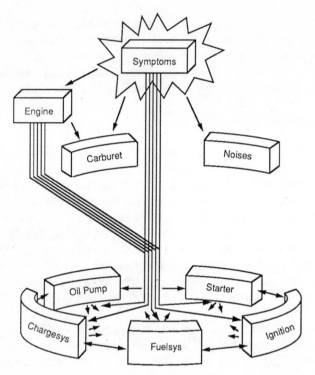

Figure 3-1 Representation of the Symptoms rule base of the auto repair system example.

to-one exercise. Because of the heavy emphasis on cause and effect, the diagnostic paradigm is easily represented as a decision tree and/or decision table.

Some examples of diagnosis are:

1. PUFF diagnoses respiratory illnesses by examining output from respiratory analyzers and asking questions via a terminal. PUFF is popular among doctors who have used it because it pursues the diagnosis task with an effective strategy and provides a service that saves the doctors time.

2. The auto repair system example (Figure 3-2) used frequently in this book contains several diagnostic rule bases (CARBURET, CHARGSYS, FUELSYS, OILPUMP, IGNITION, STARTER, NOISES) which may be invoked if the inference engine suspects that a particular auto subsystem is at fault. In a few

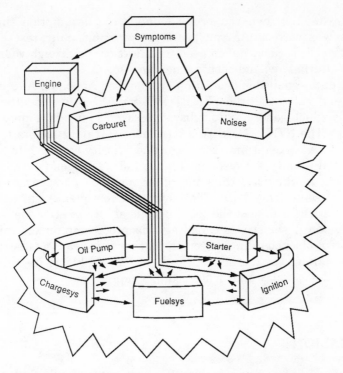

Figure 3-2 Representation of the Diagnostic rule bases of the auto repair system example.

circumstances, the SYMPTOMS rule base can diagnose a fault without transferring control to a subsystem rule base. Therefore, the SYMPTOMS rule base of the auto repair demonstration system contains hybrid paradigms.

HYPOTHESIZE AND TEST

Hypothesize and test is a paradigm to identify the best course or courses of action, then to evaluate whether or not the action produced a desired result. If the desired result is not achieved, the paradigm may continue to try new strategies. Operationally, hypothesize and test functions as a hybrid between classification and diagnosis, using certainty judgments as a navigation aid. In a hypothesize and test situation, you make the best possible judgment you can with the facts available, then you proceed under the assumption that your choice was correct. As you proceed, you continually test your assumption. If it turns out to need modification, you weigh your subsequent alternatives and choose a new course.

The auto repair demonstration system (see Appendix A) contains a front end rule base (the SYMPTOMS rule base) which attempts to classify which general auto subsystems are at fault in a malfunctioning car. The SYMPTOMS rule base uses certainty factors to set up an "agenda" to determine the order and priority by which to examine potentially faulty subsystems (Figure 3-3). An agenda manager (or queueing mechanism) calls the other modules as separate experts and requests their advice. The advice of subsequently called experts may alter the course of the session. This ability to alter the course of the session is sometimes called agenda processing, mixed initiative, or control blackboarding. If you think that it is really just structured programming, you're right. Control blackboarding is discussed further in the complex knowledge coding chapter.

COLLISIONS

"Collisions" is a constraint identification paradigm to find patterns you *do not want*. Collision analysis is essentially what *testers* are supposed to do, according to the ideas advanced by testing authorities such as Glen Myers [4] The collision approach is invaluable when the patterns you do *not* want to happen are fewer in number and better defined than the permutations of events that are acceptable. The kinds of business activities that typically fall into this category are testing, editing, and configuration. You might want to think of collisions as a vehicle to do **configuration or design by constraint**.

A typical example involving editing and configuration might be selecting phone service for your home. Phone companies now offer a dizzying array of services and options to their customers. As you might expect, the phone company wants you to sign up for as many options as possible, and has made every effort to allow you to pur-

---

4 Myers, Glen, *The Art of Software Testing*. John Wiley and Sons, Inc., 1979.

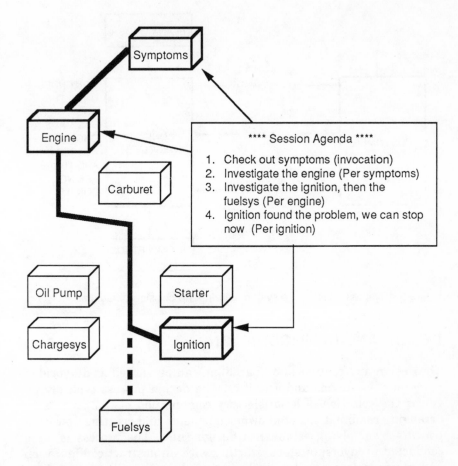

Figure 3-3 Based on weighted factors within each subsystem, an agenda is set up illustrating the hypothesize and test paradigm.

chase as many options as possible. There are only a few options which conflict with each other. A knowledge system can easily assist a customer by making finding a conflict in the order its goal. The knowledge system must offer every service option in order to seek a conflict. If a conflict is found, the knowledge system provides an explanation and allows the customer to choose again. When the order is complete and correct, the inference engine is unable to apply any rules. Figure 3-4 represents conceptually how collision paradigms work.

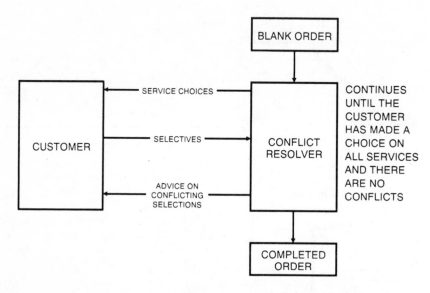

Figure 3-4 Representation of a system utilizing the collision paradigm.

DESIGN AND CONFIGURATION

The design and configuration paradigm can be viewed as a hybrid of numerous paradigms and activities. The design process typically involves the selection of a satisfactory combination of components by arranging combinations of known components and creating new components by applying established design rules. The process is often conducted in layers, or steps, starting with an abstract configuration and ending with a detailed configuration. A design system, therefore, must also contain knowledge about how to refine an intermediate design stepwise. Design may be accomplished by combining all of the paradigms already discussed. Another example of design and configuration is MICON.

MICON (*M*icroprocessor *CON*figurer) is an OPS-5 system implementation able to design custom single board computers using a variety of microprocessors. It accepts basic high level requirements from a user and applies a series of steps to transform and refine the abstract design into a detailed component specification.

MICON is composed of:

Logic knowledge — functional knowledge of the different subsystems to be designed and their interrelationships (e.g. I/O bus, processor, and memory). Also included is vendor/processor specific functional knowledge, including proprietary nomenclature and the necessary support logic.

Refinement knowledge — how to perfect structural relationships for a given design. This includes intelligence to actually construct microprocessor subsystems and to interconnect the subsystems.

Component knowledge — this includes facts associated with physical components such as signals, power, temperature range, and exception rules to match components to specific processor families and protocols.

Problem-solving knowledge — intelligence to direct and sequence the design strategy. This knowledge base prioritizes design tasks for a given design situation.

The process MICON goes through to perform its functions includes, in simplified terms, the *specification* of requirements for each subsystem. These are provided by the user and include, for example, the type of processor, clock speed, and memory size. Then *selection* takes place. Components are selected from a database, some by simple matching, others are chosen by applying selection rules. Finally *instantiation* occurs. Chosen components are inserted into design templates and support components (necessary but not specified by the user) are added. If a problem is noted in the developing design, the system backtracks to select an alternate component mix.

PLANNING AND SCHEDULING

Planning and scheduling paradigms generally involve a network of many other paradigms. The final result desired in these circumstances is not the "one" right plan or schedule, but one which accommodates all constraints stipulated by the user and is "good enough" to satisfy the user.

An example of a planning and scheduling application is the COCOMO project costing model developed by Barry Boehm[5]

---

5 Boehm, Barry W., *Software Engineering Economics*. Englewood Cliffs, J.J.:Prentice Hall, 1981.

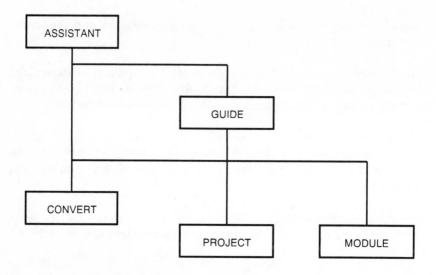

Figure 3-5 The COCOMO1 network of knowledge bases.

(*CO*nstructive *CO*st *MO*del) has proven very popular in the industry for estimating large computer software projects. The results that can be derived include cost, people required, and a proposed schedule.

Unfortunately, manual use of COCOMO represents a productivity bottleneck. Estimating 3 modules of a large system might take 1 to 1.5 days. In response to this bottleneck, Level 5 Research implemented a subset of COCOMO in their Insight 2+ rule-based system shell. The Level 5 implementation is known as COCOMO1. With COCOMO1, estimating the same 3 modules would take approximately 1.5 hours instead of 1.5 days.

COCOMO1 is constructed as a network of knowledge bases working together (Figure 3-5):

The diagram and following descriptions are based on information in *Project Costing With COCOMO1*.[6]

---

6   Williamson, Mickey, *Project Costing with COCOMO1*. AI Expert, 1986.

ASSISTANT — This knowledge base collects preliminary data about the project and gives the user choices about reports.

GUIDE — This knowledge base examines the project at a high level and determines which other knowledge bases should be visited and in what order. This knowledge base may be bypassed by an experienced user.

CONVERT — This knowledge base determines how to factor in existing lines of code that will be reused in the project. It selects (diagnoses) the appropriate algorithms to apply to the existing lines of code, calls the algorithms, then returns the result to GUIDE for use in selecting the next knowledge base to be called.

PROJECT — Based on a few additional interview questions and an average effort assumption, PROJECT generates reports including total cost, total person-months required, and time and person-months by project phase.

MODULE — MODULE's report expands on PROJECT's report by including cost driver information.

IMPORTANCE OF CLASSIFICATION AND DIAGNOSIS PARADIGMS

Rule-based knowledge systems are strongly biased toward classification and diagnosis by the cause-and-effect architecture of if-then-else rule expressions. Fortunately, this is good news, not bad. *All other paradigms* can be defined in terms of classification and diagnosis, and in terms of each other. The cause-and-effect bias of rule expressions facilitates validation, testing, and maintenance of rule-based knowledge systems.

Rule-based shells have been around a while, and many have been optimized for conventional machine architectures. Therefore, knowledge systems coded as classification/diagnosis in rule-based shells tend to perform better than the same system coded in other forms of representation. These assertions will become clearer as you gain experience in building your own systems. If you did not read the chapter about how rule-based knowledge systems think, please do so now.

SUMMARY

Paradigm is the term used to describe the representation for the internal model that humans use to think about something. While a variety of paradigm types have been suggested, this book concentrates on six of them: classification, diagnosis, hypothesize and test, collisions, design and configuration, and planning and scheduling. These can be used as guidelines to help you identify how an expert thinks.

Classification is the process of grouping objects into classes.

Diagnosis is the process of identifying the correct cause-and-effect pattern relationship in a wide range of possibilities.

Hypothesize and test is a problem-solving strategy that explores the set of possible solutions and selects the best.

Collisions paradigm makes use of the exclusion of patterns that are not wanted.

Design and configuration paradigms select a satisfactory combination of components by arranging combinations of known components and creating new components according to design rules.

Planning and scheduling entails finding a plan or schedule that accommodates all constraints specified and is good enough to satisfy the user.

"A new paradigm makes thoughts thinkable," said Charles Bachman.[7] Every well-executed project starts with a plan or strategy. In the case of a knowledge system project, a major subplan is to obtain the knowledge necessary for the system from human experts. Recognizing and exploiting paradigms (yours and the expert's) is an effective way of capturing and validating that essential knowledge. If you are an experienced analyst and/or programmer, you have been doing it all along, but you may not have paid this much attention to the concept of paradigms. To be an effective

---

7   *Future(s)*, Feedback '86 issue. Topeka, KS: Ken Orr & Associates, Inc.

Knowledge Engineer, you will use paradigms as a key to acquiring knowledge.

As you can see from the discussions above, knowledge problems that are worth automating are seldom solved with a single, simple line of reasoning. Do not be surprised if a typical project involves *all* paradigms. Don't be surprised, either, if you create an entirely new paradigm out of some novel combination of the ones you already know.

Look at the examples of the Uneeda Phone Company and of the Auto Repair Demonstration throughout the book. Could you have implemented these applications with a single line of reasoning? Would the application be useful to anyone if you simplified the lines of reasoning?

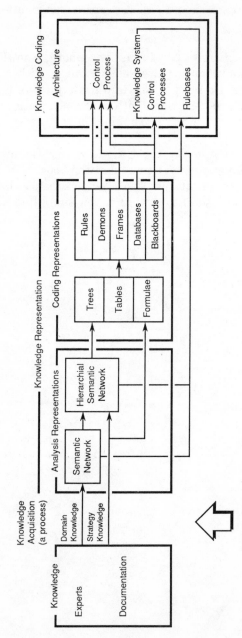

4

Knowledge Acquisition Techniques

Knowledge acquisition is the **gathering** of information, decisions, and relationships from any resource available. What you gather will be used to create and implement a model of a domain in the computer. Your acquisition approach will depend on the nature of the problem, available information, and, perhaps, your inventiveness. This chapter describes techniques for finding information sources and assimilating their knowledge. It also explains why some sources are better than others and how to get the most from each type. Detailed information on iterative knowledge acquisition technique, information sources, resources, and gathering techniques, conducting personal interviews, observing experts at work, organizing printed material, and tools for organizing information is provided.

ITERATIVE APPROACH TO KNOWLEDGE ACQUISITION

An iterative approach to knowledge acquisition can be extremely effective and is highly recommended. It consists of gathering data, validating it, refining it, and then repeating the entire cycle (Figure 4-1).

It is important that you not begin your knowledge representation too soon during the initial phase of knowledge acquisition. You need to learn about the domain before modeling it. During this early stage

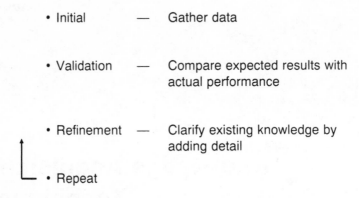

- Initial   —   Gather data

- Validation   —   Compare expected results with
                        actual performance

- Refinement   —   Clarify existing knowledge by
                        adding detail

- Repeat

Figure 4-1 The iterative process of knowledge acquisition.

of information gathering, you should gather any and all kinds of information available. You will have a variety of knowledge sources. Put off any temptation to begin representation until you are very familiar with the nature of the problem, the vocabulary of the experts and their domain, the processes, and the personnel involved with the project. Your perception of the most efficient means to a solution will change with time. After gathering as much background information as possible, you will be ready to model the problem domain by using the techniques described in Chapter 5.

After the initial model has been built, use your interviews with the expert and formal test plans as a knowledge base feedback and correction mechanism (see Chapter 13).

Subsequent stages of knowledge gathering help to refine your initial perception of the problem by adding more detail to clarify what is already known. Divide the domain information into units or "objects" which are logical groups of data. For example, when discussing a "car," you may think about the object called the "engine" as a single object. The attributes and functions of an engine should be treated as a single logical entity. The "engine" is also part of another object called "car." When your point of view shifts from the "engine" to the "pistons" or the "oil pump," stop thinking about the "engine" object. It is no longer the object under consideration. Frame your thoughts around the new object.

Decomposing the problem domain into discrete objects will help you and the expert to concentrate on a single part of the domain at any given moment and will create logical domain modules which will be used during the representation phase.

INFORMATION SOURCES, RESOURCES, AND GATHERING TECHNIQUES

The information sources and gathering techniques outlined below are effective when applied at the appropriate time. However, they do not all apply for every case. Take any information when you can get it and determine whether or not it will be needed at a later time. Remember the Cardinal Rule of information gathering: write it down! Concepts that seem crystal clear one moment (because you have a temporary, deep understanding of a portion of the domain) are forgotten quickly if you are not the expert.

Information is everywhere. Personal interviews with your domain expert(s) will be your most valuable resource. However, interviews are not the only information source available. Alternative sources to personal interviews include, but are not limited to, observing experts at work, personal notebooks, trade journals, books, questionnaires, etc.

Personal Interviews

The personal interview is the most effective way to gain expertise and receive immediate feedback. Since your communication with the expert is of paramount importance, you should begin by acquiring as much of the expert's "domain vocabulary" as you can. While you need not become an expert yourself, your command of some of the expert's terms will help you communicate with the expert.

At the outset of each interview, set your goal(s), identifying what you expect to accomplish during your session. As you question the expert, convey your understanding of the problem at hand (usually some subdomain of the overall problem). The expert will either correct or refine your perception or reinforce it. Do not concentrate all knowledge-gathering interviews within a single week. You will need time to structure the knowledge for expert review and verification. The expert will need time to unwind (avoiding burnout).

You are better prepared for the interview than the expert because you know what you are looking for (anything and everything pertaining to the domain). Tell the expert what type of interview you are going to conduct. It is wise to obtain verbal permission before intellectually stretching someone's psyche. You are about to force the experts to think about parts of their everyday life which they felt were quite sorted out. They will soon discover their "understanding of their understanding" falls far short of your expectations. Interviews are strenuous for both the expert and for you. Your challenge will be to keep the expert from overloading their senses. When you notice a loss of enthusiasm, it is time for a break.

At the first meeting, the expert may want to talk about topics in which you have no interest. Their initial reaction is often "I know you can computerize Job ABC, but you'll find mine much too difficult for the **computer** to comprehend." Allow them to chat for a short time to unclutter their mind. What they have to say is important to them, and they will feel that they are already contributing to the project. Let them get it out of their system. Without wasting too much time, steer the conversation around to the topics in which you are interested. *Note*: This is where the communication skills of a good knowledge engineer are invaluable.

Begin by gathering high-level information only. Ask broad questions like "What are the names of the major **things** you work with?" or "How would you **categorize** the different **parts** of your job?" You are looking for the names of the major components and their immediate subparts. Chapter 5 will provide further details about **what** information to gather.

Use the expert's "natural" approach to the problem. They have developed their own heuristics for practical and valid reasons. Encourage the expert to describe the domain in any fashion. Some experts are more comfortable drawing pictures or making charts than they are forcing themselves to think in terms of if-then rules. Acquire as much written material as possible for later reference. If you cannot remove it from the expert's premises due to logistics or its overwhelming nature, determine when access is available to you.

After the initial meeting, begin to gather detailed data. Pick one part of the domain and grab everything you can. You will take the information back, model it, and return to the expert later for verification. If, during the course of your discussion, the topic turns to some other part of the domain, grab the information while it is pertinent, for use later. Then steer the discussion back to the original topic.

If the expert can handle the pressure, you may be able to extract high-level information very quickly by not allowing the expert enough time to formulate a complete solution to a problem. This technique uses rapid-fire questions to elicit information from the expert and should not be used for extended periods of time.

Let's try an example with you as the expert being interviewed.

In 30 seconds; How do you do your taxes, and what material is required? . . . . Time's up!!

In 30 seconds; What are your options and which is the best, if you are missing some of your data? . . . . . . Time's up!!

Neither question gave you enough time to answer completely. You have probably already thought of alternatives you missed during the 30-second limit.

The first question was goal-oriented. The goal was to determine what resources and input data are required to prepare an individual tax return. The second question was decision-oriented. Given some uncertainty about which data was missing and how to handle the problem, the expert (you) determined some of the alternative paths to a complete decision.

The kind of information gathered with this technique is the easiest to recall. This knowledge is sometimes difficult to gather if the expert has enough time to think. Why? Because, if given sufficient time, experts tend to think the problem through to its "best" solution. They will ignore alternative solutions and will not know "why" the solution is valid. They are unaware of the high-level decisions they just made to reach the conclusion. A good interviewer can use this approach, without the expert's knowledge, by generating a sense of urgency during a normal interview (quickening the pace), asking three or four rapid-fire questions, then retreating to a more leisurely pace.

Observing Experts at Work

Observing an expert on the job is an excellent way to gather initial data and obtain the general flow of the expert's thinking. You can also use observation to verify a partially working system. When performing a task, people do things that feel natural. Certain actions will surprise you, and those surprises help to refine the problem.,

A simple example:

While constructing a system about finding trouble in a computer network, the knowledge engineer observes an expert attempting to isolate the problem to a particular network component. The expert is interviewing the person who reported the problem. The expert asks some questions about terminal symptoms. Then, unexpectedly, the expert switches context and asks a question about a lamp on the user's modem. After the lamp question, the expert continues with terminal questions!

During a subsequent interview session (later) the knowledge engineer asks the expert why the "modem" question was asked at that particular moment. The expert explains that the question was pertinent to identifying which part of the circuit was in trouble and that pursuing terminal questions would have been fruitless if the problem was on the computer's end of the circuit. The answer to the "modem" question led the expert back to the terminal for further study.

Knowledge about how to "**use**" subparts of the domain knowledge is called "meta knowledge." Meta knowledge can be used to manipulate and control the overall search for the system goal. Even though each system component (subdomain) has a list of faults which pertain to how to isolate a problem within itself, individual items on that list may be pertinent to a "larger" problem (one that investigates another object).

In this case, the larger problem was to find the trouble in the overall collection of components called a "circuit." The modem question was applied to the larger circuit problem first, to help prioritize the search among competing subdomains (MODEM or TERMINAL). If interviews were used as the sole source of information, the problem-solving approach taken by the expert might not have been discovered. By observing the expert, the system developer discovered a discontinuity in the existing system model which was corrected in a subsequent interview. Keep observation notes about the domain and, especially, the surprises. They greatly help in creating a system which acts "naturally" to the ultimate user community.

Do not interrupt when observing someone during a live situation. Questions should only be asked when the expert is free to think about the knowledge system without regard to the immediate problem. If you do not wait, the expert may become confused about whether to think in terms of the knowledge system or the problem at hand.

Personal Notebooks

Personal notebooks (knowledge gold mines) tend to document two types of information: information which is not documented elsewhere and abbreviated procedural information. The first type of information documents new ideas, insights, or tricks. People know when there is a good chance they will not remember a new item, and they write it down for later recall. They also know when this information is not available in other texts. They draw pictures. They make important references to other knowledge sources (where to find it) when alternates are available.

The second kind of information kept is usually in the form of abbreviated procedural information. Here, the expert keeps "high-level" information. They note the most important concepts and procedures as memory aids.

Do not overlook this resource. If you do not see a notebook at the expert's work location, ask for it!

Role Playing by Experts

20 Questions — During 20 Questions, one expert considers a problem and its symptoms, while the other asks about symptoms to determine the problem. This technique should not be used for the "long haul." It would be too slow and agonizing to bear for long. It can, however, be effective for finding specific solutions to very specific problems.

The Expert as the Computer — A novice has unorganized data which is pertinent to a particular problem. An expert, sitting behind a curtain, is allowed to ask the novice about the data. The expert is only allowed to ask questions, not to view any data the novice has in front of him/her. The expert is playing the role of the knowledge system and the computer. As the expert asks questions of the novice, detailed notes are kept by the knowledge engineer. It is important to note, specifically, which questions are asked and in what order they are asked. Primary decision questions are asked before secondary decisions can be made. When the session has ended, the knowledge engineer performs an in-depth interview with the expert to determine what "decisions" were being made and to which subdomains the decisions applied.

STARTER

Starter system troubles are relatively easy to isolate. The following are common symptoms and causes.

1. <u>Engine cranks very slowly or not at all</u> — Turn on the headlights. ┃If┃ the lights are very dim, the battery or connecting wires are probably the cause. Check the battery as described in Chapter Seven. Check the wiring for breaks, shorts, and dirty connections.

┃If┃ the battery and connecting wires are not at fault, turn the headlights on and try to crank the engine. ┃If┃ the lights dim drastically, the starter is probably shorted to ground. Have it tested or install a rebuilt unit.

Figure 4-2 Text for diagnosing a starter problem. From Ahlstrand, Alan, *Datsun 510, 610, 710 1968-1977 Shop Manual.* Clymer Publications, 1978. Used with permission of Clymer Publications.

Written Information Sources

Any source of written information may be used as input to the system. Suggested sources include, but are not limited to trade journals and books, government publications, "historical results" information used on the job, forms used by the organization or work group, and questionnaires.

When inspecting written material, you should be looking for decisions, relational information, and procedures in the text. Remember that decision statements contain domain representation facts as well. Decisions can be found by looking for "decision words" such as those found in Figure 4-2.

Other parts of the text will describe relationships (facts) about the domain and procedures (algorithms) for manipulating those facts. Figure 4-3 shows how to extrapolate rules from text. The text is

---

Material discovered in the text:

Decision Words	Objects Mentioned	Possible Values or Relationships	Procedures Described
	Engine		Crank
	Crank		
If	Headlights	Dim (Drastically)	Crank
If	Headlights	Dim (Very)	Turn on
If	Battery		Check
	Wiring	Shorts	Check
	Wiring	Breaks	Check
	Wiring	Connections	Check
	Connections	Dirty	Check
	Starter	Short	Test/Detail
	Starter	Grounded	Test/Install

Figure 4-3 Text example and relational material and procedures "discovered" in the text. From Ahlstrand, Alan, *Datsun 510, 610, 710 1968-1977 Shop Manual.* Clymer Publications, 1978. Used with permission of Clymer Publications.

straight from an auto repair manual, from a section that describes procedures for locating starter troubles.

Each object has the potential to become a separate knowledge base. By carefully inspecting the text, you have identified subdomain areas which may require more detailed investigation. Figure 4-3 shows at least three rules (the Ifs) and several procedures to be employed, depending upon the "truth" of any individual rule.

A Picture is Worth a Thousand Words   People do not keep their entire domain representation as a set of verbal descriptions of domain relationships. It is often easier to extract information by using some form of visual representation. Let the subject matter expert use any visual form which helps them to communicate.

Flow diagrams are wonderful bits of knowledge engineering. Someone has already taken the trouble to organize the decisions and procedures for you. In many cases, you may be able to directly code rules from the diagrams. However, often the person who creates a flow-chart makes assumptions about implicit knowledge which is common to the expert and himself. These assumptions leave gaps in the knowledge base which must be accounted for when represented in the computer.

"GOODS FLOW"
ENTITY DIAGRAM

CLOSED CURVE DIAGRAM
(SPECIAL OR CONCEPTUAL RELATIONSHIP)

Charts and tables generally represent relationships or decisions. When they represent decisions, you may either code rules directly from the chart or "feed" the chart into an induction tool (which will generate rules for you).

Graphs seldom represent decisions. They show relationships. The headings show object relationships and the datapoints represent facts. While some fact are discrete (as in histograms) others are represented as some continuum.

GRAPH

Frequently, the most difficult part of using a graph is either recreating the formula that produced the data or interpreting the raw data as a formula. Why (you may ask) would you want to do that? To efficiently implement the data in the final program. Computers perform math functions much more efficiently than they can implement "lookup" functions in a database (of the charted line points). Also, the resulting knowledge base will be more comprehensible.

Entity diagrams and closed curve diagrams: Experts do not always think in terms of verbalized concepts. Some relationships such as inheritance, space, patterns, or time are better represented visually. These concepts are often impossible for the expert to describe any other way and must be acquired by indirect methods, which may include the use of tables as well as pictorial representation.

Questionnaires and Forms

Questionnaires and forms may be used as aids in gathering information for implementing the initial knowledge base. In one company, a questionnaire was used in the client interview process to make sure all parts of the domain were covered when novice or intermediate interviewers obtained data from clients in remote locations. The questionnaire was part of the normal business process.[1] The company took great care to construct a tool to aid in gathering succinct and pertinent information. Information structured in this fashion can be quite valuable. A knowledge engineer can take advantage of this kind of information by using the questionnaire or form data as either input to an induction tool or as test material for the resulting knowledge base.

Note: The same data should *not* be used for both input and verification. That would be asking the data to verify itself (a no-no in certain circles such as statistical analysis).

Using More Than One Expert

It is preferable to use information from more than one expert. In some applications, cooperating experts might specialize in different, but overlapping, parts of the system domain. Use as many experts as necessary.

You should be aware of certain problems that can arise when using multiple experts. Experts do not always agree about the interpretation of available data. For example, two doctors may disagree about the possible causes of an identical set of symptoms (though they probably will agree about the plausibility of the other's conclusions). Each may place more or less importance upon certain criteria for their own conclusions.

Two simple rules will help keep **your** system sane:

1. When there are only two experts providing input to the system, one must be considered "the" expert. That person's opinion will override the other's at all times. The additional expert is used

---

1 Newquist, Harvey (III), *The Making of a Tax Expert*. AI Expert Magazine, v.2, no.3, Miller Freeman Publications, March 1987.

as alternative input for consideration by "the" expert. If an impasse occurs, use a third opinion to decide between the first
two.

2. When more than two experts are providing input to the system, use a consensus approach. No individual expert should
   override the majority opinion of their peers.

Knowledge Acquisition Tools

A variety of tools are available for recording the knowledge acquired
from an expert. While simple tools are often the best, you should
consider alternative and imaginative uses of tools which were not
specifically designed for knowledge acquisition. Any tool is appropriate if it works when you need it to work.

The interview process should be natural and smooth-flowing. If
you are using any computer program to aid the interviewing process,
be sure **you** are skilled in using it. A person looking for keyboard
keys or instructions distracts both the expert and themselves from
concentrating on the problem at hand.

With the exception of domain literature, your personal notes of interviews with an expert are your single most valuable resource. Consider them an extension of your memory. They are also used to aid
the expert when reviewing and verifying your understanding of the
expert's domain. DON'T LEAVE HOME WITHOUT THEM !!

Tape recorders make some people nervous. To remove an expert's
jitters, get the expert's permission before using a tape recorder. During the interview, place the recorder in an inconspicuous place and
turn it on. Do not pay any attention to the recorder other than
changing the tape when needed.

Generally, tape recorders have limited utility. You probably will
not use the information recorded on a recorder unless you transcribe
the recorded session, and transcription is very labor intensive. It will
take you as long to transcribe the tape as it would have taken to
make detailed notes during the interview. There is a place for recorders, however, when a time constraint is imposed upon the interview process. If the expert's time is **very** valuable, or the expert
needs uninterrupted time to describe some area of the domain, a
recorder is useful. You will still need to do a transcription of the
session, but the interview can proceed at a faster pace.

Often the expert will prefer **drawing** relationships such as inheritance, space, patterns, or time. You will use these pictures to keep
your discussions centered on a topic and, later, to translate the
expert's pictorial knowledge to machine-understandable code. Use

any tool that helps the diagramming process. If more than one expert is being interviewed at the same time, use an easel. The easel is better than notepaper because it communicates ideas simultaneously to each member of the interview group and provides space for "global" thoughts and ideas.

Other Knowledge Organization Tools

Tree design tools —   There are several tree design tools that can be very useful in organizing the knowledge *as it is being collected*. The following paragraphs describe several of them.

Mind mapping is a powerful method to help relate "free associations" and "ideas" of one or more people. It is a good tool for acquiring high-level information at a very fast pace — so fast, in fact, that some people find the process quite stressful. You must keep this stress in mind when using this technique because those who are made uncomfortable may volunteer better information by using other interviewing techniques.

The process is quite simple. A topic is placed at the center of a large, blank writing space (Figure 4-4a). This topic will become the root node of a tree which branches out in all directions from the center. Anyone may offer a new "connection" to the tree by naming any node and a relationship (which also becomes a node). The new node is placed on the drawing and a line is drawn between the original node and the new one (Figure 4-4b).

Each new idea is added to the picture whether it seems relevant or not (Figure 4-4c). Ideas that are not relevant can be judged and acted upon later. Sometimes, a seemingly strange association can

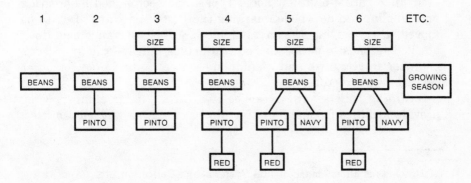

Figure 4-4 Growth of a tree from mind mapping.

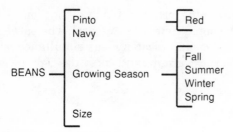

Figure 4-5 Restructure of the BEANS project into Brackets™ form.

lead to creative new ways to apply domain-specific information. Drawbacks to this procedure include the lack of detail which will be required for the final system, as well as non-normalized and redundant data. But, the quality and utility of the information usually far outweighs its lack of **total** organization.

Tree design tools (i.e., Brackets™[2] and Sourceview[3]) are tools which aid the developer when organizing and manipulating data trees on a VDT screen for later printout. The tools were intended to be used for organization and coding of "conventional" programs by supporting structured design topologies and methods. A knowledge engineer can use these tools to organize any structure that can be represented as one or more trees. For example, in Figure 4-5 the mind map of the BEANS project has been restructured into a Brackets(TM) document.

Looking at the tree, it is clear that Pinto and Navy fall into the same class and can be moved to a lower level on the tree. The tree can be easily manipulated whenever new relationships are discovered. In Figure 4-6, a new node, Types, has been added by creating and labeling the new node, marking the Pinto and Navy block to be moved, then moving the marked block. (This rearrangement took about 8 seconds to perform.) The tool makes it easy for a knowledge engineer to recognize and manipulate classes, inheritance, or other related data structures.

Outlining tools — These can be used in a similar manner. They provide facilities for manipulating blocks of text as "tagged" entities.

---

2   Brackets is a trademark of TLA Systems and Education Ltd.

3   Sourceview is a product of Heartland Systems.

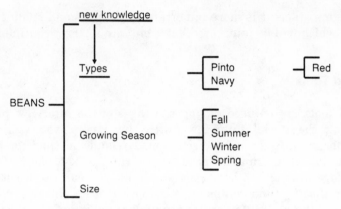

Figure 4-6 Rearrangement of BEANS tree.

A disadvantage of using outlining tools is that patterns do not stand out as much when they are not represented graphically (Figure 4-7).

Word Processors — If you lack formal software engineering tools, you may use your word processor to organize knowledge. Word processors are good general purpose tools. They can be used to aid in representing almost anything that can be written or drawn. However, they have the same nongraphical representation drawback as outlining tools. They also lack the logical "tags" to manipulate data relationships as simple blocks.

USING EXPERT SYSTEM SHELLS TO ORGANIZE KNOWLEDGE

Using a shell to gather knowledge can be useful because the shell will help structure the knowledge and keep your discussion centered around a single topic during the interview. Be careful that you do not rely on the structure too early in the project. During the knowl-

```
1       BEANS
1.1     Pinto
1.1.1       Red
1.2     Navy
1.3     Growing Season
1.3.1       Fall
1.3.2       Summer
1.3.3       Winter
1.3.4       Spring
1.4     Size
```

Figure 4-7 The BEANs example in outline form.

edge-gathering stage, it is more important to gather small islands of knowledge which will be integrated, later on, into a larger continent.

Rule-Based Tools

Rule-based tools can be used during all stages of the interview process. During the initial interviews with the expert, you will be searching for a basis for later discussion. A simple method for acquiring this initial information is to "throw rules at the tool." After the knowledge system has been partially built, you can use a set of rules for verification and refinement. Using a tool for the interview also gives you the ability to verify your understanding of the knowledge with the expert "on the spot" by executing portions of the knowledge base while the expert observes the program.

Throwing rules at the tool is the process of letting the expert name as many rules as can be easily remembered. While **not recommended as a long-term solution** to knowledge collection, the process does have the advantage of giving you an initial (fragmented) look at isolated parts of the data. It also helps define both terms and other topics for discussion. Be careful — the process may produce garbage which you will have to strip from the knowledge base. In any event, this type of knowledge will not be reusable without major restructuring. Your goal should be to collect sufficient information for a "best representation" to become evident. You will reorganize the data (away from the expert) and return with a new representation for verification. During subsequent interviews, your strategy should switch from this somewhat random approach to a more structured one (see Chapters 6 and 7).

Induction Tools and Decision Tables, or How to Deal (Sometimes) with Expert Uncertainty

Experts cannot **always** describe their knowledge as an explicit set of rules. When this happens, they often **can** state that they "know" some fact to be true if they are given a set of attributes (preconditions) that relate to that fact. It is the knowledge engineer's responsibility to determine which attributes are important by asking the expert what items they consider important when making the decision. The expert answers with a list of attributes which they feel contribute to their decision.

The attribute list is prioritized from most to least important and configured as a set of table headings. Each row in the table is filled in with cases for the expert to make a decision about. Values for the attribute headings are varied for each case. The expert makes a decision about each, which is then associated with the instance. When enough examples have been acquired from the expert, the resulting table, with the expert's decisions, is fed into an induction tool. It is the induction tool's responsibility to synthesize (make sense of) the data and output a decision tree which becomes part or all of the final expert system. The whole process makes the expert's uncertain knowledge quite simple to convert to usable rules.

Databases are already in table format. They often have the results of decisions hidden in their data. Consider the EZ2 Geta Loan Company. EZ2 Geta keeps records about all customers and loans which have been approved by their loan officers. The database records include information about how long the customer has had his present job, the customer's earnings, whether the customer owns a home, how much money was approved for the loan, etc.

Hidden in this data is the collective expertise of the company's loan officers. If each record is fed into an induction tool, we might learn the appropriate questions, parameter ranges, and loan amounts for a given customer "type." The output of the induction tool could be used to build a knowledge system for use by novice loan officers.

INDUCTION CAVEATS

You must take care when using an induction tool to collect knowledge. Tool makers use various induction methods in different tools. Some tools create very simple trees with the data. Others attempt to organize the data by weighing the importance of each attribute and structure the output accordingly. Still others throw away data which does not seem pertinent to the problem at hand. Take time to understand the internal induction algorithm of your tool, or your rules may not make sense.

Another failing stems from the expert's view of what seems important to the problem at the moment. The expert may leave out important attributes which should be considered before any conclusion is drawn from the system. The induction tool has no way to guess that there might be missing attributes and will faithfully build a set of rules with the available information.

A third kind of problem happens when the tool weighs the importance of the data. Some tools attempt to average ranges of data instead of finding threshold (cutoff) criteria. For example, you might have never answered "customer earnings" with a value greater than $30,000 or less than $10,000 for a "loan amount" of $2500, whereas that may be the exact range that is appropriate for a loan of $2500. You may be surprised when the resulting rule states:

```
IF customer earnings          > $12,000
   and customer earnings       < $28,000
THEN loan amount                 $2500
```

What is wrong with that? It's true that you will not give any loans to any one who should not have one. But you also will be disallowing some loans which you should be approving. YOU ARE LOSING CUSTOMERS!!

Whenever you use any induction tool, be sure to **carefully** scrutinize the output rule base for missing or approximate information. Use the induction tool as part of your knowledge acquisition process, not the *only* acquisition process.

SUMMARY

Any technique that "works" is appropriate for gathering knowledge. Knowledge can be acquired from interviews, text analysis, observation, role playing, group interaction, or by any inventive approach you can imagine. Make sure you use an iterative approach to gathering information. Gather the data, validate it, and clarify and refine the data through additional research.

There are a variety of tools available for recording knowledge. Your notes, of course are critical. But in addition, you may want to employ a tape recorder or have the expert draw pictures. To organize your knowledge, you may want to employ mind mapping, outlines, tree design, and organizing tools such as Brackets™ and Sourceview, or an expert system shell. Induction tools and decision tables may also be useful, but you must be careful in choosing the tools you wish to use.

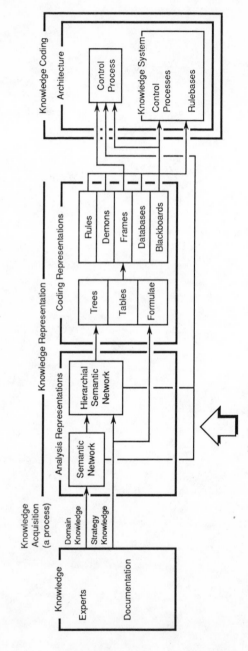

Knowledge Representation and Structuring Techniques

"Experience has shown that designing a good representation is often the key to turning hard problems into simple ones."[1]

Paradigms describe **how people think** about a problem. Knowledge representation and structuring are tools for illustrating **what people know**. Paradigms describe the ways people use or process their knowledge, but not the details of a specific domain of knowledge. The details become explicit through knowledge representation and structuring tools, which are needed to capture, illustrate, and inspect the information.

"A picture can be worth a thousand words." Would you rather read 1000 words of project specification or look at an illustration containing the same information? There is an obvious preference for and benefit to illustration-oriented methodologies, such as Ganes and Sarson, Yourdon, and Data Structured System Design (DSSD™). The following benefits represent some of the utility of pictorial representation in computer projects, and especially knowledge systems development:

---

1 Winston, Patrick Henry, *Artificial Intelligence*, 2nd ed. Addison-Wesley Publishing Company, 1984.

1. Validation through enhanced/uniform communication between development team and users
2. Testing and debugging system logic because of clean design and documentation
3. Completeness because methodologies encourage complete documentation and quality assurance reviews with users
4. Accuracy of solutions because of documented and tested logic
5. Ease of maintenance because reduced effort is needed to understand/interpret someone else's code
6. Programming productivity through enhanced/uniform communication and documentation
7. Ease in coding system because of structured approach

The purpose of representing/structuring knowledge for expert systems is to develop structures that assist in coding knowledge into programs so that they can exhibit intelligent behavior. This book concentrates on techniques for structuring knowledge so that it may be coded into production rules. Throughout this chapter the term *knowledge representation* is used to mean the combined process of representation and structuring.

Whatever the problem selected, the knowledge representation techniques you use must codify the knowledge in a form that best satisfies the system's ability to produce the desired result. Pictorial tools make the job easier and facilitate reviewing and fine tuning of the expert's knowledge. It is necessary to first agree on scope and emphasis of a domain, then gather information using one or more of the techniques. The kinds of knowledge you need to represent include objects, events, performance (cognitive behavior), and meta knowledge (general knowledge that may indirectly affect the subject area).

It is possible to represent a domain of knowledge, i.e., subject area, in different ways. Knowledge of wine, for example, can be represented in at least three ways:

1. The physical universe of wine, i.e., the physical/organic composition of wine.
2. The digestive universe of wine, i.e., how wine interacts in the human digestive tract.
3. The cultural universe of wine, i.e., how humans perceive combining wine with food.

Only the third form would be a primary focal point for building a knowledge system that recommends wine for meals, but 1 and 2 are valuable in scoping the application, validation, and testing. The scope represented in 2, for example, might tell us that sweet wines might cause stomachaches if combined with rich main courses.

As knowledge is gathered, it must be translated and stored in forms that facilitate good knowledge system design and quality assurance review practices. The three most popular techniques for representing/structuring knowledge are semantic networks, rules, and frames. In addition to these, this chapter will also discuss decision tables, decision trees, and demons. All of the techniques can be grouped into two categories: analysis techniques and coding techniques.

The knowledge **analysis** representation techniques — semantic networks, decision tables, decision trees — are best used during scoping and initial knowledge gathering. They provide a pictorial view of the domain and can ultimately be coded into a system with additional structuring.

The knowledge **coding** representation techniques (production rules, frames, demons) are the actual code used to transform the pictorial diagrams of knowledge into the working code of a knowledge system. This can be done via a tool or programming language with the necessary capabilities. The analysis representation techniques as defined in this book are easily translated to code forms; decision trees are readily converted into production rules which can be executed by rule-based shells. In addition, there are tools that assimilate decision tables.

Hybrid techniques, those combining one or more of the above, are extremely useful when dealing with complex subject areas. For example, representing a collisions paradigm involves a combination of techniques. This is described in more detail later in this chapter (see the Uneeda Phone Company example). The technique or combination of techniques you choose to use will depend on several factors, including:

1. Knowledge engineer's/systems analyst's preference
2. Expert's paradigm(s)
3. Domain knowledge structure and complexity
4. Implementation requirements
5. Maintenance and enhancement requirements

It is necessary to utilize a technique that is comfortable for both the developer and the expert. There will be many conversations and interviews using diagrams to represent the domain. Make sure the diagrams are understandable and functional in order to facilitate the knowledge engineering process, not hinder it.

If the domain knowledge lends itself to a particular technique, take advantage of it. Diagnostic applications are easily diagramed using semantic networks and decision trees, whereas configuration applications may be more easily represented using decision tables.

System requirements, such as implementation and maintenance needs, may influence your representation method. These factors will ultimately point to a best overall representation technique. Of the implementation needs, the greatest influence will be from the tool(s) you select. Do not hesitate to change your representation scheme if your current choice is not working. Changing the representation can provide valuable validation of design and requirements. It can be favorable but also take extra time. It's your call to make. A project manager's goal is to develop the best system for the least cost in the shortest time.

This chapter explores several popular techniques. They are defined using examples. In some cases, a sample of an expert's dialogue is structured using a specific representation technique. How to make use of the diagrams will be explained in much more detail in Chapter 6.

SEMANTIC NETWORKS

Semantic networks, also referred to as semantic nets, are a contextual, intransitive map of relationships utilizing nodes and links. The nodes represent objects, events, or concepts. The links show the relationships between the nodes. Although there are no formal rules on structuring semantic nets, the classical approach is to represent nodes by circles or boxes and the links by arrows connecting the nodes. A semantic net is meant to be examined/validated by looking in all directions from any one point. The mammal-dog-human semantic net (Figure 5-1) is a simplified structure which could become very complex given the many possible relationships that could be represented.

The advantages of semantic nets are that they easily represent inheritance, and they are flexible. Inheritance is the process by which one node derives characteristics from another node in the hierarchy. In the mammal-dog-human example, the COCKER node inherits the attributes of the dog node. Likewise, if you examine the SANDI node, you will know that SANDI is a DOG and has all the characteristics of "dogs in general" that have been catalogued in the

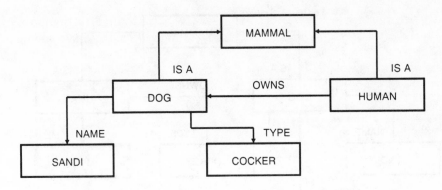

Figure 5-1 A simple semantic network.

dog node. Because of the inheritance characteristics of a semantic net representation, many things can be assumed about an object. In this case, humans and dogs have some common characteristics because they are both mammals.

Because of the simple syntax and flexibility of a semantic net, it is easy to modify the diagram by adding, deleting, or changing a node or link as necessary. Remember, there are many possible ways to represent something. The goal is to find a representation that accurately describes your subject area. In the example above, it may be necessary to add a node to represent the sex of the dog and the name of the human. This could be added in several "correct" places. It is the expert's choice when representing the expert's knowledge (Figure 5-2).

Although the representation of semantic nets is flexible, its tendency toward a lack of formal structuring can be a disadvantage. The branches of complex semantic nets often become intertwined, and the resulting semantic nets may be referred to as tangles or meshes. These involved diagrams are usually hard to work from and even more difficult to validate. The Warnier/Orr approach solves most of these problems. It is a representation technique used to aid in conventional coding by encouraging the representation of semantic nets as hierarchical data models which are much easier to validate by data normalization.

Rearranging a semantic net into a hierarchy is a technique of normalization. You can see why the hierarchical diagram is the preferred representation for coding rule-based systems (Figure 5-3). It lends itself to transformation into cause-and-effect relationships. Be-

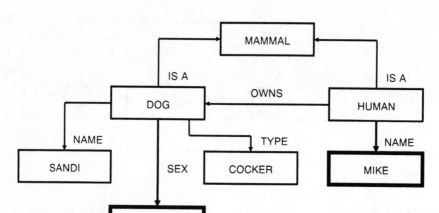

Figure 5-2 Modification of semantic net.

cause it is untangled and simple to validate, diagrams are easy to create and edit. Some high-performance inexpensive tools exist that support this kind of diagraming. Ken Orr & Associates is a supplier of these tools. In Chapters 6 and 7 we'll learn more about normalization.

In conventional software engineering practices, semantic networks are known as data models. Their purpose is to model objects and relationships in the universe of your systems and then normalize the relationships to produce a clean representation. This should be done when initially scoping an application. It is a valuable road map for

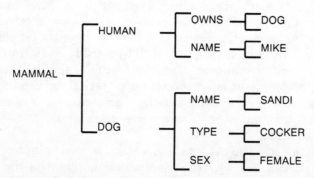

Figure 5-3 The hierarchical version of a semantic net (this is a recasting of the previous network).

keeping relationships among things in the domain clear. Semantic nets are usually converted into a decision tree before coding. This flattens out the complexity of the diagram and makes it easier to code the knowledge into a tool.

Example 1 — Uneeda Phone Company

The following example is presented in detail here and used several times throughout the rest of the book.

Design-Your-Own Phone Service from the Uneeda Phone Company[2]   The Uneeda Phone Company offers many options and features for its customers. Most of the combinations of features that a customer could choose are feasible, but certain patterns would result in an invalid order. Uneeda customer representatives work with a customer by explaining the options and features and steering the customer away from invalid combinations.

Uneeda options and features available to a customer include:

1. Type of service:

    • Standard service — every call is timed and measured
    • Unlimited service — local calls are not measured
    • Low-income service — standard service at a discount for qualifying customers

    Design constraints:

    • Standard service is required for most options that result in special, timed billing, such as call diverting.
    • Standard service is generally more economical for customers who make fewer than 20 minutes of local calls per month.

---

2 Uneeda Phone company features resemble the kinds of features you might find at your local phone company. Features change over time, so we have used a fictional phone company is fictional, rather than run the risk of misrepresenting any particular real company.

- Low-income service is a courtesy service. If a customer wants most of the other features and options, she) will have to forfeit low-income service.
- To qualify for low-income service, total income in your household must be less than $15,000, and there may not be any other phone lines on the premises.

2. **Call diverting**: This service allows you to enter a command on your phone which makes calls placed to you ring on some other number. The caller is unaware that the call has been diverted. You pay the charges for the forwarded call as if it was placed from your phone.
   Design constraints:

   - You must be on standard service.
   - You must have touch tone service.
   - You have to be at home, at your phone, to turn call diverting on and off.
   - This service cannot be selected in addition to anywhere call diverting.

3. **Anywhere call diverting**: This service is like call diverting, but you can control it from anywhere you have access to a phone that can call your home.

   Design constraints

   - You must be on standard service.
   - You must have touch tone service.
   - You have to use a touch tone phone to turn call diverting on and off.
   - This service cannot be selected in addition to regular call diverting.

4. **Toll discount**: This option gives subscribers a toll discount on calls to neighboring communities.

   Design constraints:

   - You must be on standard service.
   - You must make toll calls totaling more than twice the monthly service charge in order to save money.

5. **Personal trunk line**: This option gives subscribers a discount on long distance calls to selected communities.

   Design constraints:

   • You must be on unlimited service.
   • You must make long distance calls totaling more than three times the monthly service charge in order to save money.

6. **Incoming call**: This option beeps your handset if a second party is trying to call you while you are already on the phone. You can tap your switch hook to put the first call on hold and receive the second call. You can return to the first call again by tapping the switch hook.

   Design constraints:

   • Not recommended if you plan to use your phone line for a computer or terminal dial-up connection; the "beep" will drop your computer connection.

7. **Electronic phone book**: This option allows you to store up to six frequently called numbers "in your phone." Any phone on your premises can dial a simple code to automatically call a stored number.

   Design constraints:

   • You must have touch tone service.

8. **Conference calls**: This option allows you to phone two different numbers at the same time and establish a conference call.
   Design constraints:

   • You must *not* have low-income service.
   • You must *not* have the incoming call feature.

A hierarchical semantic network describing the Uneeda Phone Company options and features is very "flat" and has few contingent relationships (Figure 5-4). The "flatness" suggests that this problem may be suited to a Collision paradigm (see Figure 3-4). The Uneeda

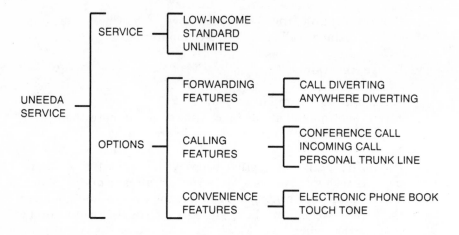

Figure 5-4 Hierarchical semantic net for the Uneeda Phone Service.

Phone company is discussed further in the examples of decision tables later in this chapter.

Example 2 — Warnier/Orr Approach

The following example will illustrate the benefits of using the Warnier/Orr approach to developing and representing semantic nets. We begin with a classic semantic net using the node-link representation for automobile information (Figure 5-5).

The tangled net is accurate but could easily get out of hand. The Warnier/Orr approach flattens the diagram out so that it can be easily interpreted and validated (Figure 5-6).

It is easy now to separate out the diagnostic/repair domain view for automobile as shown in Figure 5-7. This one is appropriate for troubleshooting, because it represents the systems that may be in trouble (i.e., the number of doors on your car doesn't help you figure out why the car won't start). This is the same information present in the semantic net, recast as a hierarchical semantic net.

Further acquisition and refinement of the auto repair domain might lead to the structure shown in Figure 5-8. This hierarchical semantic network drawn in perspective is the structure selected to implement the auto repair example in the book.

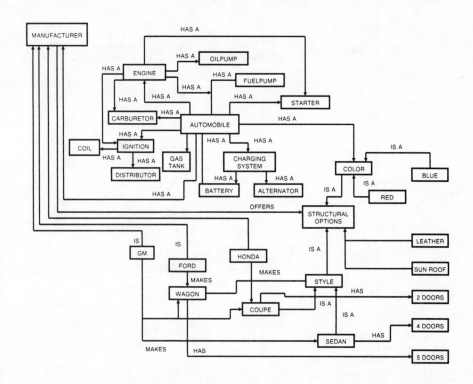

Figure 5-5 Tangled semantic net for limited domain of an automobile.

A careful reader will question the redundant references under EN-GINE. During knowledge acquisition, it became apparent that the SYMPTOMS domain can fix some problems, but could also recognize and delegate investigation of more specific problems in all of the automobile subsystems (domains). ENGINE can also recognize and delegate problems in subsystems that are components of the ENGINE. ENGINE's knowledge is more specialized than that of SYMPTOMS, however, and ENGINE will have different reasons for delegating investigations.

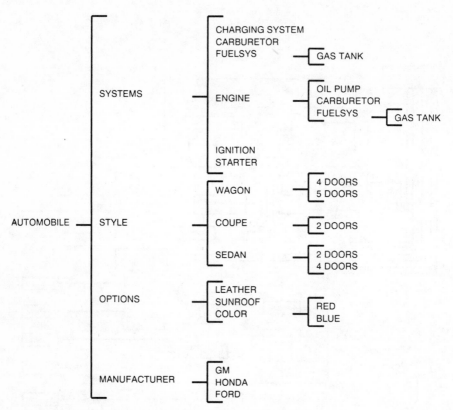

Figure 5-6 Warnier/Orr semantic network for automobile.

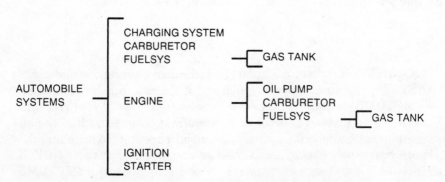

Figure 5-7 Automobile semantic net as a hierarchical semantic net.

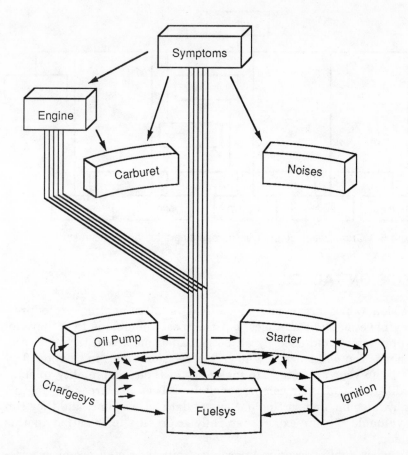

Figure 5-8 Refinement of domain view to a hierarchical semantic network in perspective.

Once the domain representation has been made hierarchical, you are at liberty to choose a style of hierarchical representation that best suits your needs. Under certain circumstances, the representation shown in Figure 5-9 of the same information may also be useful, especially in discussions with nontechnical persons. All three representations in Figures 5-7, 5-8, and 5-9 are logically equivalent. The ability to present hierarchical information in a variety of forms is a major advantage.

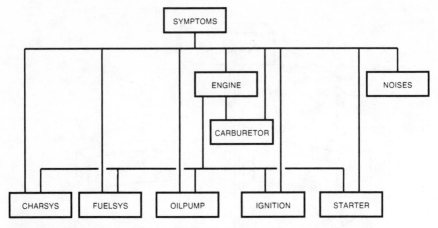

Figure 5-9 Organization chart style representing a hierarchical structure.

DECISION TABLES

Decision tables are a proven method for documenting procedures. They have many advantages, but the most valuable is that they can be understood and used by all both management and technical professions. You will learn how to create decision tables in Chapter 6. It will be to your advantage to make use of their adaptability to standardization and their comprehensibility. They are great for capturing, cataloging, and sorting out lots of data at one time, and they can be valuable if your expert naturally expresses information in this fashion

Decision tables describe knowledge, but they may not clearly describe a decision process. This is one of the disadvantages of using decision tables. They lend themselves to a specific type of inference engine called an induction tool. The input to most induction tools is tables (see Chapter 4). Tables can be converted to trees by running them through an induction tool. This is acceptable as a step in refining knowledge, but it should not be used to deliver a production system unless it is carefully validated.

As you will see in Chapter 6, decision tables can also be used as input to semantic nets and decision trees. This is valuable when multiple representation techniques are needed. Multiple techniques might be needed when building a complex knowledge system or when the subject area contains a lot of information that must be used in different ways to solve a problem or reach a goal. The "collisions" example portrayed in the Uneeda Phone Company is an example of an application that is facilitated by se of decision tables.

ATTRIBUTES									
shape	round	round	round	round	oblong	oblong	oblong	oblong	
smell	acid	acid	sweet	sweet	sweet	sweet	acid	sweet	
color	yellow	orange	yellow	red	yellow	yellow	orange	green	—>>
taste	sour	sweet	sweet	sweet	sweet	sweet	sour	sweet	
skin	rough	rough	smooth	smooth	smooth	smooth	smooth	smooth	
sees	yes	yes	yes	yes	yes	yes	yes	yes	
CONCLUSIONS									
grapefruit	x								
orange		x							—>>
apple			x	x					
banana					x				
pear						x		x	
kumquat							x		

Figure 5-10 Decision table based on dialogue with fruit expert.

Example 1 — Dialogue on Identifying Fruit

Typical dialogue between Expert (E) and Knowledge Engineer (KE) on identifying fruit:

KE: **Tell me how I can recognize a fruit.**

E: Do you want me to just tell you about fruits?

KE: **Yeah, in fact I have some in my lunch box over here.**

E: (*picks up grapefruit*) Well, this is a grapefruit. It's round, has an acid smell, yellow color, kind of sour, the skin is rough, and it is full of seeds.

KE: **So you consider shape, smell, color, taste, skin, and seeds. Is that right?**

E: Yeah.

KE: **Tell me about these other fruits. Would you consider the same criteria?**

E: That's all I think about, I guess.

KE: **OK, let me make up a decision table (Figure 5-10), and let's fill it in.**

E: OK, what's a decision table look like?...and so on....

Example 2 — Uneeda Phone Service

The decision table (Figure 5-11) is perfect for depicting the combinations of options and features for the Uneeda Phone Service. The reason the table is preferable to a tree in this case is because there are

	TYPE OF SERVICE	CALL DIVERTING	ANYWHERE CALL	TOLL DISCOUNT	PERSONAL TRUNK	INCOMING CALL	ELECTRONIC PHONE	TOUCH TONE	CONFERENCE CALLS
CALL DIVERTING	S		−					+	
ANYWHERE CALL DIVERTING	S	−						+	
TOLL DISCOUNT	S								
PERSONAL TRUNK LINE	U								
INCOMING CALL	(1)								
ELECTRONIC PHONE BOOK								+	
TOUCH TONE®									
CONFERENCE CALLS	−L					−			

Legend:

(1)	Use of a personal computer on this line "not recommended"
−L	Must not have low income service
S	Must have standard service
U	Must have unlimited service
+	Must have this service
−	Must not have this service

Figure 5-11 Decision table based on Uneeda Phone Service example.

only a few entities, and a few significant relationships. From the Uneeda example, it would be relatively easy to generate rules. In Chapter 6 you'll learn how.

DECISION TREES

A decision tree may be thought of as a hierarchical semantic network bound by a series of rules. It couples search strategy with knowledge relationships. The nodes represent *goals*, the links *decisions*. When using the tree, it must be examined left to right (root to leaves). It may be reentrant left to right at several node levels. All terminal nodes except the root node are instances of a primary goal.

Decision trees depict a strong sense of cause and effect, just like rules. That's why they convert so well into rules and why they are easy to validate. For ideas on how to validate cause and effect, see *The Art of Software Testing.*[3]

Example 1 — Dialogue on Identifying Fruit (Continued)

This example continues the dialogue that took place in the decision table example in Section 5.2.1.

KE: **This is a great decision table!**

E: Yeah, but it's kind of wordy and not really how I think about the problem.

KE: **Is there a strategy to the way you identify fruit?**

E: Now that you mention it, I think there is.

KE: **What is your first impression when you look at this pile of fruit?**

E: Well, some are citrus and some aren't. That is easy to figure out because citrus fruits have an acid smell, and once I know that I have narrowed the possibilities a great deal. Are these the only fruits we are going to consider?

KE: **Yes. This is the scope of the problem. Imagine these are the only fruits in the universe (grapefruit, orange, apple, banana, pear, kumquat). OK, take a "for instance,": let's assume it is a sweet-smelling fruit. What do we need to consider?**

E: Let me see, they all have seeds, so that's out, and it's kind of confusing because banana seeds are so small and not noticeable. These particular sweet-smelling fruits have a smooth skin, so that's out. I know, all we really need to consider is shape — apples are round and bananas and pears aren't.

KE: **Is it that easy with citrus fruits too?**

E: Well, not exactly, because we have two round citrus fruits in the universe and they all have seeds . . . . I've got it! It's their color and shape that tell them apart.

---

3 Myers, Glen, *The Art of Software Testing.* John Wiley, 1979.

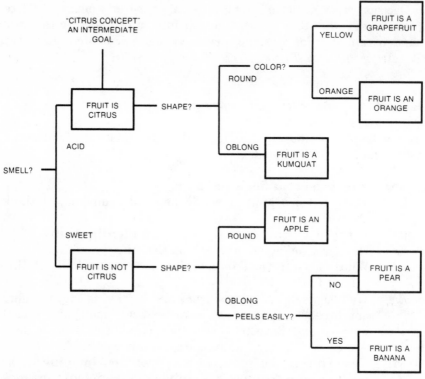

Figure 5-12 Decision tree based on dialogue with fruit expert.

KE: We still need to distinguish between a pear and a banana. Color doesn't work because a pear is yellow when it is ripe.

E: Since color doesn't buy us anything, we will have to differentiate based on how easily they peel. A banana is very easy to peel, and a pear is not. This could be kind of vague but since our universe of fruits is so small it works! . . .

Now we revise the decision tree based on the discussion with our expert (Figure 5-12).

Example 2 — Uneeda Phone Service

Having completed and validated the semantic network of the Uneeda Phone Service example, the authors decided that a decision table is the appropriate choice to depict collisions. However a related activ-

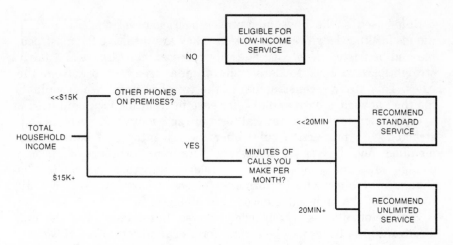

Figure 5-13 Part of the decision tree for phone service selection.

ity, the strategy for selecting a type of service is a simple diagnosis problem and is more easily represented in a decision tree (Figure 5-13).

Note that this tree only represents the part of the knowledge dealing with deciding the type of service. For a representation of all of the knowledge in the domain, see Figure 5-11. When the application is finally built the diagnosis for type of service and collision test will "work together" to complete a customer order.

PRODUCTION RULES

Production rules or rule-based knowledge representation utilizes **"if condition then action"** statements. Given a situation the inference engine seeks to satisfy the condition in the if part of the rule. A true condition results in an action. The action could involve initiating a command to a system process or directing program control by causing a set of rules to be checked.

Rules are easily created from tables and trees. They are a powerful tool for coding knowledge into a form to be executed by a rule-based shell. Rules are inappropriate during knowledge acquisition. They require too much detail too early and distract you from considering general requirement issues. Therefore, their use is not recommended during initial representation activities.

Rule-based shells have advantages over some of the other techniques for knowledge representation. They are intuitive for most people and heuristic knowledge is easily represented. Also, it is a fairly straightforward task to derive the original tree network from the rules. This static reconstruction of the tree has value when validating the knowledge base and also for ease in creating documentation.

In addition to being a natural form of representation, systems constructed with production rules offer the advantages of being easily modified and having a consistent rule-base structure. You can change rules independent of their relationship to other rules. The change may affect the performance of the system but will not directly affect the knowledge encoded in other rules.

The use of rules as a knowledge representation technique also has disadvantages. Rules can be a rigid form of representation. However, if you maintain a modular approach to development, the flow of inference and control should not be hard to follow. In a complex production rule system, rule bases can be split into modules that interact in a manner similar to frames, or rules sets may be viewed as objects. Some of the guidelines for coding production rules will be presented in Chapter 6.

Example 1 — Rules for Identifying Fruit

Let's look at part of the tree from Figure 5-12. The path representing the rule is highlighted (Figure 5-14).

The rule can be stated as follows:

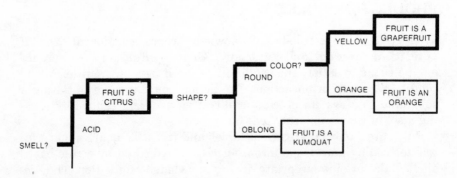

Figure 5-14 Path used to create a rule from the fruit decision tree.

```
IF smell     = acid
and shape    = round
and color    = yellow
THEN fruit   = grapefruit
```

Another way to do the same thing:

```
IF smell     = acid
THEN type    = citrus
IF type      = citrus
and shape    = round
and color    = yellow
THEN fruit   = grapefruit
```

Example 2 — Diagnosing a Starter Problem

The following example illustrates the ability to construct rules from manuals and documentation. The partial paragraph of domain expertise (Figure 5-15) is for diagnosing a starter problem with an automobile. The information is an example of well-organized knowledge from an automotive shop manual.[4]

Starter.   Starter system troubles are relatively easy to isolate. The following are common symptoms and causes.

Engine cranks very slowly or not at all — turn on the headlights. If the lights are very dim, the battery or connecting wires are probably the cause. Check the battery as described in Chapter Seven. Check the wiring for breaks, shorts, and dirty connections.

If the battery and connecting wires are not at fault, turn the headlights on and try to crank the engine. If the lights dim drastically, the starter is probably shorted to ground, Have it tested or install a rebuilt unit.

If the lights remain bright or dim only slightly while trying to start the engine, the trouble may be in the starter, solenoid, or wiring. To isolate the trouble, short the 2 large solenoid terminals to-

---

4 Ahlstrand, Alan, *Datsun 510, 610, 710 1968-1977 Shop Manual.* Clymer Publications, 1978.

STARTER

Starter system troubles are relatively easy to isolate. The following are common symptoms and causes.

1. Engine cranks very slowly or not at all — Turn on the headlights. If the lights are very dim, the battery or connecting wires are probably the cause. Check the battery as described in Chapter Seven. Check the wiring for breaks, shorts, and dirty connections.

If the battery and connecting wires are not at fault, turn the headlights on and try to crank the engine. If the lights dim drastically, the starter is probably shorted to ground. Have it tested or install a rebuilt unit.

If the lights remain bright or dim only slightly while trying to start the engine, the trouble may be in the starter, solenoid, or wiring. To isolate the trouble, short the 2 large solenoid terminals together (not to ground). If the starter cranks normally, check the solenoid and wiring up to the ignition switch.

If the starter still fails to crank properly, inspect brushes as described in Chapter Seven. If the brushes are good, have the starter tested or install a rebuilt unit.

Figure 5-15 Text for diagnosing a starter problem. From Ahlstrand, Alan, *Datsun 510, 610, 710 1968-1977 Shop Manual*. Clymer Publications, 1978. Used with permission of Clymer Publications.

gether (not to ground). If the starter cranks normally, check the solenoid and wiring up to the ignition switch.

If the starter still fails to crank properly, inspect brushes as described in Chapter Seven. If the brushes are good, have the starter tested or install a rebuilt unit.

By pulling out the sentences containing an if-then structure we can construct rules. It is critical to maintain the flow of the information to preserve the order of troubleshooting.

IF	the lights are very dim,
THEN	the battery or connecting wires are probably the cause.

IF	the battery and connecting wires are not at fault,
AND	you turn the headlights on and try to crank the engine.
AND	the lights dim drastically,
THEN	the starter is probably shorted to ground.

IF	the battery and connecting wires are not at fault,
AND	you turn the headlights on and try to crank the engine,
AND	the lights remain bright or dim only slightly,
THEN	the trouble may be in the starter, solenoid, or wiring.

IF	you suspect the starter,
AND	you short the two large solenoid terminals together,
AND	the starter cranks normally,
THEN	check the solenoid and wiring up to the ignition switch.

IF	you suspect the starter,
AND	you short the two large solenoid terminals together,
AND	the starter still fails to crank properly,
AND	you have checked solenoid and wiring up to the ignition switch,
THEN	inspect brushes as described in Chapter Seven.

| IF | the brushes are good, |
| **THEN** | have the starter tested or install a rebuilt unit. |

Would you believe that just by typing these rules into an expert system building shell this will work? Try it!

FRAMES

Frame-based tools use a relational table approach to knowledge representation. A frame describes an object by containing all of the information about that object in "slots." Slots are more commonly known in conventional programming as field/attribute names with an associated value. The collection of attribute names can contain actual values, pointers to other frames, rules, or procedures for obtaining a value. Frames are similar to spreadsheets and databases in conventional programming. A spreadsheet consists of object names (rows), attribute names (columns), and values for the attribute data. These values sometimes require a calculation or look-up into another table. Frames are similar to databases because database records are snapshots of knowledge, like frames in a movie.

One of the biggest advantages of frames is that you can attach procedures to attribute values instead of being restricted to a static (constant) value. This means that the slot can contain instructions for invoking a procedure to determine the value of the entry, as in a calculation field in a relational database. Frames are recommended when any of the following are true about your application.

1. Knowledge is described succinctly or mathematically
2. Significant portions of the knowledge already reside in databases
3. Real-world simulations are being modeled

Although Frames might sound like a departure from the ideas in this book, in reality Frame oriented tools usually rely on rules to facilitate interaction betweenframes.

Example 1 — Sales Performance Assessment

Figure 5-16 is an example of a spreadsheetlike application. A manager completing this form must rank the employee on subjective general categories and document the employee's performance on target goal figures. The target goal calculations are an example of a spreadsheetlike application. While this could be implemented as a spreadsheet, doing so would not relieve the major risk factor facing the sales manager, i.e., justifying the evaluation to the employee. The manager's dilemma rests with the general categories rankings. These are subjective, and would profit from a consistent and documented approach to the decision process.

DAEMONS AND DEMONS

The final form of knowledge representation we'll discuss is one used when coding a knowledge system. Daemons and demons are functions which are not invoked explicitly, but hibernate until a predefined condition occurs. This technique allows you to represent knowledge at a global level without following the protocol of rules within a knowledge system. This is a nice capability but also dangerous, because the process is not directly related to any given program and it can be computationally expensive.

Daemons and demons either run in the background or can be reactivated at any time by a previously defined event. The terms daemon and demon are often used interchangeably, and the distinction is not clear; the meanings and pronunciations of these words seems to drift. The majority of the literature considers demons to be processes within a program (internal process) and daemons to be programs

```
Sales Performance Assessment                    page 1
For:         J. Smith
Date:        10/10/92

GENERAL CATEGORIES          RANKING
 attitude                      91
 client                        92
 satisfaction
 (additional general categories)


OVERALL       87
-------------------------------------------------------------------

TARGET GOALS  OBJECTIVE    ACTUAL  MET  %
 gross sales    $2M         $2.1M   Y   105%
 (additional target goals)
```

```
Sales Performance Assessment                    page 2
                Instructions to sales managers
Fill out the form on the reverse side as part of your evlauation
of sales personnel.

Assign a number between 0 and 100 for each general category,
then calculate the average and place it in the overall line.

Use the following scale when assigning the rankings:

   90-100      excellent
   80-90       good
   70-80       barely acceptable
   0-70        unacceptable

Enter target and actual performance values in the target goals
section. If the goal was met or exceeded, enter a Y in the met
column, otherwise enter an N. Calculate the percentage of tar-
get and place this figure in the percentage column.

Back up the assessment with written comments! You may be re-
quired to justify your decisions in case of disputes.
```

Figure 5-16 Sales performance evaluation sheets.

running on an operating system (external process). We will use the terms internal demon and external demon here. The *external processes* cause actions to happen at a global level in parallel or sequence with a system. When demons are used as *internal processes* they represent reflexes in the system. They act like rules that are continually tried and used as needed. This allows demon knowledge to have priority at all times.

Internal demons are most commonly used to attach procedures to data, so that if a data value changes, it causes a procedure to be executed. Essentially they are a process invoked when an object is referenced, like Macintosh ICONs. By definition, all references must be performed by the act of the inference engine examining the rules. The procedure that is invoked may be internal or external and usually performs functions such as halting or restarting the session, looking for external interrupts, calling a program to get an answer, sampling data, or telling the knowledge system to "forget what you know about. . . ."

External demons react to dynamic data stored in files or to system calls in the database instead of reacting to live data values in a program session. It is possible to have an external process called by an internal demon that is capable of reacting to its own demons, which are external to the rule base. For example, you might call a database requesting a value in a table. Upon accessing the database, instead of finding a value, you find a call to another program which must be executed in order to return the value.

The following diagrams help to depict the concept of demons and how they relate to the other system processes. Figure 5-17 represents the environment.

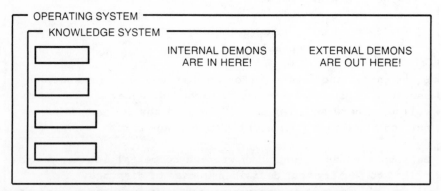

Figure 5-17 Environment showing the relationship of internal demons and external demons to the knowledge system.

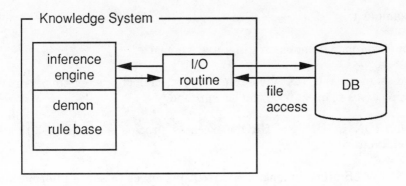

Figure 5-18 Illustration of a call to an internal demon.

To demonstrate how an internal demon works, let's say that a rule in a rule base requires information from a database. The inference engine calls an internal demon, (a database I/O routine), to retrieve the data (Figure 5-18).

To illustrate how an external demon works, let's assume that a knowledge system requests information which must be obtained by running an I/O routine. Without the knowledge system knowing, this I/O routine invokes another external process (the demon) beyond the knowledge system's control. In Figure 5-19, either of the demons illustrated would satisfy the scenario.

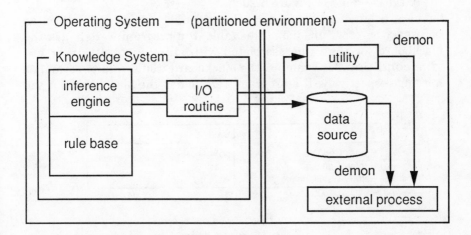

Figure 5-19 Example of external demons.

Example 1

Some common demons existing in systems are:

& sign is a UNIX shell command special character that causes processes to execute in the background

CHRON in UNIX, CHRON executes processes at specific times and dates

SIGNALS allow independent UNIX processes to share information and affect each other

"Swappers" in multitasking systems

GUARD FILES in the Burroughs, Operating System. GUARD FILES are security programs bound to data files, which demand passwords if any process attempts to open a guarded data file.

Example 2 — Data Blackboard

The following is an example of a demon implemented in a data blackboard. (Data blackboards will be explained in Chapter 7.) Data Blackboards are data base systems with "demon" features. Consider the database table in Figure 5-20.

The attributes and values can be added, changed, and deleted as necessary by programs using this table. If a program were to ask the blackboard for the value associated with **starter condition** or **engine condition**, for example, the blackboard would return normal or missing respectively. If a program were to ask the blackboard for the

ATTRIBUTE	VALUE
Starter Condition	normal
Engine Condition	missing
Battery Condition	!sensor1

The exclamation point denotes
that this value is a demon

Figure 5-20 Generic Data Blackboard database table.

value associated with **battery condition**, however, the blackboard would not return a value because it would find a demon posted there. It would, instead, invoke an external program process called **sensor1**. It is sensor1 that will return the answer to the original calling program, using the blackboard as a conduit. The original calling program has no idea that an external demon was invoked to obtain the answer.

SUMMARY

Knowledge representation encompasses the techniques available for translating and storing knowledge as it is gathered in forms that facilitate a good knowledge system design. This chapter describes several **analysis** and **coding** representation techniques for structuring domain knowledge. The ones you choose to use will depend on your application needs, the knowledge engineer, and the expert's paradigm. The techniques available include:

Semantic networks – maps of relationships utilizing nodes and links.

Decision tables – matrices of conditions that are to be considered in the description of a rule along with the actions to be taken for each set of conditions.

Decision trees – a hierarchical structure of information wherein the nodes are decision points and the branches are alternative decisions.

Production rules – knowledge representation that utilizes the cause and effect format IF (premise) THEN (conclusion) ELSE (conclusion).

Frames – representation of an object utilizing a relational table approach.

Demons – a coding technique that provides the ability to only trigger a code or a function when certain conditions have been met.

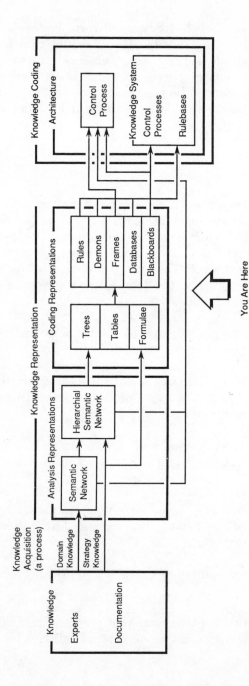

Figure B-1

6

Knowledge Coding Techniques

We'll begin this chapter with a procedure we suggest you follow in converting (engineering) knowledge representations into code. This procedure is only a recommendation, however, so you will see examples of coding knowledge from all forms of knowledge representations. The examples here relate very closely to the material presented in Chapter 5, so plan on looking back. Also, Appendix A contains a detailed accounting of the development of the auto repair demonstration.

The examples in this chapter are fairly simple and limited in scope. You probably will not be inspired with visions of the world class system you would like to build. That's OK . . . . you have to learn to walk before you fly. Chapter 7 will explain how to take on larger, more complex problems. At this point, you need to concentrate on learning the basics of coding knowledge structures.

The recommended procedure consists of seven steps that will take you logically from a semantic network through to the coding of rules.

1. Review the semantic network and be sure that the domain view represented in it will support pursuit of the system goals.
2. Acquire additional knowledge as necessary to fill in any gaps in the semantic network
3. Convert tangle/mesh semantic networks to hierarchical semantic networks.
4. Convert hierarchical semantic networks to decision trees or decision tables

5. Acquire additional knowledge as necessary to fill in gaps in the decision tree.
6. If the application contains multiple domains of knowledge, split the tree into appropriate pieces and use the modular system techniques discussed in Chapter 7.
7. Convert knowledge representations into rules.

You learned a little about semantic networks and hierarchical networks in Chapter 5. We'll learn more about them now, including how to get from this form of knowledge representation to the rules that your shell will use.

SEMANTIC AND HIERARCHICAL SEMANTIC NETWORKS

Semantic networks are the preferred high-level representation for domain knowledge. Hierarchical semantic networks, which can be derived from semantic networks, provide an opportunity to organize the knowledge in a strategic fashion which facilitates creation of decision trees and tables. The authors recommend converting semantic networks to other forms of representation before using the knowledge to code a working system. A step-by-step example is provided here.

1. Let's start with a tangle-type semantic network depicting knowledge about fruits (Figure 6-1). We will assume that the knowledge represented here is considered to be complete and within scope by the expert and knowledge engineer:

2. The next step is to "normalize" the tangle into a more useful, structured representation of knowledge, the hierarchical semantic network. The process for making the conversion is illustrated with a smaller example (Figure 6-2).

   Readers may perform the process shown in Figure 6-2 on paper using the tangled semantic network for fruits to arrive at the hierarchical diagram shown in Figure 6-3. Since the subject of the domain is fruit, the object *fruit* is placed at the highest level of classification, in this case, on the left side of the diagram. Then the general attributes that classify types of fruit are grouped as subclasses of related categories.

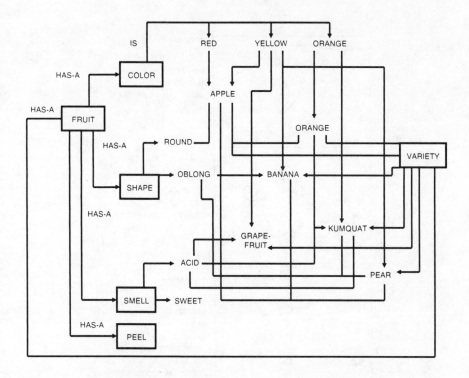

Figure 6-1 Tangled semantic network depicting knowledge about fruits.

3. After the hierarchical semantic network is completed, it is time
    to document the underlying relationships. The cause and effect
    diagrams presented in *The Art of Software Testing*[1] *are an
    ideal first step. To construct a cause and effect diagram (Figure
    6-4), the high-level object, fruit,* is repeated on the far right side
    of the page. Then each low-level attribute is associated with
    the other attributes that will yield a value that can be assigned
    to the high-level object. For example, the low-level attribute
    "sweet" smell may be associated with the low-level attribute
    "oblong" shape and peels "easily" to yield banana, which is a
    type of fruit.

1   Myers, Glen, *The Art of Software Testing*. Wiley, Inc., 1979.

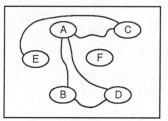

STEP 1

Think of the tangled semantic network as a bunch of balls connected by strings.

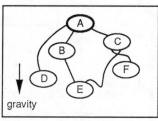

STEP 2

Decide which "ball" represents the highest order of importance. Pick this ball up, dragging the others, so they "dangle" below.

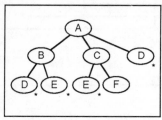

STEP 3

Untangle the strings and spread the dangling balls out in neat groups. In order to finish the untangling, it may be necessary to make duplicate copies of some of the balls and strings.

(*) denotes duplicates

If you cannot untangle your original semantic network, you may have to rework the original diagram based on the following issues:

1. You may not have used enough objects (balls) in your original network to adequately represent the subject area.

2. The relationships (strings) you have defined may not be appropriate for the purpose of your application.

3. You may have picked up the wrong object (ball) to use as the top level.

Figure 6-2 Normalizing a tangled semantic network.

4. Myers' book provides guidelines for mathematically analyzing the cause-and-effect diagram, if desired. Once you are satisfied that the cause-and-effect diagram is complete, converting it to a decision table or decision tree is a straightforward task. A detailed explanation of the paradigms associated with that conversion is not provided here. Readers who have experience with

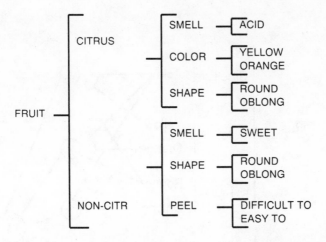

Figure 6-3 Hierarchical semantic network depicting knowledge about fruits.

any of the structured methodologies mentioned in this book should already know how to perform the conversion; inexperienced readers should read some of the methodology books recommended in the bibliography. Conversion of the cause-and-effect diagram of Figure 6-4 led to the decision tree shown in Figure 6-5. This decision tree is ready to be converted to production rules and coded into a shell. You'll learn how to do this shortly.

DECISION TABLES

Let's look at the fruit decision tree from Chapter 5 (Figure 6-6).
You could generate the following rule from the table:

IF shape	=	round
and smell	=	acid
and color	=	yellow
and taste	=	sour
and skin	=	rough
and seeds	=	yes
THEN fruit	=	grapefruit

We do not, however, recommend coding directly from decision tables. You should at least construct a semantic network and validate

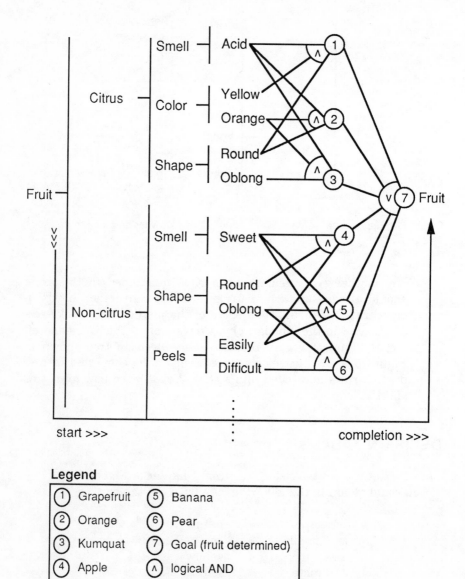

Figure 6-4 Cause and effect diagram.

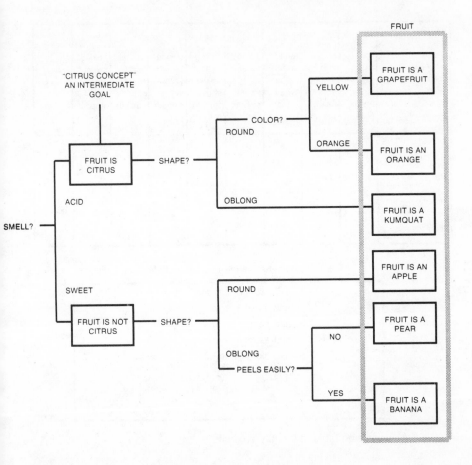

Figure 6-5 Decision tree based on cause and effect diagram.

the table data against the decision trees derived from them. The problems with coding knowledge directly from decision tables can be illustrated by the fruit example.

As defined, this knowledge structure cannot distinguish between a banana and a pear. The table could be restructured to accommodate pears, but the optimal way to do so is not as obvious as it would be in a tree. As the table gets larger, it is increasingly difficult to discover, locate, and resolve this kind of problem.

Some of the knowledge represented is not really necessary in the analysis. You'll notice that every fruit has seeds, making it a useless bit of information. This will result in unnecessary questions. Perhaps

ATTRIBUTES									
shape	round	round	round	round	oblong	oblong	oblong	oblong	
smell	acid	acid	sweet	sweet	sweet	sweet	acid	sweet	
color	yellow	orange	yellow	red	yellow	yellow	orange	green	—>>
taste	sour	sweet	sweet	sweet	sweet	sweet	sour	sweet	
skin	rough	rough	smooth	smooth	smooth	smooth	smooth	smooth	
seeds	yes	yes	yes	yes	yes	yes	yes	yes	
CONCLUSIONS									
grapefruit	x								
orange		x							—>>
apple			x	x					
banana					x				
pear						x		x	
kumquat							x		

You could generate the following rule from the table:

```
IF                    shape = round
                 and smell = acid
                 and color = yellow
                 and taste = sour
                 and skin = rought
                 and seeds = yes

THEN             and fruit = grapefruit
```

Figure 6-6 A decision table to identify six fruits.

it is something that will be useful later, but it is harder to extract it from the structure than it would be in a tree representation. If the table was much larger, it would be difficult to confirm that it was removable.

There is no clear way to optimize the relationships of the knowledge in the table: Relationships are not explicit as they would be in a semantic network or a decision tree. Therefore, you cannot depict any "strategies" in the knowledge base to clue the inference engine in on the best order to ask questions.

If you are faced with coding from complex or large numbers of decision tables, consider using an induction rule tool to create a decision tree to help you sort out cause and effect in the information. Optimize the decision tree, *then* convert the information to production rules (see the discussions of decision trees and rules, below). Induction rule tools were discussed in Chapter 4.

DECISION TREES

Decision trees are the easiest means of generating complex diagnostic style knowledge structures that are easy to maintain and validate. In the following example, we will generate rules from a decision tree (Figure 6-7) for identifying a fruit from among a closed domain of six fruits — grapefruit, orange, apple, banana, kumquat, pear.

You'll remember that when we interviewed our expert in Chapter 5, he mentioned that the first thing he noticed is that some fruits are citrus and some aren't based on the smell. The concept of a fruit being citrus or not citrus has been represented as an *intermediate goal*. When the inference engine examines the rules, it will ascertain the answer to the intermediate goal and then **chain** the appropriate rules together in order to identify the fruit. A complete listing of the rules that may be derived from the tree is shown in Figure 6-8.

As a result of coding the rules from a well-structured decision tree, the system will ask questions in a logical fashion, pursuing the goal

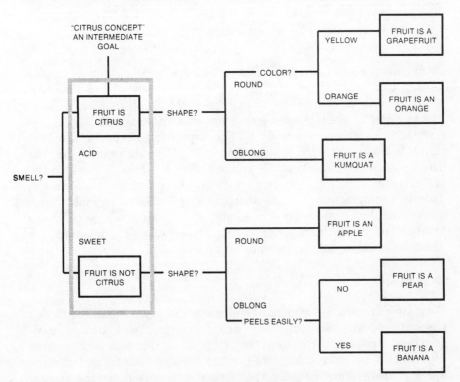

Figure 6-7 Example of decision tree based on dialogue of fruit expert.

SYSTEM GOAL: Determine the fruit

If   the type of fruit is citrus and the shape is oblong THEN   the fruit is a kumquat

If   the smell of the fruit is acid THEN   the type of fruit is citrus

IF   the smell of the fuit is sweet THEN   the type of fruit is NOT citrus

IF   the type of fruit is NOT citrus and the shape is round THEN   the fruit is an apple

IF   the type of fruit is citrus and the shape is round and the color is yellow THEN   the fruit is a grapefuit

IF   the type of fruit is NOT citrus and the shape is oblong and it does not peel easily THEN   the fruit is a pear

If   the type of fruit is citrus and the shape is round and the color is orange THEN   the fruit is an orange

IF   the type of fruit is NOT citrus and the shape is oblong and it peels easily THEN   the fruit is a banana

Figure 6-8 Rules that may be derived from the fruit decision tree.

by hypothesis and deduction. The logical flow of the rules will make it easy to recreate the decision tree if it is ever lost and makes it relatively easy to change the knowledge and rules, if necessary.

Was an intermediate goal for citrus/not citrus essential? No. It is just the way we decided to do it. The expert felt that it was important to make the citrus/not citrus distinction prominent in the process of identifying fruits. If you add the question of smell to the last five rules, you can do away with the first two rules altogether. This is a judgment call **you and the expert** have to make. In a more complex system, intermediate goals can keep your rules smaller and make them easier to read, especially if the intermediate goals make important concepts more apparent.

COLLISIONS

Collisions are a novel and powerful means of generating knowledge bases that can **configure or design a product under constraints**. The use of the term "collision" here refers to two or more aspects of a design coming into conflict with one another. Collisions are knowledge relationships that are characterized by the importance of exceptions rather than regularity. In a typical scenario, the object is to find out what you are *not* allowed to have, rather than to find, the goals/things you can have. In many situations, identifying the collisions or constraints in a system is more productive than trying to identify every combination that is acceptable.

Let's go back to the Uneeda Phone Company example. The "collisions" between options and features could be represented in a variety of forms, including decision trees and decision tables. In the case of collisions, decision tables may be preferable over trees because there will be relatively few entries (the minimum entries are the conflicts, not the accepted cases). Sifting through the Uneeda option descriptions in the knowledge representation chapter, we found that the following simple table describes all collisions between products (Figure 6-9):

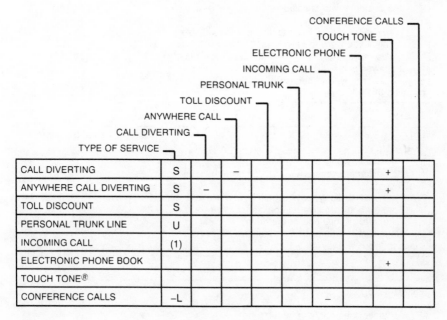

Legend:

(1)   Use of a personal computer on this line "not recommended"
−L   Must not have low income service
S   Must have standard service
U   Must have unlimited service
+   Must have this service
−   Must not have this service

Figure 6-9 Table describing collisions in Uneeda option descriptions.

Rules would be coded from the horizontal rows in the Uneeda decision table. Remember that we want to code only those rules that describe what is *not* permitted, where a conflict exists. By default, if no conflict exists, then the options and service selected are fine. Some examples for column 1 might be:

System goal: find out if conflict = true
               reexamine rules if a conflict is found
               write order data if no conflicts are found

Rule U-1

IF   customer does not want standard service
    and customer wants call diverting
THEN conflict = true
         advise "I'm sorry, but call diverting is available
         only if you were to select standard service.
         You may change you mind about service if you wish."
forget answer to call diverting question
forget answer to type of service question
examine this rule again

Rule U-2

IF   customer wants call diverting
    and customer wants anywhere call diverting
THEN conflict = true
         advise "I'm sorry, but it would be a mistake to sign
         up for both call diverting packages. You
         need to choose one or the other."
forget answers to call diverting question
examine this rule again

Rule U-3

IF   customer does not have touch tone®
    and customer want call diverting
THEN conflict = true
         advise "If you want call diverting, you must sign
         up for touch tone®-service. You can decide
         now . . ."
forget answer to touch tone® service question
examine this rule again

FORMULAE/AUTOMATIC CALCULATIONS

Encoding automatic calculations in a knowledge base is fairly obvi-ous and similar to defining calculations in a spreadsheet. Shells that allow math calculations generally allow you to define any one math variable in terms of others. You simply define a variable to hold the final result, then define the necessary work variables to support the final result. To make the calculation "happen," you need to use the final result variable as a **goal**. *Note*: In this way, math variables will chain backwards in a formula in the same fashion that rules chain together to pursue a goal. If the need for formulae is extensive, you may be better off calling external processes to perform calculations and passing the results back to the knowledge base.

Let's use the sales employee performance assessment from Chap-ter 5 to illustrate the point (Figure 6-10).

A manager completing this form must rank the employee on sub-jective general categories and document the employee's performance on target goal figures. The target goal calculations are an example of a spreadsheetlike application. While this could be implemented as a spreadsheet, doing so would not enable the sales manager to justify the evaluation to the employee. The manager's dilemma rests with the general categories rankings. These are subjective and would profit from a consistent and documented approach to the decision process. A rule-based tool would provide such an approach and offers the following advantages:

1. Automatic calculations are supported as goals.
2. Once the company generates a standard list of appraisal ques-tions, the tool can conduct the interview and calculate the gen-eral rankings in a consistent manner.
3. The tool can print out a list of the interview questions, the manager's responses, and the calculations performed.
4. The tool can capture spontaneous comments from the manager and insert them in the evaluation.

Let's see how a rule base could be built to perform the sales per-formance assessment.

First we'll define the ground rules. We want to automatically gen-erate the average of the scores on the attitude and client satisfaction so that we have one score for each category. To generate the overall score, we'll take the average of the two averages (Figure 6-11).

The following rule forces the interview questions to be goals by chaining them to the system goal:

```
Sales  Performance  Assessment                page 1
For:         J. SMith
Date:        10/10/92

GENERAL  CATEGORIES            RANKING
 attitude                        91
 client                          92
 satisfaction
 (additional  general  categories)

OVERALL        87

-----------------------------------------------------------------

TARGET GOALS   OBJECTIVE      ACTUAL   MET   %
 gross sales      $2M          $2.1M    Y    105%
 (additional target goals)
```

```
Sales Performance Assessment                page 2
                Instructions to sales managers
Fill out the form on the reverse side as part of your evlauation
of sales personnel.

Assign a number between 0 and 100 for each general category,
then calculate the average and place it in the overall line.

Use the following scale when assigning the rankings:

   90-100       excellent
    80-90       good
    70-80       barely acceptable
     0-70       unacceptable

Enter target and actual performance values in the target goals
section. If the goal was met or exceeded, enter a Y in the met
column, otherwise enter an N. Calculate the percentage of tar-
get and place this figure in the percentage column.

Back up the assessment with written comments! You may be re-
quired to justify your decisions in case of disputes.
```

Figure 6-10 Sales employee assessment form.

```
System declarations:

Automatic Average = Attitude, Client satisfaction

Overall = automatic average of (attitude, client satisfaction)

System goal = 1. complete the evaluation

                2. call report generator
```

Figure 6-11 Declaration of the calculations to be performed and the goal.

```
Rule 1(chain control rule)

    IF sales percentage has been calculated
    and attitude questions have been asked
    and client satisfaction questions have been asked

    THEN evaluation is complete
    and call report generator and display results
```

The following two rules assure that the sales data is gathered and then calculate sales achievement.

```
Rule 2

    IF gross sales objective is known
    and actual sales results is known
    and actual sales results >= gross sales objective

    THEN sales target met = YES
    and sales percentage = actual sales results/
                            gross sales objective * 100
```

```
Rule 3

    IF gross sales objective is known
    and actual sales results is known
    and actual sales results is known
    and actual sales results < gross sales objective

    THEN sales target met = NO
    and sales percentage = actual sales results/
                            gross sales objective * 100
```

Any number of questions can be used to generate the attitude and client satisfaction ratings. The inference engine will attempt to apply

them all. To get an idea of the kinds of rules (questions) that might
be used to assign values to the ratings, look at 4–9.

Rule 4

> IF the emplyee's general attitude is "the customer
> is always right"
>
> Then attitude = 100

Rule 5

> IF the emplyee's general attitude is "I can talk
> the customer into anything"
>
> Then attitude = 75

Rule 6

> IF the emplyee tends to keep quiet in meetings and
> not ideas and suggestions
>
> Then attitude = 25

Rule 7

> IF customers always request the employee by name
>
> Then client safisfaction = 100

Rule 8

> IF a significant percentage of the employee's sales
> are repeat orders
>
> THEN client satisfaction = 90

Rule 9

> IF customer complaints have been received regarding
> the employee
>
> THEN client satisfaction = 0

If rules 4 and 6 are true, for example, then attitude would be assigned a value of $(100 + 25)/2 = $ **62.5**

SUMMARY

This chapter has emphasized the steps by which to convert knowledge into the rule syntax of shells, but no specific examples of shells and shell syntax have been given. This is because all shells operate in essentially the same way, with major differences only in syntax and control linkages. The means by which to enter rules into a given shell are, with few exceptions, well explained by the vendor.

The procedure we recommend consists of seven steps. They are:

1. Review the semantic network and be sure that the domain view represented in it will support pursuit of the system goals.
2. Acquire additional knowledge as necessary to fill in any gaps in the semantic network.
3. Convert tangle/mesh semantic networks to hierarchical semantic networks.
4. Convert hierarchical semantic networks to decision trees or decision tables
5. Acquire additional knowledge as necessary to fill in gaps in the decision tree.
6. If the application contains multiple domains of knowledge, split the tree into appropriate pieces and use the modular system techniques discussed in Chapter 7.
7. Convert knowledge representations into rules.

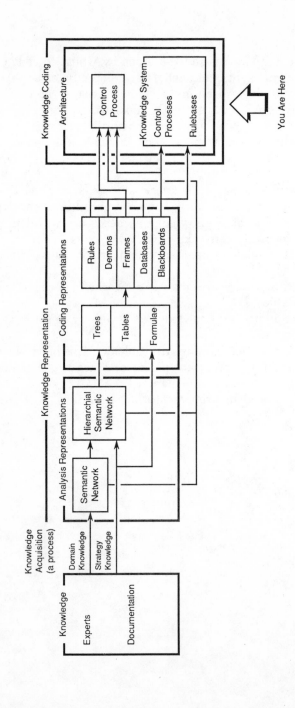

7

Complex Knowledge Coding Techniques

As you delve deeper into knowledge systems technology, you will find that some applications become too big to fit into a single rule base and still be maintainable. In the authors' experience, an application becomes complex if any or all of these situations occur:

The knowledge acquisition and representation cannot be completed in one day or less.

There are several subject areas involved. For example, a knowledge system to deal with a car's oil pump will be relatively simple, but a system that understands the relationship and expertise of all of the subsystems of an automobile will be complex.

The outcomes are probably not reachable by a simple cause-and-effect goal strategy alone, i.e., you may have to use several paradigms.

The system will have to obtain information from sources other than the user.

In this chapter, you'll learn about the concept of certainty and how to apply it, blackboards, and other methods of dealing with complex applications. The auto repair demonstration (Appendix A) uses the techniques explored in this chapter. It consists of more than eight knowledge bases that network together like a team of experts to work out the solution to complex automobile problems.

CERTAINTY

Most shells offer a means of attaching a *judgment of certainty* to your knowledge. This is commonly called certainty, certainty factor, confidence, confidence factor, or probability. Certainty can be attached to the information you provide to the system and to the conclusions that are drawn by the system. Certainty is another mathematical property that the shell maintains in association with the system knowledge variables. It quantifies how probable the conclusions reached by the system are. When rules are used by the system, the conclusions that are reached in the then or else clauses have their "certainty" calculated from the composite certainties of all variables in the if clause. The calculation of certainty can be based on simple averaging, Bayesian probability, or other algorithms.

Attaching certainty to conclusions or goals in your system has great value in the creation of complex applications. It is an additional tool that helps to prune the scope of the search for the goal to a reasonable size. However, attaching certainty to input data almost invariably results in a system that is difficult to validate and maintain. Our discussion of certainty therefore will break down into two separate tracks: a dead end for input data certainty, and a host of possibilities for conclusion certainty.

Input Data Certainty

Input data certainty might sound like an interesting idea, but often it gives rise to systems that reason poorly. For example, sev-

A rule:		
IF	effectiveness of mailed surveys	confidence factor > .6
THEN	consider mailed surveys	confidence factor = 1

Figure 7-1 Example of rule that uses certainty in input data.

```
SYSTEM:  On a scale of 100, how sure are you that you
         smell smoke?

USER:    I am 50% sure.

SYSTEM:  I am 50% certain that your house is on fire.
```

Figure 7-2 How expert systems cope with certainty in input data.

eral shells are supplied with demonstrations that make judgments on a par with the example in Figure 7-2.

This rule was reached through other rules that have "chained" to this rule to find out whether mailed surveys should be investigated in more detail. The shell would present the question to the user thus (Figure 7-3).

The user would be expected to move the "x" to a place on the ruler which expresses their confidence in mailed surveys.

So what's wrong with this technique? The problem is that the question is asked in vague, undefined terms. The user is not aware of the 60% threshold in the system and its impact on the consultation, and the term "effective" is not defined. Is effectiveness measured in sales revenue versus survey cost, number of returned surveys, etc.? If the question had been well planned in the first place, certainty would not have been needed at all. In this case, input certainty was an easy way out for a lazy knowledge engineer.

The question that should have been asked leaves no guesswork to the user. The question is self-defining and explicit. A far better question to have asked is shown in Figure 7-4.

You have at least a fighting chance of isolating the effect and validating your system.

There are more complicated messes that can be created with certainty in input data. Some shells will collect all the rules that may be about to fire and take a private vote on which one to fire. The

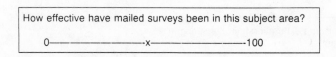

Figure 7-3 Method of requesting certainty in input data.

How effective have mailed surveys been in this subject area?

1. Greater than 60% revenue versus cost payoff

2. Less than 60% revenue versus cost payoff

Figure 7-4 Example of a well-defined question.

decision would be based on which rule's conclusion can inherit the most certainty from the items of its if section. As you might guess, the amount of certainty of the items in the if section was probably gathered on the fly from uncertain user input, directly or in chains from other rules. The result is simply that it is impossible to validate the rule base short of throwing a battery of test cases at the system and hoping you didn't miss anything. How many of us can afford to take those kinds of risks?

Asking yourself certain questions before relying on input data certainty (Figure 7-5). They will help you avoid making mistakes like those we've just discussed.

Attaching Certainty to Goals/Conclusions

Attaching certainty to conclusions is a powerful technique that will make your systems decision process more reliable. Assuming you have taken our advice about avoiding uncertainty in input data (above), then the only way that certainty may be assigned is if a rule

1. Are you asking the right question?

2. Are you clearly explaining the intent and impact of the question and the response?

3. Can you take control of input certainty by offering multiple choice responses?

4. If you decide to employ uncertainty techniques, are you willing to put significant extra effort into attempting to validate the system?

5. Avoid making fact of fantasy.

Figure 7-5 A survivor's checklist on input data certainty.

assigns it as a decision. The first technique that may be used is to **make the uncertainty obvious and let the user interpret the result**. Provide a series of alternatives with certainty ratings and let the user decide how to act on your recommendation.

Let's look at an example. A rule base has been designed to recommend several films to a photographer based on lighting, etc. Each film recommended will be accompanied by a confidence rating, but the photographer is at liberty to use any of the films. The system offers confidence solely as evidence of which film *it* favors the most. A typical consultation might look like this:

> *SYSTEM:*　Hi. I am going to help you pick out a roll of film.
> *SYSTEM:*　What kind of lighting will the picture be taken in?
> *USER:*　**Sunlight**
> *SYSTEM:*　Is "publication quality" required?
> *USER:*　**No**
> *SYSTEM:*　Is the final product prints or slides?
> *USER:*　**Slides**
> *SYSTEM:*　Here are your film options (the final choice is yours)
> 　*RECOMMENDATION:*
> 　　Slide film, ASA 400 probability 7/10
> 　　Slide file, ASA 64 probability 6/10
> 　*NOTES:*　Since camera movement is a major cause of missed photos, the higher speed film is more desirable if publication quality is not required.

The system goals are to rate the advisability (probability) of using various films. A system listing (Figure 7-6) illustrates the system goals of rating the advisability (probability) of using various films and displaying any relevant text (in quotes). The comments in parentheses are not displayed to the user.

The second technique is to **make an agenda** for navigation which enables the system to process uncertainty in a consistent fashion. Putting uncertainty to work within the system is a much more realistic approach than asking the user to intervene with more subjective interpretations. A convenient way to do this is to let your knowledge system identify a list of possible alternatives at appropriate points in an investigation and use this list of alternatives as an agenda by which to navigate through subsequent areas of knowledge. For example, the SYMPTOMS knowledge in the auto repair advisor may make an initial agenda that says "I am 80% sure that your problem is in the ignition and 40% sure that your problem is in the alterna-

Systems Declarations

Determine type of film
apply all possible rules
produce formatted status report

Rule 1:
   IF
            The lighting is bright indoor or dark
            indoor or night
   THEN
            Print film, ASA 1200 - Probablility 9/10
            Slide film, ASA 400— - Probablility 9/10
            Print film, ASA 100 - Probablility 9/10
            Slide film, ASA 64   - Probablility 9/10

Rule 2:
   IF
            Publication quality is required
   THEN
            Slide film, ASA 64   - Probablility 9/10
            Print film, ASA 100 - Probablility 9/10
            Slide film, ASA 400 - Probablility 9/10
            Print film, ASA 1200 - Probablility 9/10
   ELSE
            Slide film, ASA 400   - Probablility 9/10
            Print film, ASA 1200 - Probablility 9/10
            Slide film, ASA 64   -   Probablility 9/10
            Print film, ASA 100 -   Probablility 9/10

            Display:
            "Since camera movement is a major cause
            of missed photos, the higher speed film
            is more desirable if publication quality
            is not required."

Rule 3:
   IF
            The desired final product is slides
   THEN
            Print film, ASA 100 - Probability 0/10
            Print film, ASA 1200 - Probability 0/10

(this rule removes the above films from
probability consideration by declaring them
to be unconditionally false).

Figure 7-6 (1 of 2) System listing to recommend which type of film should be used.

Rule 4:
 IF
        The desired final product is prints
   THEN
        Print film, ASA 100 - Probablility 8/10
        Slide film, ASA 1200 - Probablility 8/10
        Print film, ASA 64   - Probablility 5/10
        Slide film, ASA 400   - Probablility 5/10

        Display:
        "Prints can be made from slides, but if
        the final results desired are prints, a
        print film is more desirable."

Rule 5:
 IF
        The lighting is night
   THEN
        Print film, ASA 1200 - Probablility 9/10
        Slide film, ASA 400 - Probablility 8/10

        Display:
        "Low light conditions will require the
        use of a strobe."

Rule 6:
 IF
        The lighting is NOT sunlight
        and publication quality is required
   THEN
        Display:
        "For best results, please use a strobe."

Figure 7-6 (2 of 2) System listing to recommend which type of film should be used. *Courtesy of EXSYS, Inc.*

tor." The system would next consult the IGNITION knowledge. IG-NITION might say, "Well, it's not me but I think it's the fuel pump." The system would next consult FUELPUMP, keeping ALTERNA-TOR in queue. If FUELPUMP says, "I found the problem, we can stop now," then the agenda is closed and the system comes to a stop without looking at the ALTERNATOR knowledge. You will recognize this technique's relationship to the hypothesize and test paradigm described in Chapter 3.

The agenda concept is a form of meta control, i.e. control outside of the activities of the inference engine. Agendas are really stacks of pending operations. The pending operations are visits to various knowledge bases and processes. Agendas may be sorted by certainty, and any entry on the agenda, while executing, has the power to modify what can happen next in the agenda. You may find it easier to conceptualize as similar to a meeting agenda. The items to be discussed correspond to the stacks of pending operations. The discussion of each agenda item corresponds to visits to various knowledge bases, while the course of the discussion may prompt you to move items on the agenda around to make the flow of the discussion more appropriate, modifying what happens next. Utilities that provide agenda processing go by many names, the most appropriate of which is blackboarding, discussed below. The agenda technique is implemented in two steps: modular knowledge base design and blackboarding utilities.

MODULARIZING KNOWLEDGE BASES

Modularizing rule bases has the same advantages as using modular programming in conventional systems. You are splitting up the subject area into logical pieces. As a general rule, if you require more than 50 rules to complete a rule base, you may have a candidate for multiple modules. Each distinct module is a semi-autonomous expert in its own right. A high-level knowledge system module surveys the situation and sets up an initial agenda. The system consults the agenda to determine which modules to call in what order. The modules, in turn, have their own say in the agenda. Any module can add, change, or delete entries on the agenda.

The decision of how to partition your knowledge bases into modules will probably rely heavily on how you break your domain into classes and subclasses in your semantic networks. Consider the Auto Repair Demonstration System as an example (Figure 7-7).

The symptoms rulebase and each of its subclass objects may be coded as separate rule bases. Each rule base will contain knowledge that is pertinent only to its own domain and provide referrals (i.e., navigation) to other subject areas when appropriate. The outcome of any rule base will be either:

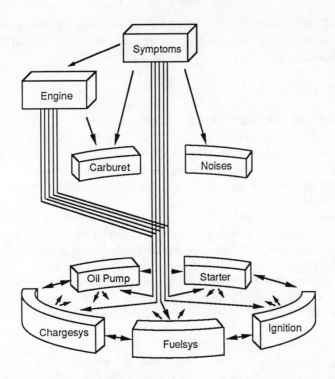

Figure 7-7 Auto Repair Demonstration System.

1. I found the problem (It is: _____)

   We can stop looking and close the agenda.

or

2. I am going to refer you here next: _____

   with certainty: _____

   because: _____

The modular approach is advantageous for development, validation, and maintenance. Appropriately bounded modules are inherently easier to build and maintain. In spite of the advantages, however, modularization is more work and adds system I/O overhead. If
you have an application where the selection of modules at runtime is

straightforward and the total number of modules is less than 7, you can place all of the modules in one big rule base and switch them on and off in banks with control rules and premises.

Control Rules and Premises

Control rules are procedural code placed in a rule form. They direct the attention of the inference engine to a specific place in a specific order. An example of a control rule was found in the formulae example in Chapter 6.

The goal in this rule (Figure 7-8) is *evaluation is complete*. To reach that goal, the three premises in the if part take on the power of goals, causing the inference engine to seek sales percentage, attitude rating, and client satisfaction in sequential order. The rules that deal with these three subjects know nothing about each other's subjects and do not interact with each other's data. Therefore, they have the autonomy of modules. The rule does not participate in analysis of the domain. Rather, it forces the inference engine to examine the domain in a specific sequence.

Control premises are placed in the if part of rules and act as switches to prevent them from firing unless selection criteria are met. Control premises may actually be useful knowledge or they may be limited to control purposes. Recall the example of fruit identification from Chapter 6. Four rules from the listing are given in Figure 7-9.

The third and fourth rules contain a control premise in their if sections: the concept of **citrus** versus **noncitrus**. This control premise acts as a switch to a particular bank of knowledge. For any given fruit, only one of the banks will apply. The first and second rules are

```
Rule 1 (chain control rule)

    IF sales percentage has been calculated
    and attitude questions have been asked
    and client-satisfaction questions have been asked

    THEN evaluation is complete
    and call report generator and display results
```

Figure 7-8 Control rule found in the formulae example.

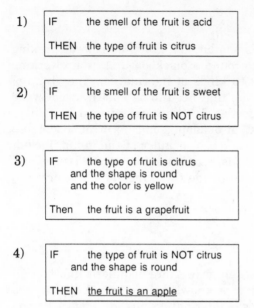

1)

IF   the smell of the fruit is acid

THEN   the type of fruit is citrus

2)

IF   the smell of the fruit is sweet

THEN   the type of fruit is NOT citrus

3)

IF   the type of fruit is citrus
          and the shape is round
          and the color is yellow

Then   the fruit is a grapefruit

4)

IF   the type of fruit is NOT citrus
          and the shape is round

THEN   the fruit is an apple

Figure 7-9 Rules from fruit identification example.

control rules in a sense, but they are also valid knowledge rules, because smell and citrus/noncitrus are useful things to consider when identifying the fruit.

The problem with using control rules and control premises is that they may become extensive and confusing as the rule base becomes more complex, because more and more protection is needed to keep the rules from interacting. In some systems, it can become necessary to bind control premises on top of every knowledge rule in order to prevent an aggressive inference engine from wandering into the wrong rules. It is amazing to see how fast the actual knowledge in the system becomes clouded and unmaintainable due to the influx of procedural code hiding in the control rules. Why is procedural code a hassle? Because the inference engine has its own procedure to follow. Forcing it to do something else has a lot in common with lion training. Slip up just once in your control rules and you will get an unwelcome surprise.

If you find that more than 10% of your rules become control rules, then you should break your rule base into separate modules and use the agenda techniques.

BLACKBOARDS

The concept of a blackboard is similar to a group of experts working out a problem while standing around a blackboard. A group working around a blackboard shares two kinds of information. The group of experts share bits of information that need to be known by everyone involved. Utilities that provide this function are referred to as data blackboards. The group must also adopt some form of leadership which moderates the activities of each member of the group, including: order of speakers, digressions, reexamination of the issues, and when to wrap up. Utilities that provide this function are referred to as control blackboards.

Data Blackboards

Data blackboards are databases used to share or inherit information between different components in a knowledge system. A typical use for data blackboarding is to pass information already known by one component in the knowledge system to another component so that it will not need to pursue the information separately. Data blackboarding is used extensively in the auto repair demonstration system listed in Appendix A. For example, when the engine rule base decides, in rule 3 (Figure 7-10), that the ignition rule base is to be consulted next, it places the engine symptom on the data blackboard before calling IGNITION. ENGINE does this so that IGNITION will know what the symptoms are without asking the user a second time.

```
ENGINE Rule 3

IF
        engine symptom              = WILL NOT START
        and spark getting to plugs  = NO

THEN
        post "engine will not start" to global data blackboard
        queue IGNITION rule base in control blackboard
```

Figure 7-10 Example of rule posting data to a data blackboard.

Control Blackboards

Control blackboards may be thought of as queue managers for knowledge systems. They strongly resemble the job schedule managers in conventional operating systems. Control blackboards let the knowledge system schedule and prioritize access to modules. When a particular class or subclass of knowledge is invoked, a queue of instructions (command script) is loaded and executed. The control blackboard provides meta control to supervise module interactions and operations including initialization, data to be obtained from other knowledge sources (inheritance), access to the rule base, data to be inherited by someone else (bequest), and iteration.

The following diagram in Figure 7-11 provides a detailed anatomy of a control blackboard network.

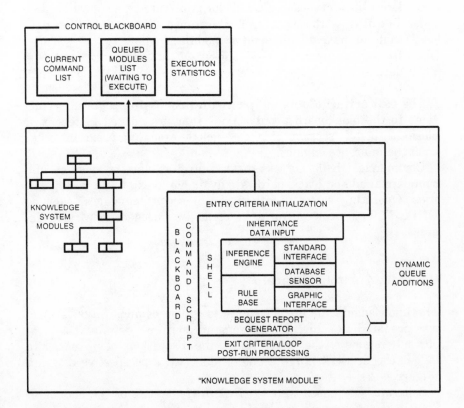

Figure 7-11 Detailed anatomy of a control blackboard network.

Let's analyze this diagram in detail. The *control blackboard* manages the queue of modules waiting to be run and executes the command scripts associated with the module that is currently running. You can see from the expanded *knowledge system module* that it is a composite of control blackboard commands and utilities. It contains the *blackboard command script* that tells the control blackboard how to use this particular module. *Entry criteria and initialization* instructions tell the blackboard about actions that are needed to set up the module session. This may include executing programs other than inference engines. The rule-based shell contains pre- and post-processing functions that are documented for the shell as well as the blackboard module. These functions include:

1. **Inheritance** — preexisting data available to the module/shell at start up time.
2. **Data import** — specific calls for information
3. **Bequest** — the reverse of inheritance. New information data that will be available to other modules/shells
4. **Report Generator** — A subsystem for exporting formatted data

The **exit criteria/loop** and **post-run processing** contain instructions to the blackboard about actions that are needed to repeat or close the module session. This may include executing programs other than the inference engines.

Commercial shells possess meta control to varying degrees and commercial add-on blackboards are available to extend these capabilities. Operating systems with powerful script languages, such as UNIX®, allow meta control to be created as needed, to varying degrees.

Use of the Control Blackboard

The knowledge structure for the auto repair demonstration system was prepared as a hierarchical semantic network defining the various subsystems of the car. To make the discussions below easier to follow, the network is represented here with a perspective diagram (Figure 7-12).

Separate rule bases were created to treat each of the classes of knowledge. Symptoms can refer troubles to any of the other rule bases; Engine can refer troubles to the rule bases below it, and Chargsys, Fuelsys, etc. can call each other if necessary. (Names are

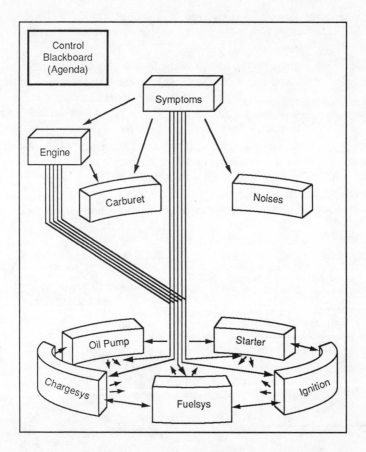

Figure 7-12 Perspective diagram of the Auto Repair Demonstration.

shortened to eight characters or less because of operating system limitations.) Each rule base may be thought of as a "class" of knowledge, "module," or "object." The system was integrated using a control blackboard which schedules access to and interaction between each rule base module and a data blackboard to allow modules to share information. A picture library is also shown as a repository of graphic images of automobile parts.

Control Blackboards in Operation

The following discussion is a step-by-step explanation of the actions taken by the control blackboard during a simple operation of the auto repair knowledge system. Review of this material will assist you

Explanation of vocabulary in the command scripts:

cls	clear the user's screen
echo	put following text (or blank line) on the user's screen
display	display a bit mapped graphic picture on the user's screen
do	queue commands in the control blackboard
include	synonym for "do"
pause	halt execution until user presses a key
type	display a text file or test graphic image on user's screen
if exist	execute statement if file is present
if not exist	execute statement if file is not resent
run	execute program
!	execute statement/program at operating system level

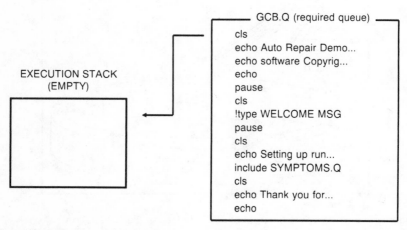

EXECUTION STACK
(EMPTY)

GCB.Q (required queue)

```
cls
echo Auto Repair Demo...
echo software Copyrig...
echo
pause
cls
!type WELCOME MSG
pause
cls
echo Setting up run...
include SYMPTOMS.Q
cls
echo Thank you for...
echo
```

Figure 7-13 Queue as it is invoked.

in implementing a working Auto Repair system using the examples throughout the book and the source listing in Appendix A.

When the system is first invoked, the control blackboard sets up a queueing list or stack to keep track of all other activity that will occur during the session. The control blackboard then loads and begins to execute the master queue file, pictured in Figure 7-13 as "MAIN.Q." MAIN.Q and all other files to be discussed ending in "Q" are blackboard command scripts. Please review the following vocabulary listing so that you'll be familiar with the terminology used in the command scripts that follow.

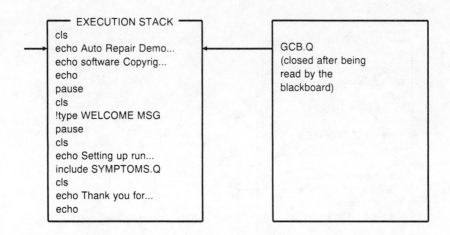

Figure 7-14 Execution control stack after initial include.

After the initial **include** operation of MAIN.Q, the Control Blackboard's internal control stack contains the commands to be executed and MAIN.Q is closed (Figure 7-14).

When MAIN.Q encounters the "Include Symptoms" command, processing of MAIN.Q is suspended, and the SYMPTOMS.Q file is brought into the stack (Figures 7-15 and 7-16). Processing continues with the SYMPTOMS.Q file. SYMPTOMS.Q performs the housekeeping and execution of the symptoms rule base.

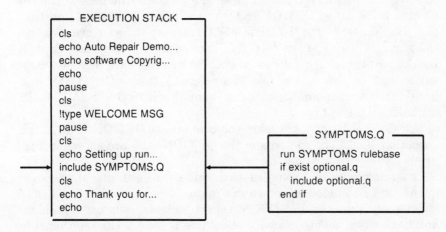

Figure 7-15 New queue to be added.

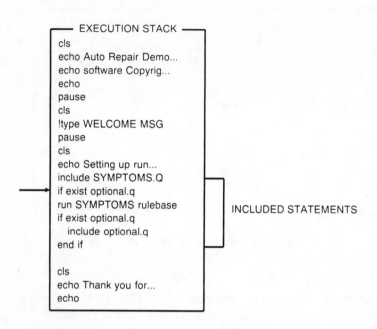

```
┌──── EXECUTION STACK ────┐
│  cls                       │
│  echo Auto Repair Demo...  │
│  echo software Copyrig...  │
│  echo                      │
│  pause                     │
│  cls                       │
│  !type WELCOME MSG         │
│  pause                     │
│  cls                       │
│  echo Setting up run...    │
│  include SYMPTOMS.Q        │
→  if exist optional.q       │
│  run SYMPTOMS rulebase     │─────┐
│  if exist optional.q       │     │  INCLUDED STATEMENTS
│     include optional.q     │     │
│  end if                    │─────┘
│                            │
│  cls                       │
│  echo Thank you for...     │
│  echo                      │
└────────────────────────────┘
```

Figure 7-16 Stack after the inclusion operation.

Let's say that the symptoms expert has recommended that you look next at the IGNITION rule base and then at the CHARGSYS rule base. If this has happened, the SYMPTOMS rule base will have written a file called OPTIONAL.Q. You will note in Figure 7-16 that the final lines of the SYMPTOMS.Q file say "if you see the optional.q, include and execute it." You can tell when the Control Blackboard is executing a new queue, because we have included messages that say something like "Transferring to the IGNITION rule base" in the beginning of each queue below the SYMPTOMS QUEUE.

The Control Blackboard adds the contents of OPTIONAL.Q to the execution stack. The contents of the OPTIONAL.Q are shown in Figure 7-17.

The stack will be expanded to include the contents of the new queues to be included as shown in Figure 7-18.

Let's say that the IGNITION expert isolates your car's problem and knows that no other advice should be pursued. The ignition rule base will write an OPTIONAL.Q containing the statement "disallow

```
optional.q

do ignition
do chargsys
```

(do and include are synonyms)

Figure 7-17 Contents of OPTIONAL.Q.

all," which means disable the pending inclusion of all further queues. When the Control Blackboard sees this, it will continue to process any suspended commands from queues already processed, other than **include** or **do** commands (include and do are synonyms). The only commands really left to process in our example are the implied exits from IGNITION, SYMPTOMS, and the two **echoes** and a **clear screen** statement from MAIN.Q. As these finish, you are returned to the DOS prompt, as shown in Figure 7-19.

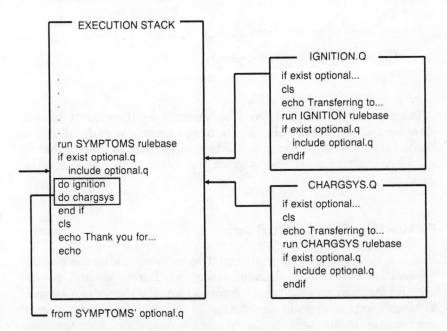

Figure 7-18 Expansion of stack with new queues.

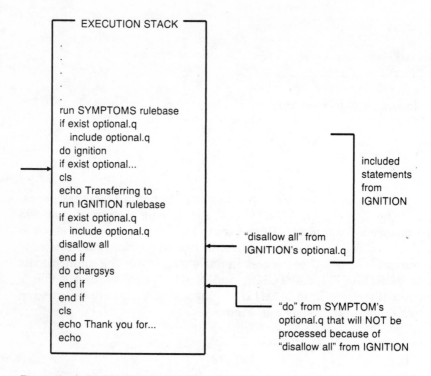

Figure 7-19 Conclusion of execution of stack.

The Control Blackboard frees up memory as it executes queued statements. Therefore, a blackboard can be enormous and still run in limited memory. It is also possible to design cyclic processes that do not have a finite start and stop as the auto repair demonstration does.

EXTERNAL DATA SOURCES

In any system design, one goal should be to avoid asking the user for information that can be obtained elsewhere. Databases and sensors are an ideal way to obtain such information. Databases can be used as blackboards to provide communication between knowledge system components. Databases can also be used as repositories for transient details and to store historical and audit data, patterns, and trends.

In many applications, the details of the facts are transient, but the basic reasoning about the facts doesn't change. An example might be a system like MICON, cited in Chapter 3, which designs computer boards. Over time, vendors will change the minor electronic components used in the design. Tolerances and performance characteristics of specific component types will change. As long as MICON is kept informed of changes in component details via a database, its ability to design systems will not be impaired. This is because the rules in MICON understand the basic behavior of the components and how to select the best match from the details currently available in the database. Physical component details are avoided in the knowledge base whenever possible.

Knowledge systems can profit from access to historical data about their domain. Historical data may be posted by the knowledge system itself, as well as by other applications and sensors, then read back as needed. An example might be a knowledge system used as an online monitor for a computer site. The knowledge system would periodically connect to the various computer hosts and examine the console log (saved in a database). If the online monitor recognized a pattern of activity in the host which would lead to a system failure, it could take corrective action. It might also check its own history database, to determine if it was seeing this problem regularly. Any problems which seemed to be recurrent would be reported to the system operator.

It may be useful for your knowledge system to know physical details about the domain environment. When you are prototyping, it's OK to ask the user to describe the physical environment. When you go into production, however, inputs such as temperature, voltage, lights, etc. should be automated as much as possible to speed system operation and remove subjectivity.

BACKTRACKING

Backtracking allows an inference engine to retreat from the current hypothesis in order to examine another. This effect is essential to the implementation of design and configuration applications. The means of implementing backtracking includes forgetting information and asserting new alternatives at dead ends. This is also known as "truth maintenance."

Let's go back to the Uneeda Phone Company to look at an example of forgetting information. The rule below detects a problem in the design of a customer's phone account. The conflicting information is discarded (forgotten), which causes the inference engine to seek new data in order to complete the service order.

Rule: U-1

IF   customer does not want standard service
and customer wants call diverting

THEN *conflict = true*
advise "I'm sorry but call diverting is available
only if you were to select standard service. You may
change your mind about service if you wish."

forget answer to call diverting question

forget answer to type of service question
examine this rule again

Note that after forgetting the answers to both questions, we must invoke the rule again to get new answers.

Another example of forgetting can be found in the STARTER rule base of the auto repair demonstration. The forget feature is used in the following situation to implement multiple skill levels (Figure 7-20).

The STARTER rule base needs to know whether the car's battery has sufficient charge to crank the engine. Obviously, if the battery is dead, this is not a starter problem. There is a chance, however, that the user is not familiar with hydrometers which are used to test batteries. Therefore, the answer to the question "Check the battery with a hydrometer. Is the battery OK?" has **three** answers:

Yes, No, and How (do I check?)

If the user answers "How?," then the inference engine displays a picture to teach the user how a hydrometer is used. After the picture is displayed, the forget commands cause the inference engine to forget that it had ever considered this rule. The user will again be prompted for the battery condition and can continue the session by answering Yes or No.

If a major chain dead-ends and fails, use an intermediate goal to start a new chain in a different section of the rule base. In our auto repair demonstration, the ENGINE rule base has a series of rules to determine an action or referral based on the misfiring of a running engine. The investigation is complex, and the expert's strategy is not "airtight" for every possibility. One of the potential "dead ends" is

Rule 3 (from theSTARTER rule base)

IF:

STARTER SYSTEM: What symptoms are evident? ...Engine
cranks very slowly or Engine does not crank at all.

and STARTER SYSTEM: Turn on the headlights and isnpect them.
Are they VERY dim? ...NO (or only slightly dim).

and STARTER SYSTEM: Check the battery wiring for breaks,
shorts, or dirty connections. Does everything appear to be
OK? .. YES

and STARTER SYSTEM: Check the battery with a hydrometer. Is
the battery OK? ...HOW (do I check?)

THEN:

display the HYDROMTR.TST picutre

and forget answer to the last question

and forget that this rule fired

NOTE:
SHOW "HOW" TO PERFORM A HYDROMETER TEST AND ASK THE QUES-
TION AGAIN.

Figure 7-20 Example of forgetting information. (The rules that expect the YES
and NO answers are not illustrated here. See the complete source code listing
in Appendix A for further information.)

illustrated in the rule below (Figure 7-21) taken from the ENGINE
rule base. If the user's information causes the investigation to reach
an impasse, however, the expert does not want to give up on the
user's problem. Thus, the rule below and several others give the user
a second chance to try a slightly different interpretation of the misfiring behavior of their engine. The alternatives available at this particular dead end include erratic miss, miss at idle only, and miss at
high speed only. The new subgoal that the user selects will cause
new branches in the tree to become active. This is an explicit example, because the user chooses the new direction. The rule itself could
have made the decision just as easily, in the background, using
available information, sensors, certainty factors, etc.

IF:

> ENGINE: What proglem are you experiencing? ...Engine misses.

and   ENGINE: How does the engine "miss"? ...steadily.

and   ENGINE: What happens if you disconnect a spark plug wire (ONE PLUG AT A TIME) and ground it while the engine is running? Replace the last wire before you try another. ...Disconnecting any plug has the same effect; the missing gets worse.

and   ENGINE: All of your cylinders seemto be functioning so my strategy for "steady miss" is exhausted. Think again about the nature of your problem and choose the most appropriate of the following: ...Engine misses erratically at all speeds.

THEN:

> assert ENGINE: How does the engine "miss"? ... erratically at all speeds.

NOTE: THE USER HAS INDICATED AN ENGINE MISS. WHILE THEY MAY HAVE PICKED THE WRONG ATTRIBUTE FOR ENGINE MISS, WE CAN'T ASSUME THERE IS NO MISS AT THIS POINT. LET'S USE "NONMONOTO-NIC REASONING" AND ADD TO THE INFORMATION ALREADY KNOWN ABOUT THE MISSING ENGINE.

Figure 7-21 Example of a dead-end situation.

SUMMARY

There are times when applications are too big to fit into a single rule base and still be maintainable. A variety of techniques are available that will provide you with the means for dealing with complexity. The most important of these are:

Certainty — a mathematical property that attaches a confidence factor to the conclusions reached by rules.

Modularization — similar to modular programming. Partitioning the rule base into modules.

Blackboard

Control blackboard — a means of controlling the flow of a knowledge system by allowing modules to schedule and prioritize processing.
Data blackboard — a means of passing information from one module of the system to another.

External Data Sources — making use of sensors, historical data, databases, etc. to avoid asking the user for data that can be obtained elsewhere.

Backtracking — the retreat of the inference engine from examination of the current hypothesis in order to pursue another.

Learning to use the techniques in this chapter will allow you to start building significant applications using rule-based systems without resorting to exotic approaches. Use the source listing of the auto repair demonstration system in the Appendix A to get more information. As you become familiar with the techniques, you will soon discover additional ways to develop complex systems.

Human Factors

Human factors is the study of how people relate to the computer and its programs "naturally." The human factors part of any design is important because it affects ease of system use, accuracy of data entry, clarity of presentation, accuracy of data interpretation, and human productivity during system use. There are several aspects to consider when determining **how** the completed knowledge system will interface with the user. We will discuss human/machine interaction, screen display guidelines, user interaction with the completed system, and human acceptance of the system. Entire books have been written about computer/human interaction. This chapter provides a summary of some of the key points.

HUMAN/MACHINE INTERACTION

The user is a part of the overall system. Keeping the user updated is just as important as keeping the computer updated. Satisfying human/machine interaction requires frequent feedback to the user. When making use of special symbols like arrows, graphics, etc., if there is any possibility that the user might confuse the meaning or purpose of a particular symbol, visual help should be offered either by explanatory text next to the object or "help" menus. If you must display the text on a different screen, there should be a simple way of reaching the alternate screen and returning. The procedure to perform this simple navigation should be indicated on the current user screen. An example might be "For HELP, Press F1" or a box labeled "HELP" for mouse navigation.

System states, which consume time or make the user wait for the completion of some event, should be indicated by an active message on the screen. If the waiting time is shorter than a few seconds, the active message might be "One moment . . ." or "Working." Longer times are best represented with an estimated time (i.e., "This takes about 2.5 minutes") and a time-to-completion indicator. As the process progresses, the indicator is updated to show the proportion of time elapsed and remaining (Figure 8-1).

When providing system output, make sure that the "Output semantics", the system's ability to describe the meaning of any system output, is clear and complete. Likewise, the program should make the "actions expected of the user" explicit. This will ensure that the systems's expectations of the user will not be misunderstood.

The current problem-solving procedure or strategy being applied by the program should be made apparent to the user. This explanation helps the user to maintain an "internal model" of the system and its states. In a database application, messages such as "Deleting Old Records" or "Sorting by Key Field" are indicators to the user of what procedure is being employed and how much time an operation will take. In a knowledge-based system, messages such as "Inspecting the Engine" or "Prioritizing Alternatives" indicate what strategy the system is taking.

SCREEN DISPLAY GUIDELINES

Following some simple strategies for displaying text can greatly improve the program's interaction with the user. Some of these strategies may be applied to graphics displays also. The cardinal rule in screen display is that the **screen organization should always be consistent.**

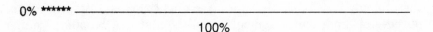

Figure 8-1 Example of a time-to-completion indicator.

1. Use the same area of the screen to display a particular type of information. For instance, do not display menus in different relative locations on the screen. If the relative location for a particular menu is to the right of the cursor, do not show it at the top of the screen. If the location is relative to the text on the screen and the date is normally shown at the bottom right corner of the screen, do not use the bottom right at one time and the upper left corner later for a new date.

2. Show the same kind of data in the same format throughout the session. You might choose to show a date as SEP-11-88, or 9-11-88 or 09/11/88, or 880911. Choose one format and stick with it.

3. Separate different "logical" parts of the screen visually. Either use blank space or (better) lines to separate the screen into logical data areas.

4. Do not display information which is not pertinent to the problem at hand. This helps to keep the user's attention centered on the current needs of the system.

5. When displaying menus, the number of items presented to the user should be eight or fewer. Also, menus should not be nested more than two levels deep.[1] The number of items and depth of nesting affect speed of performance, error rate, and ease of learning.

USER INTERACTION WITH THE COMPLETED SYSTEM

Study the user's interaction with the system after you have delivered a working program. Look for any interaction between the user and the system causing any delay or interruption in the smooth execution of the session. Input devices may include one or more of a keyboard, mouse, light pen, touch screen, or voice input. When using more than one input device, do a time and motion study to see whether the user's reaction time is faster when using a single device or when using multiple devices. For instance, it may be faster to leave the user's hands on the keyboard than to remove one hand to manipulate a mouse.

---

1 Galitz, Wilbert O., *Handbook of Screen Format Design*. QED Information Sciences Inc., 1985.

If you are using color, the colors chosen should not strain the eyes. Use colors which already mean something in the real world (e.g., red = danger, green = OK). When appropriate, allow the user to change colors to suit his personal taste. Voice output devices may be appropriate when, to perform a job, the user's attention is directed away from the keyboard/VDT combination.

System response time can indirectly affect the total time to complete a session by causing a delay in user response time. Whenever the user must wait for a response from the system, his/her attention wanders from the job at hand. There is a direct correlation between system response time and the time it takes the user to respond to a new input prompt. User response delays can amount to a significant amount of the total time to complete a session when system delays between screens are longer than one or two seconds.

Use graphics when they are an appropriate communication medium. It is often easier to *show* an idea than to *describe* it. Pictures are an appropriate communications medium whenever a fair amount of text is used to describe locations or relationships to the user. Text screens that have statements such as "Look for the third button to the left of the red nob" are an indication of a need to replace the text with a picture. Graphics displays are also appropriate for communicating the current state of large systems. It is easier for a user to see a picture of the severity and location of a blocked valve than a verbal description of the same situation.

Watch for logical stumbling blocks in the knowledge program (see Figure 8-2). If the user chooses item 2 in Figure 8-2 (at slow speeds), the program will pursue knowledge about how to find engine troubles which occur when the engine is running slowly. When all options have been exhausted, the system could abandon the user and make a statement such as "There is no further information for engines failing at slow speeds." However, this is not the time to quit! The user has indicated an engine trouble at *some* speed, but has chosen the wrong "subjective" answer. Instead of abandoning the search for the trouble, the system should restate the question. A simple solution would be to have the user select a new answer from a reduced list (Figure 8-3).

With the previous response removed, it will be easier and slightly less subjective for the user to distinguish between "running at idle" and "medium speeds."

A robust system knows how to choose alternate search strategies when an existing strategy fails. If you can anticipate these failures, you can program some of the user frustration out of your system.

```
PROGRAM:            When does the automobile engine begin
                    to run erratically?

POSSIBLE MENU
RESPONSES:          1. When running at idle
                    2. At slow speeds
                    3. At medium speeds
                    4. At high speeds
```

Figure 8-2 A poorly worded question.

HUMAN ACCEPTANCE OF THE SYSTEM

Is using the program easier than *not* using the program? Good programs are self-evident. There is no need to sell the end users on employing a tool which will make their work easier or more productive. Early knowledge system programs tended to manipulate the user instead of the data. Their use did not make a user more productive. Early diagnosis systems were (and still are) notorious for this type of action. In a typical diagnostic system, the user must supply all of the input data. Internally, the program understands what to do with a set of static symptoms (external) and is able to find a solution from a set of static (internal) solutions. This type of reasoning makes the program very rigid. It is only able to follow one line of reasoning which is either too difficult for a novice (because the novice does not understand information required for system input) or too easy for an expert (because the expert must answer many questions which seem oversimplified). This type of program **will not be used.**

A more flexible diagnostic system asks "high-level" questions first. Novice users, who do not understand the required input, may ask for more detailed guidance. Expert users may answer the high-level

```
PROGRAM:            When does the automobile engine begin
                    to run erratically?

POSSIBLE MENU
RESPONSES:          1. When running at idle
                    2. At medium speeds
                    3. At high speeds
```

Figure 8-3 Restatement of question removing wrong subjective answer.

QUESTION ->	Is the battery OK?
POSSIBLE ANSWERS ->	YES (I know how to test a battery and it is OK.)
	NO (I know how to test a battery and have found it faulty.)
	HOW (I do not know how to determine the fitness of the battery. Please tell me more or ask a question which will lead me to an answer.)

Figure 8-4 High-level questions with facility for additional guidance for the novice.

questions directly. In Figure 8-4, one method of presenting this to the user is shown.

This approach makes the assumption that people will "honestly" answer "I don't know" or "how" when they need more information. While **not appropriate for critical systems**, it works well for training or guidance in noncritical areas. This type of program **will be used**, but only if implemented in the appropriate environment.

To make people most productive, the knowledge system must do some work (manipulation and transformation) on the data. The data might be provided to the system via sensor inputs, table look ups, database access, or any source which is external to the user. Users should supply as few inputs to the system as possible. Their input should direct the system to manipulate the appropriate data. Part of the knowledge system should reason about the user's input to determine "which" data to manipulate. Another part of the program should reason about and/or manipulate the data. By manipulating data, "real work" is done for the user. This type of program **will be used** because it is performing a service for the user which they would have had to do themselves without the program.

SUMMARY

It is important to pay special attention to the interface between the program and the user. Remember that your goal is to provide your user with a system that is presented clearly and is easy to use. The system should support accurate data entry and interpretation. Human productivity during system use is most important. These goals can only be met by considering the user as part of the whole system.

9

Software and Hardware Selection

Before implementing any computer system, you must consider the factors of "best fit." You could use a Rolls Royce to haul dirt, but it would probably not be the best use of resources (What would the neighbors think?). This chapter will cover matching resources to the needs of the completed system, both during and after development. Software selection issues include:

Purchasing or Building-Your-Own System
Representation Scheme(s) Available in the Tool
Features Available in the Tool
Matching the Problem to the Type of Tool
Development and Delivery Environments
Portability

The criteria for selecting appropriate software are interdependent and sometimes conflict (e.g., software features which make the programmer's job simpler conflicting with tool cost). When choosing a tool, you should consider all costs, tool features, development/delivery environments, and problem fit. *All* selection criteria should be considered together before making a development tool selection.

Hardware issues include integration with the existing environment, cost, performance, and the software that is available for the hardware.

PURCHASE OR BUILD YOUR OWN?

There is *always* a "build or buy" decision to be made whenever you have decided to commit resources to a software project. If you have a particular need, there is a good chance that other organizations or companies have the same need. There may already be a program tailor made to fit your organization's requirements. If this is the case, you would be hard pressed to make a business case for building a program with similar functionality when the cost of the program could be distributed among several business entities.

As with the knowledge application program, you should consider whether or not to spend your resources programming a new knowledge building tool. Existing tools are quite adequate for most programming needs. Costs for knowledge systems software are not very different from those of other, more conventional, systems. PC-based tools range from $99 to $10,000 (1988), minicomputer tools (specialized workstation tools also fall into this category) from $1500 to $75,000, and mainframe tools from $25,000 to $250,000. These seemingly outrageous figures are not unreasonable when one considers both the developer's costs and the number of machines available for delivery.

Generally, minicomputer software is about 10 times more expensive than PC software and mainframe software is about 10 times more expensive than minicomputer software. A higher price does not necessarily mean more functionality. Many PC tools have the same or better functionality than their mainframe counterparts but lack a mainframe delivery platform.

It is important to match a tool's existing functions and cost to your application needs while considering both the development and delivery environments. It is perfectly acceptable to develop on a PC in one tool and deliver on a mainframe in another, provided you have included the additional training, installation, and software costs in the project estimates. Functionality is critical. Be sure to pick tools which deliver the functions required for the project. If you spend money on a tool which does not provide what you need, you are going to end up spending more, either by purchasing another tool which *will* do the job, or programming around the deficiencies in the initial tool.

There are certain circumstances under which building your own shell might be appropriate. Rule, frame, or object capture rates can be much higher using specialized tools. They might be a better fit for your particular needs. Shells that specialize in capturing knowledge about a specific type of domain often outstrip their generic counterparts in the time taken to code the knowledge. For instance, you might create a tool which specializes in factory process management. If you build a tool that "understands" factory processes (i.e., inventory, assembly queues, delivery rates, etc.), you will not have to handle those processes as special cases. They will be part of the programming environment. As such, your attention remains focused upon the important aspects of the domain instead of concepts which should be peripheral to the problem.

Another circumstance under which you might build your own tool is when existing tools do not have the internal facilities you consider important for either program development or program maintenance. Each tool maker offers a subset of possible features, but no vendor offers everything possible in a single package yet. This stems from the fact that the industry is still young. Features that will someday be considered impossible to live without either exist but have not been implemented in every tool or have yet to be invented.

The disadvantages of building your own shell are economics . . . economics . . . economics. Consider what will happen if you build a tool that is not general enough to handle "general" problems. Tools that have been built for special purposes cannot be applied to general knowledge problems without extra programming work. Spending time to build a tool for a single application will not be cost effective unless the application (and potential payback) is *very* large.

Development costs are only a part of the total cost of the tool. You will bear the maintenance burden when bugs are discovered or new features are needed to support continued use of the tool. Building any tool is expensive in terms of money and time. You should not waste either.

FEATURES AVAILABLE IN THE TOOL

The *way* knowledge is expressed is a product of the type of tool used to represent the knowledge and the features available in the tool. While some knowledge is best represented as a set of rules, other knowledge may be better expressed as frames, objects or procedures. Knowing how and when to fit a particular tool to a particular problem will help you to develop versatile, robust, and explicit knowledge bases. Throughout this chapter we will describe the features you might expect to find in knowledge representation tools, why you might want them, and how they might best be used.

Representation Schemes

Three basic inference engine types are in wide use today: induction, rule, and frame. In addition, frame representation languages, object-oriented languages, and conventional languages facilitate knowledge representation at a more fundamental (and abstract) level.

The languages are not dealt with in any detail here. However, you should be aware that using a knowledge representation tool is not a **requirement** for capturing and coding information. Capturing and coding knowledge has been done for many years (albeit with difficulty) in conventional languages. In fact, certain kinds of knowledge (i.e., procedural knowledge) are better represented in conventional languages than in inference engines.

Let's look at what you can expect to find in the various inference tools. Induction tools attempt to assimilate and place order upon tabular data supplied by the user or programmer. It is very important for the tool maker to communicate the essence of the tool's induction algorithm to you. If the induction algorithm is more than simply converting a decision table to a tree (most are), the tool maker should make clear to you how they deal with uncertain data or how dependent sets of data are combined. Without such information, you will have no means of understanding how to interpret the output data. To you, the tool will be a "black box" that says "Trust me . . . I know what I'm doing."

Rule-based tools use a treelike internal representation while frame object-based tools use an internal representation that is more like a relational data base with calculated fields. The different vendors of rule and frame-based tools use inconsistent and dissimilar nomenclature to name identical internal features and functions (e.g., goal = conclusion, slot = attribute-name, etc.). Also, several different methods are used to attach math variables and functions to rules. Be aware that these inconsistencies exist between vendors.

Internal Features

It is important that your tool provide as many features as possible. They make knowledge coding easier and provide you with greater flexibility. A review of the types of features available will give you some direction when you begin your search for a tool.

Control Language. The nonprocedural nature of knowledge-coding tools is both a blessing and a curse. Some tools make life miserable for the knowledge programmer when a procedural component is present in the knowledge. Without an internal control language, you must either use abstract control rule structures or impose control via external programs. These solutions make the program's procedural knowledge implicit and difficult to maintain. Look for a tool that has anticipated the use of procedures and has provided a control language for implementing procedures.

Class Hierarchy (Network) for Rules, Frames. Tools that allow you to group rules or frames into a class hierarchy facilitate structured design. Conceptually, you begin to think of these groups as objects or modules of reusable code which function as stand-alone or networked objects.

Network diagram. A network diagram can be presented as either indented text or, preferably, a graphic picture. The diagram helps by showing the programmer or user an overview of structure and organization of the program's logic. The ability to see a diagram of the decision network helps you to identify missing fragments of logic and unnecessary duplication in the logic. Some tools allow the programmer to directly use the network picture to add, delete, or rearrange system knowledge.

Why/How Explanation Facilities. It is often important for a logic program to give some explanation of its reasoning to the user of the program. Unfortunately, the terms "why" and "how" are not dealt with in a consistent manner across all tools. This stems from the way people use the words "why" and "how." When someone asks "why" or "how," they generally mean one of three things:

EXAMPLE 1:   Why/How — Why did I get here?
                    How did I get here?

EXAMPLE 2:   Why — Why is this question being asked?
                    Why do you need to know this answer?

EXAMPLE 3:   How — How do I do that?
                    How do "I" know? I need more detail!

In the first example, the person is interested in the logic behind the program. They may have reached the system goal or they may be somewhere in the middle of a session. In either case, the user would be satisfied with a trace of rule firings or events that led up to the current state of the system. They might also be interested in the programmer's remarks associated with the current rule under consideration by the system. Some tool vendors call this feature "Why," others call it "How."

In the second example, the system is waiting for input from the user, but the user wants the reasoning behind the current question before continuing. This is different from the first example because a single question might apply to many rules in the system (including rules which have not yet been considered for firing). The user is interested in why, at this moment, a particular attribute is important to the remainder of the session.

In the third example, the user has been asked to either perform an unfamiliar operation or use information they do not have memorized. They want more detail or deeper reasoning. This feature can be implemented by the tool vendor or the knowledge programmer by offering "How" as a possible response to a question. Tool vendors call this feature "How" or "Help."

Uncertainty. You may want to represent uncertain facts in different ways, depending upon your application. If you elect to use uncertainty in your program, you should look for a tool that offers more than one scheme for dealing with uncertainty. Most vendors offer some means of dealing with uncertainty, some more than others. For example, one vendor has three vendor-supplied types in addition to a user-defined algorithm for uncertainty.

Nonmonotonic reasoning. The way to tell whether you are going to need nonmonotonic reasoning is to ask yourself whether the truth of some assertion might change during a session. The tool should offer you a means of retracting or changing assertions when new evidence justifies such an action.

Inheritance (and Multiple Inheritance). Every object has a set of properties. The object (parent) may also have one or more child-objects which are special instances of itself. A child is allowed to "inherit" all of the properties of its parent as well as some new properties which make the child unique. The parent may also own "private" properties which cannot be inherited. Inheritance helps the developer to define relationships in the knowledge system. It allows the programmer to treat frames or groups of rules as logical objects. Using inheritance, the programmer does not have to respecify all properties for each object in the system.

Multiple inheritance means a child-object can inherit properties from more than one parent. Using multiple inheritance, you should be able to easily represent "semantic," "mesh," or "tangle" networks. However, in practice, those networks are *very* difficult to debug and maintain.

External Program Interfaces

Embeddable? Whenever you are interested in coupling your knowledge program to existing programs, you should consider, first, whether the tool vendor allows the use of their program without encumbrances (i.e., user interfaces and machine-dependant keyboard I/O). You should be allowed the ability to have your knowledge program called from another program without active user intervention.

Control Blackboards. Control Blackboards are used as job schedulers, prioritizing and sequencing multiple goals dynamically. This enables the system to consider several alternatives simultaneously or to prune the search space with either data-driven rules or data-driven demons. Tools which facilitate these activities help the programmer to modularize and program very large systems.

Communicating with Conventional Programs. The tool should permit you to call other programs from the knowledge program simply and easily. Some tool vendors supply easy access to popular spreadsheet, database, or operating system calls. Look for a tool which permits external calls either from attribute fields or value fields.

External developer interface. At times, it may be easier to manipulate a large knowledge base via your favorite text editor than from the vendor-supplied developer interface. Some tool vendors allow exterternal text files to be imported as knowledge bases. This is helpful when transporting/translating knowledge bases between tools.

Other Features

Some features are not required for coding and running knowledge bases but are still quite useful. They are productivity and human interface tools for the programmer that make the programmer's life much easier.

Trace Reports for Debugging. When debugging a program, there is often a need for detailed trace information which goes beyond the simple explanation facilities for a single rule. You may be interested in the overall flow of the logic (what happened and when), not just the logic behind a single goal. Look for a tool that has a report that shows which rules were fired and in what order they were invoked.

Cross Reference Reports. Cross reference reports provide you with static information about where individual attributes and values are used in a rule base. The report should identify the name or number of all rules using a particular attribute or constant value. It should show whether the attribute was used in the "if" or "then" part of the rule. A sample report from a hypothetical tool is illustrated in Figure 9-1. Inspection of this information helps assure completeness of the knowledge base. If any value is not used in a "THEN" part of a rule,

-Attribute-	-Used in IF RULE#-	-Used in THEN Rule#-
COAT COLOR IS	23 44 85	21 30
-Values for-		
COAT COLOR		
RED	44	21
BLACK	23 85	30

Figure 9-1 Example of a cross reference report.

you have an immediate indication of what part of the knowledge base is incomplete.

Report Generators. Report generators allow the developer to create clean output that is tailored to your needs. It is rare that the tool vendor's generic report provides everything your environment needs in a form that is meaningful to you or your user. Find a tool that allows you to specify your system's output in a flexible manner that meets your requirements and expectations.

Text Screen Generators. Some vendors provide a single, unchangeable user interface. While this may be fine for small systems, larger systems usually require a variety of displays. It is important that the tool you select provide facilities to use displays specified by the developer. If the tool does not have a built-in screen generation language, be sure its external call features are flexible enough for your needs.

Graphics Utilities. A picture **can** be worth a thousand words . . . if only you can get the picture to the screen! Few tools have a complete graphics editing and display feature. We should see more when one of the "windows" environments becomes the defacto standard. Until then, if you require graphics, either find a tool that supplies this feature internally or call an external program that has the ability to display graphic images.

Knowledge Manipulation Facilities. An easy to use developer interface will help you to be productive. The tool should have the facility to add, rearrange, or change the knowledge base in a straightforward manner. You should be able to think about what needs to be done, not how to get it done.

Look for a tool that has simple knowledge manipulation and navigation facilities. It is helpful if your tool can support copying all or parts of rules to new rules, the ability to manipulate the text with features such as deletion, search, scan, and change, the ability to accept rule input in Englishlike text, immediate cross referencing, and the manipulation and navigation of decision nodes from graphical trees.

MATCHING THE PROBLEM TO THE TYPE OF TOOL

Here are some of the features you should look for when determining which tool might be the best fit for a particular problem (Figure 9-2). If you find a tool which has most, but not all, of the recommended properties, do not despair. Knowledge problems can be programmed using rules, frames, objects, conventional code, etc. The suggestions here are a subjective view of which properties are most important.[1]

Efficiency and Capacity. You should know whether or not program execution speed will be adequate. In addition, you must be aware of whether your system will fit into system memory all at once, or must be segmented. Questions you should ask yourself include:

- Will the program all fit in memory or will parts of the program need to be coordinated via a batch system?
- Does the tool vendor **insist** the program fit into memory all at once?
- Can the program be compiled? If so, is the compilation done incrementally? (this can affect development time)
- Does the program make efficient use of memory? (You may not be able to afford the time for the program to perform garbage collection, etc.)
- What is the program's capacity in rules/frames/objects?

(Many vendor's sales people cannot answer this one.) If you do not determine the program's capacity, you may run out of room when you least expect it.

SELECTING HARDWARE

Be sure to consider your delivery environment when choosing your development software. With the advent of powerful personal computers and workstations, the hardware and operating system used for the completed program are often different from those used for devel-

---

1   Gevarter, William B., *The Nature and Evaluation of Commercial Expert Systems Building Tools.* Computer Magazine, Computer Society of the IEEE, May 1987.

Problem to be solved	Applications	Features that would be useful during coding and representation
Classification	Diagnostics Interpretation of data Advice systems Decision support Debugging Repair	Backward chaining Forward chaining Forward reasoning Hypothetical reasoning Blackboard Induction Rules Frames Certainties Inheritance Logic
Configuration/ Design/ Synthesis	Computer aided design and configuration (using a set of constraints) for documents, materials, software, etc.	Backward chaining Forward chaining Forward reasoning Hypothetical reasoning Blackboard Frames Inheritance Induction Rules Logic Procedures
Planning/ Scheduling	Selecting from (planning) and ordering of (scheduling) a set of alternative tasks or goals	Backward chaining Forward chaining Forward reasoning Hypothetical reasoning Blackboard Frames Inheritance Rules Procedures
Monitoring/ Control	Observing events (monitor) and Taking action (control) on any system	Forward chaining Forward reasoning Objects Rules Messages Procedures
Prediction	Forecasting the future based on the use of experience, models, or formulas	Forward chaining Forward reasoning Objects Rules Messages Procedures Logic
Simulation	Modeling "real world" dynamic systems	Forward chaining Forward reasoning Objects Rules Messages Procedures Logic

Figure 9-2 Features to look for when selecting a tool.

opment. This situation is not a problem when programming in a conventional language but can cause difficulty if the knowledge tool is specific to one environment. If you choose different knowledge tools for development and delivery, be sure to include the cost of recoding the knowledge system in the feasibility study.

Many AI applications have been delivered in LISP because the developer preferred LISP, not for any strategic reasons. Naturally, LISP runs nicely on LISP workstations. As a result, there are a number of companies whose host processors are waiting because of a bottleneck caused by a tenuously interfaced LISP workstation doing its little task. Here is an example where a credit rating company contracted development of an advisor system on a LISP workstation networked to an online mainframe system (Figure 9-3).

The LISP workstation is a bottleneck for many reasons: limited message processing, additional network overhead, special training, and special programming staff. Efforts such as the Network Computing Forum and NCS distributed processing may eventually improve the throughput issue, but that is no excuse to unnecessarily use unfamiliar, poorly integrated hardware.

This is bad business for the practical MIS manager. Each new vendor's "box" on the floor pumps dollars away on extra contracts for maintenance, training, interfacing, consulting, new hires, and software.

Moral of the story: **Avoid unfamiliar, poorly integrated hardware, unless it offers a clear advantage.** You probably do not need it at all, and you will rarely need it to start prototyping your

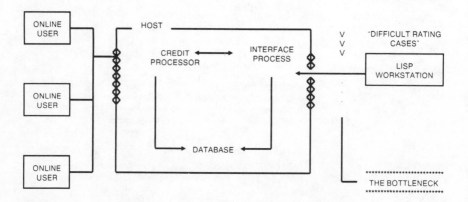

Figure 9-3 LISP workstation networked to an online mainframe.

application. Unless your application requires high-speed interactive graphics, there may be no strategic reason to consider minicomputer workstations at all. If workstation features are required, look into microcomputers hosting Intel and Motorola microprocessors first. A number of tools designed for systems using these microprocessors rival the power of some of the "AI super tools," yet offer compatibility with common operating systems such as MS-DOS and UNIX.

You should expect to be able to develop and deliver profitable AI applications in any environment you choose. If a vendor tries to tell you otherwise, seek other opinions.

Considerations

PCs are a good environment for research, development, and prototyping. The richest selection of tools exists in the MS-DOS variety of PCs, but interesting tools are also appearing for the Macintosh. We recommend that you begin your AI experience on MS- DOS/OS-2 type PCs for several reasons. PC hardware is inexpensive and plentiful, and they are a popular learning/teaching environment. Portability among PCs is not a major issue because applications are easily migrated to other tools and other hardware. There is a wide variety of generally inexpensive software tools to choose from whose quality and power rivals workstations at a fraction of the cost. Finally, the performance of 16–32 bit microprocessors rivals the high performance mini- and mainframe computers.

If your prototype environment is different from your planned delivery environment and you are absolutely certain that your need for a particular application will have a short life, consider delivering the application in your prototyping environment. Accomplishing this will require using interfaces, either automated or people, to get your prototyping environment to talk with your delivery environment.

If you are going to have to code major interface processes from scratch in order to evaluate the prototype, compare the cost and resources needed to interface the prototype against developing in the delivery environment in the first place.

If your prototype environment is the same as your delivery environment, are there sufficient machine resources available to support this project without interfering with business as usual?

PORTABILITY

Ideally, you should be able to find a software tool that can satisfactorily deliver your application in all of your intended hardware environments. In practice, however, many "portable" knowledge systems tools will fail to meet that goal. Even if you do not anticipate that your applications will have to move between hardware environments, they may still be required to move between software environments sooner or later.

Portability Across Hardware

Moving the same tool to a different hardware environment should require little more than slight changes in syntax conventions at the operating system and interface program level. These kinds of changes are generally obvious to experienced system administrators (Figure 9-4).

After you have tried out several candidate software tools for your various development and delivery environments, you will be able to develop a boiler plate procedure for porting applications. The amount of effort should play a part in your decision to purchase particular tools.

Portability Between Software Tools

Moving between different software tools is tricky because of the lack of standardization between knowledge system tools. Crucial features such as vocabulary, backward chaining, frames, certainty/confidence, control handling, efficiency, core requirements, etc. cannot be analyzed and compared by reviewing product literature and demonstrations, *you must try out the tools.*

We realize that a dose of reality is needed in subjects such as portability, therefore we compare and contrast a sampling of features of three rule based shells below. Please keep in mind that these are our opinions and we do not claim to be the ultimate experts regarding any of these tools. You should also keep in mind that tools are constantly changing and that *all three of these tools will have been upgraded by the time you read this book.*

The following comparisons are sample issues for porting systems among AION, EXSYS, and VP-Expert in the MS-DOS environment. These tools were selected for inclusion here because they are all legitimately good tools in their own right, as a whole, they span a wide

DOS to UNIX examples, using the EXSYS Expert System Shell

   DOS '/' control flags become UNIX '-' control flags

   DOS '\' directories become UNIX '/' directories

   Calls to DOS COMMAND.COM replaced with UNIX /bin/sh

   Filenames are not case sensitive in DOS, but are in UNIX. EXSYS expects certain file names to be capitalized in UNIX, assumes others are lower case.

DOS/DBASE to VM/FOCUS examples, using the AION Knowledge System Shell

   Batch calls to DBASE need to be converted to CLIST calls to FOCUS

   Field delimiters used for DBASE might need to be converted to FOCUS convention

   DOS 406K memory limit expands to VM User limit

Figure 9-4 Examples of issues to consider when porting knowledge systems across hardware.

variety of hardware delivery environments, and their similarities and differences make for a rich discussion.

Comparing Portability Issues Between Three Tools

System Architecture

AION ADS v. 12-86	EXSYS v. 3.2.6	VP-Expert v. 1.0
Designed on the concept that rule bases should be built in small sections and hooked together with a limited command protocol.	Designed on the concept that large rule bases can load and operate efficiently in a conventional environment. 3rd party products expand functionality to allow rule bases to be built in sections and hooked together with a network command protocol.	Designed with limited systems in mind that can be described in small-medium size rule bases. Offers the ability to "chain" (goto) consecutive rule bases. 3rd party products expand functionality to allow rule bases to be built in sections and hooked together with a network command protocol.

Vocabulary. All three tools represent rule knowledge in similar IF-THEN-ELSE rules. However, the vocabulary used in each tool is unique. A brief example of terminology follows:

AION ADS v. 12-86	EXSYS v. 3.2.6	VP-Expert v. 1.0
Multiple State Knowledge Base	Blackboard Rule Bases	Chained Rule Bases
State	Rule Base	Knowledge Base
Knowledge Base	Rule Base	Text of the rules
Parameter	Variable, Choice	Variable
Parameter	Qualifier	Menu Variable
Message	String Formula	Display String
Data File	Datalist	Facts File
Certainty	Probability, Confidence	Confidence Factor (CNF)
Certainty set	Sorted choice list	Sorted Variable-value-CNF triplets (see SORT command)
(feature unavailable)	CLEAR rule, variable, qualifier	RESET variable

Core Efficiency.

AION ADS v. 12-86	EXSYS v. 3.2.6	VP-Expert v. 1.0

The MS-DOS version of AION takes all available memory and uses a proprietary internal memory management schema. About 20K of RAM is actually available beyond the tool itself for processing Knowledge Bases and data bases. Careful use of the multiple rule base facilities is essential to avoid memory shortages.

AION's integrated editor and data dictionary improves core efficiency since objects need only be defined once. Objects that have not been defined may not be used. Reports of unused objects are available.

A fixed memory partition may be reserved as a DOS gateway, but doing so can seriously compromise memory needed for system operation.

EXSYS uses the standard "C" large model for memory management. 700 rule systems will fit in 320K. 5000 rule systems will fit in 640K. Memory allocation is dynamic, and unneeded memory is freed as it becomes available.

EXSYS integrated editor and data dictionary improves core efficiency since objects need only be defined once. Objects that are undefined may not be used. Reports of unused objects are available.

VP-EXPERT uses the standard small model for memory management. The small model restricts applications to a few hundred rules maximum.

VP-EXPERT uses a text editor for creating and maintaining rule bases. Misspellings spawn new objects that will cause problems. Cross reference reports are not provided. Some consistency checking is available by examining the runtime trace.

Reading a DBASE Table.

AION ADS v. 12-86

Requires a complex linking of internal system attributes, control and data parameters. The relationship of procedures, control and data parameters is not readily obvious from the tool's cross-reference report.

Because there is insufficient memory to support system calls, the entire DBASE data base must be loaded into RAM and pseudo-read by a specialized RULE BASE.

The DBASE data base must be passed into AION as a comma-delimited file, and a separate schema definition must be maintained in the tool.

Memory used by the data base must be freed up as quickly as possible. Therefore, the data base must be processed in a special, separate rule base that can be discarded when the desired record(s) are located. Selected DBASE records must be passed to a GLOBAL data array, then the special "read data" rule base is discarded from RAM.

Sample call:
  Requires 11 editor screens, and considers the low level programming. Not displayed here.

EXSYS v. 3.2.6

Every object in the system has a "definition," or text. To obtain the value of an object from a DBASE database one simply places a call to the DBASE interface in the object's definition. Whenever the object is referenced if the IF portion of a rule, a DBASE transaction will be automatically performed. (The DBASE interface is a 3rd party option.) DBASE can also be accessed from the preprocessor and report generator sections (meta control features). Access may be sequential or indexed.

Sample call:
  RUN(EXCHANGE table, index, keyname, keyvalue /C)

VP-Expert v. 1.0

DBASE tables are accessed with a simple call from the THEN or ELSE portions of rules. However, no facility is provided for invoking a procedure automatically when an object is examined in the IF portion of a rule. In order to cause DBASE to be invoked by reference, the developer must write control rules. DBASE may also be accessed from the tool's ACTIONS block (a meta control feature). VP-Expert reads the DBASE schema directly. Access is sequential; indexes are not used.

Sample call:
  GET table, key=value, field list

Binding a Procedure to an Object (a Type of Demon)

AION ADS v. 12-86	EXSYS v. 3.2.6	VP-Expert v. 1.0
Requires a complex linking of internal system attributes to control and data parameters. The relationship of procedures, control and data parameters is not readily obvious from the tool's cross-reference report. In order to have sufficient memory to support system calls, the developer is encouraged to use a stripped down version of the tool (CAES). Use of CAES requires that the developer codes replacements for all system I/O modules A series of internal procedures are available for binding, such as READ DATA and WRITE DATA.	Every object in the system has a "definition," or text. To attach a procedure to an object, one simply adds a RUN statement in the text. Any reference to the object in the IF portion of a rule will cause the procedure to be invoked. Run statements may also be invoked from the THEN or ELSE clauses and within the report generator.	Programs and script files are easily called from the THEN or ELSE portions of rules. However, no facility is provided for invoking a procedure automatically when an object is examined in the IF portion of a rule. In order to cause a procedure to be invoked by reference, the developer must write control rules.

Certainty Factors

AION ADS v. 12-86	EXSYS v. 3.2.6	VP-Expert v. 1.0
Certainty factors are allowed on all parameter objects. The User can enter certainty factors when answering questions, and certainty can be assigned in the THEN or ELSE portion of a rule. Multiple certainty expressions may be assigned to parameters in order prioritize search patterns. Attribute-value pairs asserted in the THEN portion of a rule will inherit the composite certainty of parameters in the IF portion of the rule, should it fire. A series of mathematical operators are available for combining certainty.	Certainty factors are allowed on objects called "choices" which are primarily used as system goals. Three methods for calculating certainty are provided: simple averaging, dependent probability, and independent probability. Choices cannot implicitly inherit certainty from objects in the IF portion of a rule, however, the current level of certainty of a choice may be examined in the IF portion of a rule. Assignment of certainty to input data is not directly supported but can be accomplished.	Certainty factors are allowed on all variables. The User can enter certainty factors when answering questions, and certainty can be assigned in the THEN or ELSE portion of a rule. Unique certainty is tracked for every attribute-value pair that is asserted. Attribute-value pairs asserted in the THEN portion of a rule will inherit the composite certainty of all objects in the IF portion of the rule, should it fire. The method used for combining certainties is independent probability.

Meta Control.   Meta Control is the body of procedures and processing options available in the shell that give the developer control over the activities of the inference engine.

AION ADS v. 12-86	EXSYS v. 3.2.6	VP-Expert v. 1.0
Each AION rule base (or state) has a section called "steps." Using steps, the developer directs the rule base to pursue goals, display messages to the user, and branch to other rule base states. Each rule base state can refuse to execute if entry conditions are not met. States can also iterate based on exit conditions.	EXSYS has preprocessing options to run a program prior to the session. EXSYS can receive data from the preprocessor program or from a preexisting file. EXSYS also supplies a "report generator" facility which executes a meta command script file at the end of a session, after the inference engine is finished.	VP-Expert operates from an ACTIONS block, a master command script. From the actions block, a developer has extensive control over preprocessing, calls to the inference engine, and postprocessing, and iteration.
Certainty factors may be used to prioritize navigation among a fixed set of steps.	EXSYS rules may also submit commands directly to the inference engine.	VP-Expert rules may also submit commands directly to the inference engine.

SUMMARY

The selection of software and hardware is critical to the success of your project. In selecting software, you should look for as many of the following features as possible:

Internal Features

- Control language
- Class hierarchy for rules or frames
- Network diagrams
- Why/How explanation facilities
- Uncertainty
- Nonmonotonic reasoning
- Inheritance

External Program Interfaces

- Embeddable?
- Control Blackboards
- Communicating with conventional programs
- External developer interface

Other

* Trace reports for debugging
* Cross reference reports
* Report generators
* Text screen generators
* Graphics utilities
* Knowledge manipulation facilities

Hardware selection must go hand in hand with your software selection and, in some cases, must precede it. Consider the existing environment when selecting your delivery environment. Generally, you should avoid unfamiliar hardware that doesn't integrate well with the current environment unless it offers tremendous advantages. In the vast majority of cases, there is no reason to consider such hardware.

It would be ideal if you could find a software tool that could deliver your application in all environments. In practice, however, many supposedly portable tools are not quite as flexible as their vendors would like you to believe. The more tools you try out (not just read about), the better the position you will be in to judge portability issues. Portability is a complex issue in a field of nonstandardized tools; be realistic in your expectations and investigate candidate tools carefully.

Remember that purchasing software and hardware can be costly. Make certain you get what you pay for and that it performs as expected in the environment you provide.

Part

C

Management Tools and Techniques

10

Managing the Knowledge System Project Life Cycle

Every project has a *life cycle*: a series of steps or processes, set apart by appropriate milestones. Knowledge system projects involve more uncertainty than a typical MIS project, thus the need for an orderly set of steps is crucial. Some of the concepts are similar to traditional software development practices. However, some are different and deserve special attention.

In general, the AI community has not been paying attention to efforts to refine and improve the administration of computer systems projects. For a successful project it is vital to integrate project management, quality assurance and control, software testing, and structured development methodologies into the AI technology.

According to T. Capers Jones, structured means "to use a predefined plan and predefined inputs and outputs and carry out the activities in a rational predetermined manner." This is similar to a motion picture. There is a written script which the actors and actresses follow word for word. The events in the movie are planned from beginning to end. For knowledge system projects the general plan is the management of a well-defined life cycle.

An incremental approach to project management emphasizes prototyping and phased development. Prototyping is a valuable tool for testing ideas, requirements, representation, and scoping for the development team, and it also convinces funding sources early in the project of potential success. Most knowledge systems begin with a demonstration prototype. Once the knowledge engineer and expert have structured even a small amount of information it can begin to be coded into a demonstration system. This allows the users, expert(s) and developers to see as well as test the system design. Change or refinement in approach will surface early in a project if the initial representation method does not satisfactorily portray the domain. This new approach may result in choosing another representation technique or rescoping the subject area.

Structured analysis and design are beneficial techniques for maximizing benefits and minimizing cost and time. Without the structured approach a project life cycle becomes disorganized and chaotic. Structure complemented with review practices are important to project success. To ensure proper review during the life cycle process, quality assurance procedures are essential.

LIFE CYCLE DEFINED

A *knowledge system life cycle* begins with the inception of the idea for the system and ends when the system is no longer used. This interval consists of many activities that are necessary for the development and maintenance of the system. It is important to carefully plan the life cycle. The plan will assist in creating a valuable system and estimating the resources and time necessary for development and maintenance.

There are many life cycle models, most of which are not complete for knowledge systems. A Waterfall life cycle model (Figure 10-1), described in *Software Engineering Economics*[1], *is an assembly line approach. It doesn't work with knowledge system projects because of the need for incremental development. These models want requirements static from the beginning, while in knowledge system development it is often necessary to change views and scoping several times.*

The original Waterfall model had advantages. It introduced some organization to the *process* of building software. This encouraged definition and standardization of project phases, leading to more organized software development. The disadvantage of the original model is that it did not contain any fine tuning or feedback loops for quality assurance and user certification. Several well-known consultants

---

1 Boehm, Barry W., *Software Engineering Economics*. Englewood Cliffs, N.J.: Prentice-Hall, 1981.

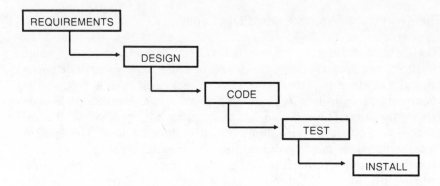

Figure 10-1 The original Waterfall model for software project life cycle.

have made fortunes by drawing review arrows on the original water-fall model and teaching companies to perform walkthroughs. Thus the "modified" Waterfall model (Figure 10-2).

The advantages of this new modified Waterfall model is that each phase of a project can be fine-tuned. This ensures that the deliverable specified in the prior project phase has been completed. Rework is minimized. The model seems to include all the necessary checks and balances. However, it only works for projects where the requirements can be frozen at the onset of the project. Massive rework and re-estimation may be required if the requirements are not completely documented.

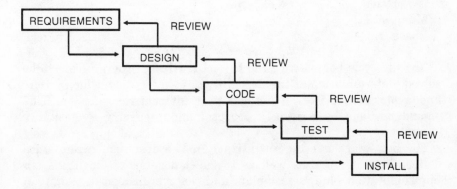

Figure 10-2 The "Modified" Waterfall model.

The Knowledge System Project Life Cycle

Knowledge system projects are "fuzzy." You cannot completely specify the product at the beginning, because the expert's knowledge is not fully understood at any point in the project. As a result, the requirements definition is a moving target and the modified Waterfall model fails. The solution is *not to expect* to freeze all of the requirements, but instead to do incremental development. The system is constructed in manageable units. The evaluation of a given unit provides validation and fine-tuning of the requirements and design and also provides early glimpses of the working product.

The *knowledge systems project life cycle* incorporates the advantages of the modified Waterfall model, incremental development, and prototyping. In large applications it may be necessary to complete the life cycle twice: once for the prototype and then again for the production system. The prototype should be carefully scoped to include as many characteristics of the final application as possible. This will allow you to test designs and validate results with the user community. In most cases, parts of the prototype system will be used as a basis for the production or final system.

There are eight stages in a knowledge system life cycle (Figure 10-3). They include:

Identification
Conceptualization
Formalization
Implementation
Testing
Evaluation
Maintenance
Phase Out

The life cycle begins with the **identification** of the problem to be solved, determination of the feasibility of using a knowledge system, and exploration of its advantages over alternative solutions. This should be done by writing a proposal and preparing a feasibility study.

The next stage is **conceptualization**. The user requirements are defined at this stage as well as the user documentation needs, an implementation plan, a test plan, and the overall logical design. In incremental development, the deliverables during conceptualization must be carefully organized into modules. For example, you will have

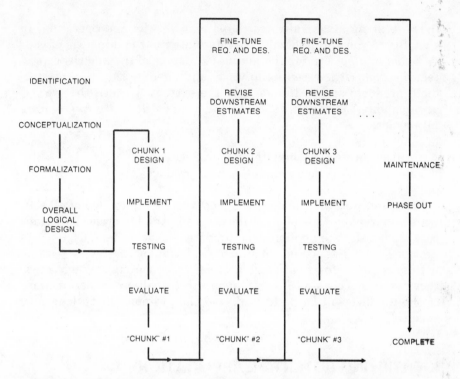

Figure 10-3 The knowledge systems project life cycle. This entire cycle occurs twice in a typical project: once for the prototype effort and again for a production system effort. The diagram was adapted from V. Basiti and A. Turner, "Iterative Enhancement: A Practical Technique for Software Engineering." *IEEE Transactions of Software Engineering*, December 1975, pp. 390–396.

overall general requirements (functions, interfaces, performance) and more detailed requirements for each of the units you define.

Formalization is the stage in which you create the demonstration prototype on a narrow unit of the domain and a physical design of the system.

The actual coding of the system will begin during **implementation**, and the internal and external documentation for the system will be produced. It is during implementation that you will be using shells, programming languages, and other tools to create your knowledge system. In addition to coding, this stage includes any integration steps necessary to implement the product or partial product. All systems or units will require some integration into the environment.

The **testing** stage validates the system results and operation. In Chapter 13 you will find valuable information for making use of your test plan and performing the **evaluation** stage of the knowledge system life cycle. It is essential to verify and validate that the intermediate products satisfy the goals of the system. We use the "verify" and "validate" terms as described in Boehm's *Software Engineering Economics*.

Verification: "Are we building the product right?"
Validation: "Are we building the right product?"

Maintenance will consume the most money (up to 70% of all software dollars) and time of all of the stages in the life cycle. This stage consists of software and hardware updates to the system. Chapter 14 provides more detailed information on maintenance.

Phase out is the final stage a project goes through. When a system has outlived its usefulness, a smooth transition of the functions of the product will be performed, and the system will no longer be used.

IDENTIFYING POTENTIAL APPLICATIONS

Conventional computer systems are doing a fine job of automating *yesterday's* manual tasks, such as accounting services. The potential applications for *knowledge systems* are *today's* manual tasks, i.e., those tasks that elude traditional automation because they require the special touch of human reasoning. If you do not already have an application in mind, pick one now (any one) and keep it in mind as you read on.

In determining whether or not an application is worth investigating, evaluate its **general appropriateness and payoff potential**. Is a knowledge system appropriate for what you're trying to accomplish? Also take a look at **the strategic fit of your knowledge system project**. How will your project fit into the existing workplace and support the existing business process? Success will require good timing, presentation, and political support.

General Appropriateness and Payoff Potential

The Gray Area Text   The first test to pass is the *gray area test* (Figure 10-4): Determine whether your application involves data interpretation or data manipulation. If your application is clearly *only* data

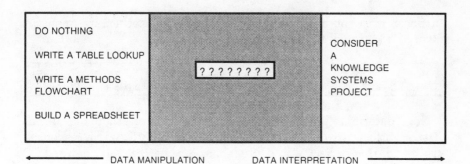

Figure 10-4 The Gray Area Test.

manipulation, then a knowledge system project is undesirable. On the other hand, if your application is clearly *only* data interpretation, then a knowledge system project is **very** appropriate. Most applications are not clearly one or the other. There is typically a mixture of manipulation and human interpretation, and therefore some uncertainty or "gray area", about the approach to use. The gray area is like a fence in the middle of the two possibilities of data manipulation and data interpretation. In order to resolve upon which side of the fence your application lies, the gray area test offers a series of criteria to consider. The areas covered by this test are by no means complete. Use it as a guideline to understanding basic feasibility issues. You may add additional criteria as appropriate for your business concerns.

In the following paragraphs, we examine the issues in the gray area test in more detail, one at a time.

First, decide if the project is worth doing at all.

DO NOTHING	<—task learned quickly <—current solution works fine <—product will have a short life	KNOWLEDGE SYSTEM PROJECT

If the product has a short life cycle or the problem is likely to go away before your project can pay for itself, you are better off not pursuing it. You won't make points by losing money. If a working, cost-effective solution already exists, you can also forget this project. You are not going to sell new technology by fixing something that's not broken.

On the other hand, if the existing application is difficult to learn and/or maintain, your project may not be redundant. Frequent staff turnover with the associated training costs is another argument in favor of a knowledge system project.

WRITE A TABLE LOOKUP	<—simple lookup; simple interpretation complex interpretation required—>	KNOWLEDGE SYS PROJ

Next, determine if complex reasoning or interpretation is required. If straightforward events occur to which straightforward responses are made, this project would probably be a waste of the power of a knowledge system. Knowledge systems are best suited to projects that require a certain amount of logic and reasoning before producing its result.

WRITE A METHODS FLOWCHART	<—simple procedure; few decision points <—stable procedure; rarely revised too complex for one page of paper —> frequently revised —> formal audit required —>	KNOWLEDGE SYSTEM PROJECT

How many times have you seen someone carrying a binder full of disorganized, dog-eared reference pages and cheat sheets? Often the copies are poor and have various anonymous notes scrawled here and there with additional ideas and opinions.

BUILD A SPREADSHEET	<—obvious, verifiable cross-calculations design stretches tool beyond functionality —-> large chunks may be conditionally n/a —> interpretation of results required —> narrative explantion of derivation required —>	KNOWLEDGE SYSTEM PROJECT

Finally, evaluate the use of a spreadsheet for your project. Knowledge system projects have advantages over spreadsheets when the **spreadsheet is stretched beyond functionality and usability.** If you need multidimensional spreadsheets or very large, formula-heavy spreadsheets, consider building a knowledge system to replace or **navigate** the spreadsheet. Overly complex spreadsheets are difficult to maintain and verify. An article by Don Shafer gives tips on the subject.[2]

If a spreadsheet contains something for everybody, it can become difficult to navigate. Some applications require large spreadsheets to cover all the possibilities, although the average user may need only small portions for a specific task. Spreadsheet vendors have included a feature sometimes used in this circumstance: the ability to "hide" cells or ranges of cells. Unfortunately, one can make mistakes when hiding cells and the user may not see something that really is applicable to him. A knowledge system is preferable if large sections of the spreadsheet are conditionally not applicable for a particular user because it will direct the user to the information that is required and hide the rest automatically, in the context of the user's need.

If your application requires interpretation or explanation of results, consider a knowledge system. A few products are now available that can figure out what the spreadsheet actually did for you, but knowledge systems have more extensive explanation facilities.

Generally, most applications **will** fall in the middle of the gray area if they really are feasible. This is because you will most often find yourself integrating a knowledge system into a conventional application environment. For example, if you are building an online consultant system, do not discard any written manuals associated with the application. Consider putting the manuals online and using the consultant as an intelligent look up facility. Then people can use the consultant system or browse the manuals directly — their choice as appropriate.

If you have a complex spreadsheet application, you might not want to port the entire affair to a rule-based system. But you *could* use a knowledge-based system to gather data in a strategic fashion, offer explanations to the user, and interpret the results on the spreadsheet[3]

The Risk-versus-Payoff Test. The next important test is the *risk-versus-payoff test*. The purpose of this test is to enable you to decide whether the penalty/likelihood for failure outweighs the rewards for

---

2 Shafer, Don, *VP-Expert: Intelligent Front End for Spreadsheets*. Knowledge Engineering, 1987.

3 Shafer, op. cit.

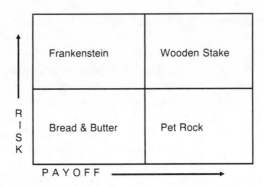

Figure 10-5 The Risk versus Payoff Test.

success. The chart has four quadrants, each representing a potential situation (Figure 10-5).

A Frankenstein project is wrong from the start. It becomes a monster, totally out of place. Typically, a Frankenstein project may address an unpopular subject area, be politically sensitive or controversial, suffer from a bad image due to prior experiences, or not be well defined.

A Wooden Stake project (i.e., as used to kill a vampire) will have a blockbuster payoff, but typically your job is at risk should it fail or be delayed.

A Pet Rock project is the best bet for your first attempt. Pet rocks are characterized as having a significant and visible benefit for a very low investment of resources. A typical first project can be delivered on the sidelines as a throwaway and used to capture the imagination and support of users and management without first having to say "May I?" These types of project may be hard to find but they are worth it! (If you are not familiar with pet rocks, see Appendix D.)

Bread and Butter projects are good to have in your hip pocket at all times. Bread and Butter will bring work to you on a slow and steady basis. They help to fill the gaps between big projects, and are generally safe to use as training projects for bringing new staff up to speed. This type of project might include small systems for limited tasks, such as assisting clerical personnel with following complex office procedures.

Moral: Go for Pet Rock and Bread and Butter projects.

The Strategic Fit of Your Project

Some projects will stand alone, but most will have to integrate with existing computer systems and manual business processes. In any case, somebody has to pay for it and somebody is going to use it. From the start, it is essential that you attempt to identify all persons, processes, and systems that will interface with your final product and **get them informed.** Determine if the project will be well received by all parties who have to be involved. If not, evaluate if it is worth it to convince them.

Determine if the project will have to interface with other computer programs or computer systems in order to share process control and data. If so, do a quick check to see how difficult that's going to be. Cautious discussion with vendors may be helpful.

Make sure that your application really addresses the right user and that the user will want to keep on using it. Take the auto repair demonstration system cited throughout the book. It is feasible, it provides valuable advice, and it might save people money. But who would really use it? Professional mechanics don't need it. The average car owner would not appreciate having to crawl out from under the car with greasy hands in order to continue a piecemeal consultation on their computer in the house. You can see that to make the auto repair demonstration system commercially viable we would have to develop it for a specialized audience by raising its expertise significantly and making it specialize in the most elusive and expensive diagnostic problems. Sensors would have to be designed into the car to allow the knowledge system to conduct the investigation as quickly as possible, with a minimum of human intervention. *Put yourself in the users' place* when you evaluate how the system will serve the user.

DELIVERABLES AND PRODUCTS

Each project stage has deliverables that are by-products of the work in the phase. Now that you've determined that you want to do your project, the next step is to develop a proposal that can be used to formally approach the person(s) in your company who can fund it.

The Project Proposal

The project proposal outlines all of the key areas of a development project including the problem definition, proposed solution, justification, and estimated risks and costs for management. This document must almost always be in hand before support or funding will be offered. This step is not only reasonable to expect, but valuable to the developer as well. Many times the information gathered while writing a proposal will help to verify that you have chosen an appropriate application, begin scoping and requirements definition, and outline the most efficient and cost-effective solution.

Proposals are frequently necessary to provide documentation when proposing to do a feasibility study, demonstration prototype, or production system. It should be short, succinct, and contain sections for all of the following:

Management summary or executive overview
Background information
Problem identification
Proposed solution
Justification
Outline of incremental development approach
Personnel — roles and responsibilities
Schedule
Cost
Risks vs. benefits

Let's look at each of these a little closer.

The management summary should summarize the contents of the proposal so that upper management doesn't have to read the entire document to understand what is being proposed. It should be made clear that the project will not necessarily be an overnight success. due to the limitations of the technology and critical issues regarding personnel and implementation. They should be made aware of the importance of the expert's role, the long-term benefits, and the fact that there will be a monetary investment necessary.

Background Information should contain only information that directly relates to the proposed application. A brief description of the environment and personnel trends will set the stage and provide the necessary background to the problem. This section should also serve as an introduction by defining terms, concepts, acronyms, etc.

Problem identification must be factual and complete. Describe exactly what it is that you're proposing your system will resolve. This must be represented in an objective fashion in order to avoid offending the user community or management.

The Proposed solution, like the problem identification section, should be objective. Justification should not be included here — this section describes only *how* you are proposing to resolve the problem. After you feel you have clearly outlined your solution, try to find its weaknesses. It is better that you find the holes and fix them before giving your source of funding the opportunity.

Justification will be your strongest marketing section. This should itemize each and every reason for which you have chosen your particular solution. An explanation and some promotion of the technology to be used may provide some flare. Explain why a knowledge system approach is being proposed over the use of a conventional system.

The outline of the incremental development approach as described in this chapter will assist the proposal recipients in understanding the schedule and cost of the project. Emphasize the need for user involvement and the benefits of prototyping, but be brief.

The next section should contain the roles and responsibilities of the personnel who will be involved with the system development. This should include managers, developers, expert(s), and users. You may want to refer to Chapter 12 and Appendix E for some guidelines. In addition to the roles and responsibilities, it is necessary to estimate the amount of time needed from the experts and users. In most cases you will not need the experts and users full time. Therefore, you may wish to determine the percentage of time you will need the resources. This section should also outline the project management and ultimate project responsibilities.

A schedule of the project phases should not be too detailed. It is difficult to arrive at exact dates. Refer to general time frames and mention any contingency factors such as availability of resources.

Itemized costs are best represented in simple tables. There should be a logical breakdown of the costs by phases of the project and/or related to personnel and capital expenses. Do not forget to provide the grand total.

In any project, there are always risks. The risks vs. benefits section should honestly compare them with the benefits of proceeding with the proposed approach. Pointing out the risks and describing means of dealing with them, if possible, will demonstrate how well you've thought out the project.

The proposal will be your initial documentation for a project. It outlines many of the key areas which need to be addressed before you begin development. You should use the proposal to gain support for doing a detailed feasibility study.

The Feasibility Study

The purpose of a feasibility study is to estimate the potential for long-term success of a project. There are usually three types of feasibility to be studied: economic, operational, and technological. Because this is such a critical task, Chapter 11 is devoted to the subject.

Requirements Definition Document

The requirements definition document is produced during the beginning of the conceptualize stage of the development life cycle. It is a detailed document describing what the system will do, including performance needs, interfaces, and what specific functions the system will perform. At this point, make sure not to consider detailed information on how the system will accomplish its task;[4] you want to present only what it's going to do.

The requirements for a knowledge-intensive project can be difficult to define because the knowledge is not fully understood at the beginning of the project. However, they can be estimated reasonably well and fine-tuned using the iterative life cycle techniques.

Logical Design Document

The **logical design document** depicts the functions and operations of the system without physical considerations. This can be done using techniques such as Yourdon's Data Flow Diagrams (DFDs).[5] Without consideration of the implementation devices, the logical design of a system will specify the inputs to the system, outputs produced by the system, the functions to be performed, the domain knowledge model, and the components of the system.

The analysis knowledge representation techniques described in Chapter 5 should be used when developing your logical design. You need to represent well-structured knowledge from your validated semantic network or other representation. We recommend converting

---

4   Vick, Charles R., and Ramamoortny, C. V., *Handbook of Software Engineering*. Van Nostrand Reinhold Co. Inc., 1984.

5   De Marco, Tom, *Structured Analysis and System Specification*. Yourdon Inc., 1978.

semantic networks to decision trees where possible, but you can proceed from other representations as well. We show several examples in Chapters 6 and 7.

Physical Design Document

The **physical design** is a detailed specification of the control structure, data structures, and interfaces as they relate to particular hardware and devices. For example, this document will specify the particular schemes for performing operations on the different brands of hardware and software tools that you will need for the system to perform as desired. It is a realistic look at how the system is going to fit into your system architecture.

The knowledge coding and representation techniques described in Chapters 6 and 7 will be valuable tools for creating your physical design. There are numerous examples in those chapters, so physical design will not be covered in any more detail here.

YOUR FIRST PROJECT

If you are about to begin your first project, you will probably want to take an approach that facilitates learning. You should take a slightly less structured approach to development than we have presented here. Given that you limit the size of your application, your first project should provide many opportunities for you to experiment with techniques for managing and developing a knowledge system.

Before you begin your project, make sure you establish your goals. Then plan carefully so that you can optimize the time you must spend in achieving them. Select opportunities within your abilities. If this is your first project, keep it as simple as possible and make sure that your staff is trained appropriately. Clearly, a poorly trained staff will have a negative effect on your chances of completing the project successfully. Remember the knowledge system part is only a portion of the system, it must integrate well with the rest of your environment.

When you begin the project, do a piece, then refine it. Be open to throwing away your first attempt. The experience you gain just starting the project will help you rethink or validate your approach. Finally, review your goals at major project milestones. If you find yourself addressing the wrong goals, backtrack to the last milestone and begin a new path.

STAGES/PHASES	SOME OF THE STEPS	DELIVERABLES/PRODUCTS	CHAP.
Identification	Data gathering Knowledge acquisition Proposal development	Proposal Feasibility study	10 11
Conceptualization	Define requirements Interview users Create project plan Design logical	Requirement definition Logical design Test plan Implementation plan User documentation	10 13
Formalization	Design physical Build demo prototype	Physical design Demo prototype	10 13
Implementation	Program system Develop interfaces Create knowledge base Install/Integrate	Code Internal documentation External documentation Maintenance plan	6 7
Testing	Test system	Documented evaluation of test results	13
Evaluation	Evaluate test results and user feedback Refine requirements, design and plan	Evaluation documentation and revised project plan and path forward	13 10
Maintenance	Update hardware Update software	Revision documentation Updated hardware and software system	14
Phase Out	Transition of product functions	Documentation Obsolete system	

Figure 10-6 Cross-reference to project stages.

SUMMARY

Whether you are building a knowledge system or conventional system, it is important to understand and control project dynamics. The knowledge system project life cycle is a valuable tool for providing quality project management and software development. A clearly defined project life cycle provides a solid foundation for projects.

For your convenience, we provide a summary of the stages, steps, and the deliverables for each (Figure 10-6).

11

Project Feasibility and Sizing

Feasibility studies are the formal justification of a project and include documentation of the application's potential, initial project resource estimates and scheduling, cursory requirements definition, and the assumptions you've made — contingencies, and critical success factors. These provisions let you build some flexibility into the project and help protect your credibility.

The probability of project success (feasibility) and estimation of system size (sizing) are the two most critical initial estimations you will make. They will have a direct bearing on whether the project appears to be both appropriate and cost-effective. This chapter offers methods to aid in the estimation of both.

The potential for long-term success of a project depends upon a variety of factors. You must obtain support and funding in order to actually do the project. Management's support will depend on how well you identify the type and nature of the problem and present the cost/benefit calculations. The scope of the problem must be bounded realistically (knowing when to stop). In presenting the feasibility study, you must also identify the delivery environment, describe the availability of the domain expert, and size the overall system (a special problem dealt with later in this chapter).

A feasibility questionnaire is provided in Appendix F. The questions will help ensure your consideration of management support, funding, and expert availability. They will also help in acquiring initial information about the remaining issues of bounding the problem, nature of the problem, and system size. They are categorized based on the information they provide.

Use the questionnaire as a "quality" filter for potential projects. The information collected will help screen out projects that seem appropriate but need more thought. If the development team is satisfied with the results of the questionnaire, a full feasibility study (cost vs. payback) should be made before committing time and money to the project.

Strong warning: **Do your own feasibility study**! There are no hard and fast answers in the knowledge system business, and no standards either! Avoid using a product vendor or anyone else with a vested interest in a specific product as a principal consultant. You know your environment better than a consultant. Use consultants to help you learn about the technology, *not* to lead the project.

DEFINING THE SCOPE OF THE PROBLEM

Just as it is important to know *how* to construct a knowledge system, it is equally important to know when to stop construction. During cost estimation, you should determine the level of expertise required to operate the system and the quantity and quality of system outputs required for success.

Take this book, for example. Its problem was "communicating how to construct knowledge systems" to the reader. When you began reading this book, you were presented with the author's expectations of you as the consumer of this product. You were expected to have a certain vocabulary (**constraints**) so that the contents would be understandable. You were also given an outline of the information contained in the book (you received an explanation of the book's **goals**). Those opening paragraphs were a means of defining the scope of the problem.

A strict definition of the problem scope is done during the requirements definition phase. However, during feasibility, a simple definition will help keep the development team focused. When determining where to begin and where to stop the project, it is best to sum up the system expectations as briefly as possible. One sentence is best, but one or two paragraphs is acceptable.

The important elements to consider when setting the system boundaries are defined here by example. The following list gives you the variable names in parentheses and what they stand for. They are used in the example of the theoretical system that follows.

minimum entry-level user experience (WW)
function to be automated (XX)
sources of input to the system (YY0, YY1, . . .)
system goals (GO)
system accuracy and completeness (ER)
when the knowledge engineer has gathered enough detail (ET)

Let's look at a generic boundary definition.

Given the users of the system have at least "WW" years/months of experience performing job function "XX" and information source inputs of "YY0" and "YY1" to stimulate system events; the system will be considered complete when goal event "GO" occurs with an error rate of "ER" percent or less.

The knowledge engineer will stop gathering information whenever the system is able to trigger event "GO" (above). Today, the current means of determining when event "GO" has occurred is when event "ET" happens.

By phrasing the system expectations in this fashion, it is possible to substitute the variable names with some English (albeit convoluted) phrases, names, and values. This reads a little better and is more meaningful with some values filled in.

Given the users of the system have at least 1 year and 6 months of experience performing job function Head Auto Mechanic and information source inputs of customer trouble descriptions and test data from an auto analysis machine to stimulate system events; the system will be considered complete when goal event of determining which mechanic in the shop is best suited to find the trouble occurs with an error rate of 5 percent or less.

The knowledge engineer will stop gathering information whenever the system is able to trigger event determining best mechanic (above). Today, the current means of determining when event best mechanic determined has occurred is when event the Head Mechanic gives the worker mechanic a paper work order happens.

These two terribly written paragraphs have covered the essential variables concerning system completeness. The knowledge engineer knows that the goal is not to identify the resolution to the trouble but *who* should find the trouble, not *what* the trouble is.

Bounding the problem is critical when estimating the effort required to complete the system. Without a clear definition, the above knowledge engineer might continue the trouble analysis when no further analysis was necessary.

IDENTIFYING THE TYPE AND NATURE OF THE PROBLEM

The **kind** of system you create will influence both the knowledge representation scheme and the interfaces required to complete the program. The system must be broken into its component parts so that you can determine if the system will be a simple dialogue, if there are simulation or real-time components, which parts will require database access or sensor input, and what the interfaces will be.

Once you've identified the subsystem components, you will begin to get a good idea of how much effort will be involved. Every computer system attempts to model a "real-world system" at some level of abstraction. Using a top-down approach, start with high-level concepts and build the system by expanding upon the detail of each successively lower layer until the code level is reached. Early in this process, which sensor inputs, control code, and human interface features must be implemented will become apparent. Anticipate these structures and features when performing the feasibility study and constructing a preliminary design, but do not begin a detailed design until formal requirements are complete.

In evaluating the kind of system you're going to develop, you must look at the system data, which will be kept in either a database or a knowledge base. There are two basic types of data — fixed instances of objects and relational "decisions," which describe how the instances relate to each other. The primary distinctions between a relational database and a knowledge base are that the relational database has a few relationships but many instances of a particular object, while the knowledge base has many relationships with a few instances of each object.

Because of this fundamental distinction, the knowledge base component cannot be implemented easily with existing tools and requires special techniques and programs to capture and control the execution of the knowledge base. Interfaces are required for passing data and control information between the knowledge base and the other parts of the program.

When you determine the "type and nature" of a problem, you give yourself the means to estimate the development effort each component will require to produce the overall system.

THE DELIVERY ENVIRONMENT

It is important to consider the delivery environment requirements during the feasibility study and before starting the prototype. Often the prototype environment and delivery environment are quite different. The determination of the delivery environment will depend on your user community: Will the system have a single user or multiple users? Their experience level is also important. You must look at the hardware, including the network, the processor, any special data collection devices, the display requirements (graphics, etc.), and the storage requirements. And you must look at the delivery software environment — which operating system and programming languages are available, the network software, the knowledge system shells available, and the native database language.

After determining the delivery environment requirements, you may begin selecting remove development tools. Choosing prototyping tools based upon the ultimate delivery environment has a large bearing on the ease of delivery and total cost of the delivered system. Chapter 9 went into this in detail.

SYSTEM SIZE ESTIMATION

Estimating system **size** is the best way to determine the total system cost. There is a strong correlation between the system size and the effort and material required to build the completed system. An accurate estimate will also enable you to set realistic delivery dates. Conventional methods for estimating the size of a project may be used. These include:

- *Top-down estimating and similarities and differences estimating.* These methods compare the parts of the proposed project and similar portions of existing projects.
- *Ratio estimating.* This method involves estimating the effort to code specific functions then converting those functions, to modules which are combined to form the completed system.

- *Bottom-up estimating.* Here, the expected effort to produce each subpart of the system is estimated, then combined with other subpart estimates for a system total.

At least two of the above methods should be used and the results compared[1]. The results should support each other and not differ widely. If the results do differ, either use a third method (as arbiter) or carefully examine your original assumptions.

If you have a documented, in-house history of knowledge-based systems, you may choose to use the techniques above. If you have no history or are looking for another alternative, one of the authors (Carrico) has developed a method which seems to work, but is not yet supported by voluminous historical data. This is an attempt at a simple, pragmatic solution to quantify the amount of knowledge captured in any system.

The method is called the *knowledge equivalence hypothesis.* It states that:

> Knowing the average number of years (or months) it takes to become an expert helps in the estimation of the number of rules, frames, or objects which will be required for a completed system.

> Or, if the size of a system is known in terms of rules, frames, or objects, you should be able to predict its "human equivalent" performance level as years and months of human experience represented in the system.

To employ the knowledge equivalence method, follow these steps:

1. Determine the equivalent number of years and months of experience the system is to emulate by asking the question: "How long does it take (from entry-level job qualifications) for an average person to become proficient at this task?" For best results, solicit opinions from several people. The amount of time required to learn the domain will correlate with the total number of rules in the finished program.

---

1 Wolverton, R. W., *Software Costing*, Handbook of Software Engineering, Vick, C. R., and Ramamoorthy, C. V. (eds.). Van Nostrand Reinhold Company Inc., 1984.

2. Convert the number of years and months to an estimate of the number of rules to be coded.
3. Convert the number of rules to be coded to "time to code."

Bottom-Up Decomposition Method

1. Determine the number of subdomain objects in the system.
2. Convert the number of objects to an estimate of the number of rules to be coded.
3. Convert the number of rules to be coded to "time to code."

Here are some simple conversion formulas that can be used to implement the steps described above:

Years of Expert Experience to Number of Rules. For every year of expertise the system is to emulate, estimate 550 (+ or - 200) rules.

Example: If you intend to capture the expertise of a job that typically takes 1-1/2 years to learn and the person meets all entry-level qualifications for the job, the number of rules, in the completed system will be between 525 and 1125 rules with a typical figure of **825 rules.**

Note: You can also work backward to estimate the relative amount of expertise that has already been captured in an existing knowledge system by dividing the total number of rules in the system by 550.

Number of Objects in the Problem Space to Number of Rules. If you are not using an object-oriented language or frames and the objects are coded as rules, use **about 25 rules per object or subdomain.** The range is generally between 15 to 35 rules per object. Consider these objects as subdomains of a larger "system" domain.

Example: Before beginning to code the auto demo example in this book, the problem was bounded to the following objects:

- Symptoms(18)
- Starter(16)
- Fuel System(9)
- Ignition(15)
- Engine(28)
- Oil Pump(4)
- Charging System(18)

Note: The numbers in parentheses are the actual number of rules in the final demonstration knowledge bases.

Given that the problem was bounded to seven objects, a coarse estimation of the final number of rules would have been between 105 and 245 rules, with a typical number being 175 rules (the actual number was 107). Note that "Symptoms" is also an object. Abstract objects should be included in the estimate.

We can also estimate the equivalent "human experience level" of our system from the example above.

$$\frac{107 \ (\text{actual rules})}{550 \ (\text{rules per year of experience represented in the system})} = 0.19 \ (\text{years experience})$$

Our demonstration system performs at the level of a new mechanic working from memory and without supporting documentation with about 9 weeks of experience in the covered domains.

Convert Number of Rules to "Time to Code". You now have an estimate of how large the proposed system is going to be. It would be nice if you could give the management people in your firm an estimate of how much effort will be required to produce the system and how long it will be before you can deliver it. It takes about as long to code and deliver a completed system as it does for a person to learn the domain. You should estimate a delivery rate of about 550 rules per "knowledge engineer/coder"-year. This figure includes time to code user interfaces, internal interfaces, system documentation (internal and external), user manuals, etc. — a completed system or subsystem. Estimates of the cost to engineer, code, and verify a rule range from 5 to 12 person-hours per rule. So, **for every year of expertise captured, a knowledge engineer/programmer will spend about one year on the program**.

Obviously, there will be other people involved with the project. The number of people connected with the project is shown below. To capture one year of human expertise (550 rules or 25 subdomains), we can estimate:

Knowledge Engineer/Coder	12 months
Domain Expert	4 months
Project Management	2 months
End User (test & verification)	1 month
Maintenance	5 months (spread over the life of the program)

The maintenance figure assumes the use of a modular system programming approach (which this book promotes) and that you plan for maintenance during development.

SUMMARY

When estimating your project, make a simple "high-level" model of the system. Don't worry too much about the ultimate design details or structure — they are likely to change somewhat during development. Determine a reasonable model of the problem, and use that model for your estimate. Remember to use more than one estimation method. If the data is available, use at least one method based upon past projects. Be sure not to rely on your early estimates for a very large project. Large projects should be reviewed regularly for errors at the end of each phase of the project life cycle because their size makes it impossible to accurately estimate every detail.

During feasibility, size and cost estimates are the most critical early indicators of whether it is prudent to continue with a project. This chapter has provided some tools for estimating both size and cost which are unique to knowledge systems. Use these procedures along with the questionnaire in Appendix F to enable you to make those estimates reasonable.

12

Management and Staffing

The knowledge system life cycle is an excellent plan for project development. However, it is useless without the human component. Organizing quality personnel and managing their talents will add to the success of the product.

There are many simple ways to protect against failure and give your effort a fighting chance even though we live in an imperfect world. The management of a project can be its vital backbone or its crushing blow. Poor management can run a project over budget faster than any other factor[1]. Avoid the mistakes that have the greatest impact on a project. These include assigning the wrong people, failure to obtain necessary resources, failure to perform all of the steps in the project life cycle (i.e., leaving testing out), redundancy of efforts, and lack of appropriate training.

MANAGEMENT

Before you begin the actual development of a system, there are several strategies that will help to ensure a good beginning. Make sure that you've selected an application that is likely to be successful.

---

1 Boehm, Barry W., *Software Engineering Economics*. Englewood Cliffs, N.J.: Prentice-Hall, 1981.

Then perform a feasibility study and identify the user community and source of funding for the project. If you are working in a rigid company atmosphere or do not have the luxury of an independent work environment, you will need to obtain management sponsorship and user interest. This sponsorship will usually provide the fuel for obtaining the necessary resources to prototype and eventually implement the final product. Remember, your final system could be a terrific pet rock, but without the proper backing it may only attract moss.

When proposing your knowledge system ideas to management, make them aware of the advantages *and* disadvantages. Be prepared to address both. The proposal should outline the resources you will need to complete the project. Limited resource availability can turn a project manager into a hapless juggler. Plan for the resources to include the development team, experts, end-users, money, hardware, and software.

Staffing

The personnel on a project are your most valuable resources and are critical to its success. Some of the qualifications needed will be project-specific. However, there are some general attributes which every team member on a knowledge system development project should have. A project team should include the following job functions:

• Project management
• Knowledge engineering/systems analysis
• Software/system engineering
• Knowledge systems librarian
• Quality assurance and control

If your team is small, responsibilities may overlap. On large teams, several people may be assigned to perform one job function. Figure 12-1 depicts a sample of how functions might be organized in the team. Any one team player can have responsibilities in several of the areas. Appendix E contains job descriptions for each of the key job functions.

To make a cohesive, well-coordinated team, *all* members should have good interpersonal skills, a high energy level, and an enthusiastic attitude toward the work. It is important that they also have the ability to interact well with people in a user community. They should be interested in learning new technology and applying it to "real-life"

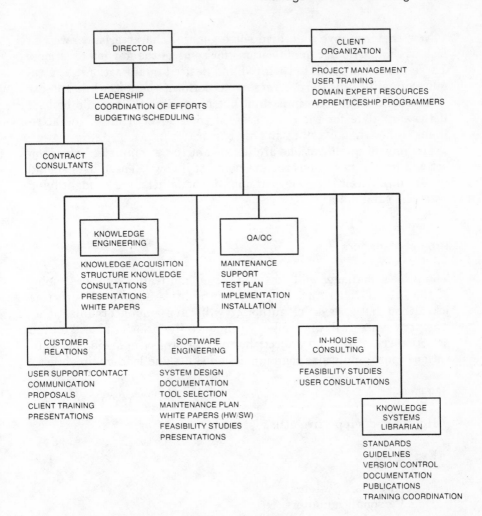

Figure 12-1 A project team and their functions.

applications. Job experience should include an assignment requiring flexible behavior, experience in a team environment, and experience outside the research environment. They should have experience with computer hardware and software and previous experience in developing projects to meet users needs as opposed to developing projects for the purpose of experimenting with new technology. Finally, team members should be able to take constructive criticism, admit mistakes, and learn from them.

Now that we have identified some general characteristics, we can look at the particular qualifications for some of the key job functions. These are organized into required and desired qualifications. The required qualifications are necessary to perform the job, while the desired qualifications are important but not essential. It would be best if the candidate for the job possessed some level of all of the attributes rather than excelling in only one or two areas.

The lists of qualifications are not meant to be complete. Your project will have other talent requirements of its own. These lists should assist you in creating your own qualifications lists and in identifying potential candidates.

Project Managers

The project manager will be the director, motivator, and focal point of the project. There are many responsibilities associated with this job although the level of authority will vary among organizations. The project size will undoubtedly influence the priority placed on the selection criteria. In all projects however, a project manager's qualifications must emphasize communication skills and leadership ability.

Required:

Honest and supportive attitude

Experience in

- AI/Expert Systems
- Personal computers
- Software and hardware selection
- Data processing programming
- Project management
- Oral and written communication skills

Political finesse: Ability to network with all levels of management and reach agreement on controversial issues

Trail blazer: Ability to work in an environment where there is no precedent or examples to utilize in arriving at a decision

Leader: Ability to capitalize on talents and earn respect and loyalty from peers and subordinates

Quality/Pride in work: No job is worth doing unless it is to the best of one's ability

Organization: Ability to sort and prioritize work to meet deadlines

Desired:

Willing to be on the team as well as leading it

Risk taker: Willingness to leverage and risk one's reputation, dollars, and resources in order to realize the achievement of high level goals

Efficiency: The work load must be handled in a cost-effective and timely manner

Creativity: Ability to think up new ways to solve problems and overcome obstacles

Imagination/Innovation: New ideas and approaches are essential to success

Loyalty: Support and contribute to others on the team

Patience

Knowledge Engineers/Systems Analysts

Knowledge engineers, similar to the systems analyst, are responsible for direct communications with the users and experts in order to structure the domain and represent the knowledge in the most accurate way. This also involves being able to properly define the problem and determine the goal of the system. The knowledge engineer usually does the majority of the work on the proposal and feasibility study. The titles for this responsibility are usually something on the order of knowledge engineer, associate knowledge engineer or knowledge analyst.

Required:

Expertise in

- Foundations of computer science
- Knowledge representation formalisms and environments
- Traditional programming skills
- Expert system shells
- Interfaces
- Structured analysis and design

Outstanding interpersonal skills with all levels of management and non management personnel as well as with team members

Programming experience in at least one high-level programming language

Programming experience in the development and delivery operating system, i.e., MS-DOS, UNIX, or VMS

Ability to take constructive criticism, admit mistakes, and learn from them

Ability to apply cost/benefit analysis to one's work so as to assure the best products are produced in the shortest possible time frame at the lowest possible cost

Knowledge and experience with data modeling

Desired:

High energy level and enthusiastic attitude toward work

Successful job experience in a team environment

Experience programming with LISP or Prolog

System/Software Engineers

The system/software engineers are responsible for the software coding, implementation, and integration of a system. They are usually involved to some extent in the knowledge engineering, because of the importance of scoping and defining the application. These engineers are AI programmers with titles something like software engineer, system engineer, AI software engineer, etc.

Required:

Experience programming in at least one low-level procedural programming language, and/or a demonstrable understanding of at least one system's internal software/hardware architecture

Experience with expert systems shell(s)

System programming and administration experience in one or more of: MS-DOS, UNIX, VM, MVS, VMS

Experience with one or more structured design/development methodologies

Advanced experience programming in at least one high-level procedural programming language

Experience with integration issues of multiple hardware types, programming languages, and network protocols

Experience with developing unit, integration and system test plans, and experience in carrying out/documenting tests

Desired:

Experience using LISP or Prolog

Good technical writing skills

Ability to communicate effectively with team members and clients working on assigned projects

Experience with end-user product ergonomics

Applied experience with any of: data modeling, logical database design, physical database design, database administration

Domain Experts

Domain experts are the individuals who possess the expertise and skills you are trying to capture in the knowledge system. You cannot do a project without them. There are all varieties of experts. However, some general qualifications will increase the success of your efforts. The domain expert

- should have expertise which has been developed over years of practical experience
- should not be threatened by the results of the system
- must be willing to communicate expertise
- must be easy to work with and able to contribute a significant amount of time
- must be willing and able to explain his or her methods explicitly

End-Users

The end-users are the people who will be interacting with the final product. They are the ones who will be utilizing the expertise or interfacing with the results of the system development. It is important that they are part of the development team and are able to provide input to the design and operation of the system. No matter how good the system is, if the users do not like it, it will fail.

The end-users or a small representative group of end-users should be:

- active participants in the man/machine interface design (see human factors)
- honest and open about likes, dislikes, and needs
- enthusiastic about potential of the system
- willing to work with development team

Consultants

Some consultants have a wide variety of experiences, but many have a limied focus from working under research budgets and exclusively with LISP machines. Shop around carefully for consultants! Take time to compare and contrast resumés to find the best fit for your company's business philosophy. Make sure the consultant has a realistic attitude about prototyping. In addition, the consultant should be able to justify all estimates.

Before you bring in a consultant, prepare an agenda for the his or her visit. Share this agenda with the consultant before he or she comes on the payroll along with background information that can be studied before arriving on the assignment. When the consultant arrives, work him or her hard. If several people need to work with the consultant, rotate them through in shifts to prevent information overload.

Key points:

* Use consultants for specific purposes, not general work.
* Remember, they are working for *you*.
* "Working a consultant" for information usually provides more value than attending a course.

HOW TO GET GOOD TRAINING

AI training courses vary from self-teaching books to elaborate several-week courses that include hands-on activities. The training you choose when developing a knowledge system should depend on the project needs, the personality and skill level of the individual to be trained, the reason for training, and other sources or alternatives available.

Your project will have specific needs related to the skills of you and your team. Assess the skills needed before you begin to look for training. This will make sure you know what you are looking for. For example,

IF   it is a small project
AND   you have a general understanding of the technology
AND   you are using a well-documented and supported shell
THEN
        you may want to take a 1- or 2- day knowledge engineering
        course
OR
        a course from the shell vendor, if one is offered

A larger application may require skills in several knowledge systems areas. Some of the areas of expertise to consider are:

* knowledge engineering — knowledge structuring, interviewing
* software engineering — structured design and coding
* hardware — to address implementation issues
* quality assurance

The personnel on a project should possess the experience and skills to successfully develop a knowledge system. Refer to Chapter 13 for more information on the characteristics and skills that will help to make a project successful. Given an individual's current skill level, outline the areas where the individual should receive training based on their job responsibilities and the expertise required of them. A description of job responsibilities appears in Appendix E.

There are many different reasons why a person receives training. Most are associated with the project or company needs. However, it is just as important to meet the individual's needs. A person must have the opportunity to expand and build upon their education in order to remain productive and interested in a field. This reason alone is sufficient to strongly recommend training when it is appropriate based on time and funding.

Training alternatives exist for even the most technical fields. There are many vendors offering courses as well as consulting companies. It would be inappropriate for us to try to list all of the choices here, because the offerings change on a regular basis. However, let's quickly look at some of the alternatives available.

Periodicals and Other Sources.   Refer to some of the periodicals mentioned in Appendix B along with the other sources of information listed. Most publications have advertisements related to training. Another good source of information is conferences. Conferences generally cover either limited topics or overview material. However, the vendor displays and distributed literature offer a wealth of information.

Consultants   A popular alternative to training is using a consultant. A consultant can be hired to perform an activity related to the project or provide customized training courses. This is usually a more expensive alternative and the one with the greatest return on your investment. Readers are encouraged to shop for consultants and to bring them into their companies for short periods to work with in-house teams. Be sure to have a list of expected deliverables before deciding on a consultant. In many cases, especially in the AI field, effective use of consultants can prove far more effective than taking courses.

The quality of training varies. On the negative side, only a few good introductory courses exist, and advanced courses are virtually nonexistent outside of graduate programs at universities. On the positive side, this situation is rapidly changing for the better. Because of the strong demand, there are more courses being offered all the time.

Be aware that the quality of most public offerings of expert systems and knowledge engineering courses is inconsistent. There is no industry agreement on what should be taught or what is *beginning* versus *advanced* information. An experienced Systems Analyst may pay hundreds of dollars for an advanced knowledge engineering course, only to be presented with remedial instruction in interviewing skills. Before you enroll in a course, ask to see the course materials and determine whether they are appropriate for you.

SUMMARY

Managing an application development group involves coordinating the job responsibilities of a team over several projects for an indefinite period of time. The size and operation of the group will depend on your demands for developing projects.

The makeup of the team should be coordinated carefully using some of the qualifications listed in this chapter. Follow the rules of your organization for planning, forecasting, goal setting. These will be important, because you should operate the development group as you would an independent business. Keep your team focused on perseverance, organization, efficiency, patience, and imagination/innovation.

A valuable reference is a book titled *Intrapreneuring*[2]. *This book provides essential ideas and guidance for developing the entrepreneurial spirit within a corporation. This includes developing business plans, enhancing creativity, and promoting excellence.*

The personnel on your project are your most valuable resource. It is vitally important that this resource is managed successfully. Start with choosing the right people for the right job and provide them with the proper training to make them successful.

---

2 Pinchot III, Gifford, *Intrapreneuring*. New York: Harper & Row Publishers, 1985.

13

Quality Assurance

Quality assurance (QA) practices are essential in any project to prevent problems before they can occur and to deliver the best fit to the users' needs. QA is essential in knowledge system projects because, as explained earlier, the requirements are a **moving target** that cannot be fully known until the project is completed.

While QA is not the primary thrust of this book, we do want to discuss the QA techniques that we have found useful in knowledge system projects. **ALL** of these QA activities must be built into the project life cycle and given priority and resources:

- Walkthroughs
- Prototyping
- Documentation
- Communication and cooperation
- Tests and test plans

WALKTHROUGHS

A number of books have been written about walkthroughs, inspections, reviews, code readings, etc., and you would do well to consult any of them for detailed information. We've listed several we recommend in Appendix C. There is considerable evidence that walkthroughs are the most effective form of testing available.[1] For our purposes, we will define walkthroughs as review meetings, convened and hosted by a presenter who has asked a group of peers to scour his or her work for defects. The purpose of the review is to assist your colleague in identifying problems in the project quickly, as they occur, so that they can be corrected with minimal trips "back to the drawing board."

Walkthroughs are most effective when the reviewers have different points of view. This is achieved by inviting reviewers who are not directly involved in the construction details of the project under review. If your group does not already use walkthroughs, it is easy to start them as an informal activity. All you really need are some simple guidelines for administration and a couple of forms.

1. Consider holding a walkthrough every 80 person-hours of effort on a particular project or at predefined milestones, whichever comes first. If the project has many tasks, apply the 80-hour rule separately to each one. This can add 5–10% overhead to the project, but it can also save hours spent in reworking mistakes.

2. Invite at least one person from the "upstream" group that supplied the information used in products under review. These reviewers have an investment in the accuracy of your work, because it is the product of their participation in the project. Also include at least one person from the "downstream" group that will have to implement this product. These reviewers have an investment in the understandability, completeness, and usability of the products under review.

3. Try to keep walkthrough meetings to an hour or less. This will force you to keep the quantity of material to a reasonable size and will encourage you to keep the discussion on the agenda topics. Review any and all project products including documentation, diagrams, code, etc.

---

1 Basili, Victor R., and Richard W. Selby, *Comparing the Effectiveness of Software Testing Strategies*. National Technical Information Service, AD-A160 136, 1985.

4. Each person on the review board has a role to play. You should assign three people to take specific responsibility for presenting the product, running the meeting, and taking notes. The role of the *presenter* is to call the meeting and request a review of his/her products. The presenter must be kept free to present the material and answer questions. The *moderator* facilitates the meeting by keeping the meeting focused on its purpose and agenda and also participates as a reviewer. It is vital that you have someone take notes on the defects detected so that the presentor can go back and fix them. The *notetaker* is also a reviewer. Depending on what is to be reviewed, you should also include some technical reviewers or users on the panel. They should have some experience in the areas to be reviewed (without having worked on this particular project) so that they can bring a fresh perspective to your work. Try to keep the total number of participants to seven or less.

5. Once the meeting has begun, the moderator must keep its focus on finding defects within the context of company standards and guidelines. Any impulses for the reviewers to start thinking up ways to fix identified problems should be discouraged. A popular slogan in this regard is "Error detection, not correction."

   It is also the moderator's job to prevent reviewers from distracting the meeting by criticizing the presenter on personal style issues. The popular slogan on this is "Check your ego at the door."

   Throughout the meeting, the presenter should move sequentially through the product, from beginning to end, asking for comments. Reviewers are expected to share their observations of problems and potential problems.

6. Copies of the material to be reviewed should be distributed to the reviewers at least two days in advance. This will give them the opportunity to examine the material prior to the meeting. Minimally, you will need a cover sheet for the review packages and a checklist to assure a consistent presentation. The reviewers will sign off on their decision about the product(s) on the **original** cover sheet, at the close of the meeting. The presenter should attach the notes from the meeting to the signed cover sheet and circulate copies to all participants. Other useful forms include checklists and test criteria that the presenter (and your company) wants all reviewers to consider. Figure

13.1 provides an example of the type of cover sheet and checklist that should be used.

PROTOTYPING

You probably noticed that the incremental model we use in our description of the project life cycle lends itself well to the concepts of prototyping. The relationship is intentional. The use of prototypes has been a great success in reducing the risk and investment in new projects. If your organization understands the value of prototyping and stepwise refinement, you can gain credibility by pointing out the relationship of a prototype to the incremental model for knowledge system's projects.

Fielding incremental knowledge system projects as prototypes can provide the end-user with early glimpses of the product which are invaluable for fine tuning of the project specification and estimates.

DOCUMENTATION

Start the user manual up front as part of or an appendix to the requirements definition. In most projects, the user manual is the last thing to be built when, in fact, it should be the first! The outline of the user manual should be completed during requirements definition and the "meat" should be added as each phase of the project progresses. Why? Because the user manual is the ultimate contract between you and the end-users and the ultimate measure of the degree to which you delivered the product that was desired. Writing the user manual forces you to explain the product's features, maintenance, and potential difficulties in detail. This can be compared to the requirements definition document to demonstrate that the product meets the specifications. Each group working on the project may refer to the user manual for guidance and clarification, adding and/or refining the sections that apply to their efforts.

When writing the user manual, make sure you use the user's terminology. All of the terms used in the project should be defined and a data dictionary should be included. Use illustrations frequently. Do not use text to describe something that can be presented simply in an illustration.

Another form of documentation that should be maintained in addition to the user manual is your detailed knowledge acquisition notes from all interviews, research activities, and preproduction trials of your system. This is the raw material on which your project is based, so treat it well.

Walkthroughs Cover Sheet

Presenter: _____   Date: _____

Product to review: _____

TO:

_____ (moderator)

_____ (notetaker)

_____ (reviewer)

_____ (reviewer)

_____ (reviewer)

RESULTS: (check one)

[   ] product accepted   [   ] not acepted

[   ] revise no followup   [   ] revise, followup review

SIGNATURES:

_____ (presenter)

_____ (moderator)

_____ (notetaker)

_____ (reviewer)

_____ (reviewer)

_____ (reviewer)

Figure 13-1 Sample cover sheet and checklist (1 of 2).

```
┌─────────────────────────────────────────────────────────────┐
│                                                               │
│                     Walkthrough Checklist                     │
│                                                               │
│                                                               │
│   Presenter:  _____   Date:  _____         │
│                                                               │
│   Product to review:  _____ │
│                                                               │
│                                                               │
│   Attached are:                                               │
│                                                               │
│   [  ] background information (optional)                      │
│                                                               │
│   [  ] full product (if not, explain on reverse)             │
│                                                               │
│   [  ] issues the presenter would like considered            │
│                                                               │
│   [  ] installation standard test plan for this type of product │
│                                                               │
│   [  ] other:                                                 │
│                                                               │
│                                                               │
└─────────────────────────────────────────────────────────────┘
```

Figure 13-1 (continued) Sample cover sheet and checklist (2 of 2).

TESTS AND TEST PLANS

You should always have a test plan in mind for any project you undertake. Elemer Magaziner, a noted QA consultant, says "A good test plan is like giving the students an outline for the final exam on the first day of a class. They perform better and learn more because they know what they are supposed to accomplish and where they could go wrong." He also said the latter about user manuals, by the way.

In that spirit, many shops have developed "generic" test plans that are tailored for use in validating traditional projects. In the following sections you'll find a generic test plan outline for embedded and stand-alone production rule–type knowledge systems. Some of the test areas may not make sense to you until you have had some experience. Start with this plan, then modify the contents and vocabulary as you gain experience with projects and tools. Remember to document the results of any testing you perform as part of your quality assurance activities.

System Test Issues

In this context, system test issues refers to the delivery environment and documentation of the system at a global level. Some of these issues are often not considered until the system is about to go into production when they can cause significant implementation delays. Make sure you examine all of the issues carefully.

1.1 *Delivery hardware*

1.1.1 *Response time*: Does the system perform at a level acceptable to the user?

1.1.2 *Reliability*: Does the product continue to perform properly after multiple cycles? Does the product perform necessary and sufficient maintenance on its own files?

1.1.3 *Visual*: Are the product displays readable and correct?

1.1.4 *Sensors and databases*: Is the product correctly accessing information sources?

1.1.5 *RAM*: Does the system have sufficient RAM to service the product, and is the product using RAM effectively?

1.1.6 *Mass storage resources*: Does the system have sufficient storage space to accommodate the application under the specified operating conditions?

1.1.7 *CPU capacity*: In a multi-user environment, is there enough CPU time available to operate the product? What is the impact on other resources?

1.2 *Optimization*: Have all rule bases been compacted with optimization utilities, if available?

1.3 *Data dictionary*: Have all of the system data, control items, and files definitions been entered into a data dictionary?

1.4   System diagrams

Verify:

1.4.1   Context diagram

1.4.2   High-level functional flow

1.4.3   Expert system/conventional system boundaries

1.4.4   High-level logical design

Integration Test Issues

When testing for a well-integrated system, you'll be looking at how data is requested and from where, how it's made available internally via blackboards, and the outputs that are produced. The program logic for manipulating the data is irrelevant when investigating integration issues.

2.1   *Blackboard content coupling*: Do units write and read the correct information on the blackboards/databases?

Verify: All I/O statements found in action blocks, report generators, rules, frames, etc. Make sure that all data constituting blackboard information must be written out at the appropriate times.

Compatible keys for the blackboard must be used by different rule bases accessing the same blackboard. If they do not use compatible keys, then a translation facility must exist in the interface.

2.2   *Blackboard control coupling*: Are the units writing, reading the right blackboards at the right time?
Verify: All I/O statements found in action blocks, command and report scripts, rules, frames, etc.

2.3   *User control*: Are options offered to the user at the right time?

This can be verified via inspections and walkthroughs. What constitutes the right time may be a matter of taste, may be a part of the specification, or both. The system should be offering the user choices to quit, continue, rerun, etc. at the appropriate points in the application.

2.4   *Audit*: Are audit trails and other reports properly created, appended, etc.?

Verify this via inspections and walkthroughs. When several programs are involved in creating an appended file, it is possible for one or more to damage end-of-file markers, etc. resulting in incomplete audit records.

2.5   *External data and control file names*: Are the names being used consistent with the product's naming conventions? Are the names documented in the system specification?

2.6   *Data dictionary*: Make sure that definitions of all system data, control items, and files have been recorded.

2.7   *Integration level diagrams*

Verify:

2.7.1   Detail logical design

2.7.2   High-level physical design

Unit Test Issues

Unit testing is most critical to the functioning of your system. You must validate the logic and the flow of the system, making sure that you've captured the expert's knowledge accurately.

3.1   *Typographical errors*: Verify rule base listing with spell checker

3.2   *Discrete subdomain errors*: Are the rules partitioned into sub-domains and/or sub–rule bases in a way that discourages mixing of unrelated information?

3.3   *Logic errors*: Verify your strategy by inspecting rule listings and graphs for anticipated problems and their solutions. This is only feasible if the rules have been partitioned in discrete subdomains.

Since the logic is so critical, we've included a number of common problems that you should look for.

3.3.1   *Undocumented control rules* which take control away from the inference engine by forcing it to follow explicit procedures.

3.3.2   *Duplicate rules* may be hard to find. Create, if necessary and inspect graphs of the rules and look for redundant paths on the graph(s). If you're using an existing tool, it may already have conflict detection mechanisms which can report on this circumstance.

3.3.3   *Contradictory rules* tend to fire together but recommend conflicting goals and certainty factors. Clearly they will cause problems in your system.

3.3.4   Look for *conditions that are not covered by rules*. Conditions that can be expressed but for which no rule will fire cause the inference engine to give up. These missing actions can often be found by examining a graphic representation of the rules.

3.3.5   *Rules covering nonexistent conditions* may exist in your system. They contain combinations of premises that cannot be input by the user, or that will never be examined because of a STOP clause which will fire in a higher priority rule.

Under other circumstances, you may have rules that examine the certainty of an attribute or goal. They will tend to fail if the goal has not been set to some real value. This is because the inference engine does not recognize "not yet specified" as a comparative value expression. You must guarantee that rules exist to set values to attributes that are used as chains to other rules.

3.3.7 *Incorrect goal priority* should be checked. most tools try to prove the first goal first, second goal second, etc. This has a dramatic effect on rule firing in the backward mode. Reorder goals, if necessary, to obtain an optimal consultation pattern.

3.3.8 *Runtime command arguments.* Make sure there are no incorrect or missing run time command arguments

3.3.9 *Rules with incorrect conclusions* may be difficult to identify, but must be uncovered. Rules require individual examination.

3.3.10 *Incomplete* chains (unreachable goals) may have several effects:

The expert system may ask questions which should never be offered to the user, i.e., should be derivable from an assertion posed by a "then" condition in another rule. If the question is asked of the user, determine what missing rule(s) needed to supply the assertion.

A conclusion is never reached even though the evidence for it is collected. This can happen when a rule tests in the "if" section for the level of certainty of a choice, but the choice has never been set by another rule.

3.3.11 *Incorrect and/or undocumented inferencing mode(s)* (forward instead of backward, etc.) can be found by examining (or preparing, if not available) a cause-effect diagram of the rule interactions. *Warning:* Preparation of documentation after the fact is very time-consuming.

3.3.12 Make sure that rule STOP commands are not interfering with chaining. Some tools allow a rule to STOP the inference process. If a rule invokes a STOP of the inference process when more chaining is desired, the session will end prematurely. Carefully examine the use of any STOP command and determine if it is really needed.

STOP should be the last assertion in any rule that employs it. Assertions following a STOP may not be activated.

3.3.13   *Use of ELSE in a rule containing more than one premise* can be tricky and should be verified. ELSE is activated if the rule does not fire for any reason. When a rule contains more than one premise, *any* permutation of "no match" will fire the ELSE statement when the rule is examined. *Be sure* that all permutations of no match on the premise pattern really supports an ELSE assertion. This is very hard to trace in maintenance if several rules use variations on the same premises.

3.4   *Coverage errors: Make sure that there are no unaccessible rule statements or incomplete chains*

3.5   Verify that *data and sensor interfaces* are supplying the correct data

3.5.1   Correct and functioning access syntax

3.5.1.1   Operating system errors may flash by and not be recognized

3.5.1.2   Nonpresence of expected return data may not be reported as error

3.5.2   Single access to outside source in one session

3.5.3   Multiple access in same session

3.5.4   Multiple access over several sessions

3.6   *Unit level diagrams*

Verify:

3.6.1   Modular rule bases

3.6.2   Conventional program interfaces

3.6.3   Database interfaces

3.6.4   Blackboard interfaces

4   Code documentation should be detailed and complete.

4.1   *Control rules*: Are control rules labeled with an explanation in their note fields?

4.2   *Command and Report scripts*: Are comments included to explain the purpose?

4.3   *Runtime options*: Are *all* runtime parameters documented?

4.4   *Filelist*: As part of the data dictionary, has a list of all files used by the system been provided, each with a paragraph explaining **how, when, and where** used?

4.5   *Legal notices*: Are copyright/proprietary notices included in all rule bases and supporting files?

4.6   *Data dictionary*: Definitions of all system data, control items, and files.

5   *Technical documentation* should be complete. Verify that the following has all been gathered into notebooks or files:

5.1   *Domain expert interview notes*

5.2   *Copies of all project management documentation*

5.3   *Copies of all approvals and agreements*

5.4   *Diagrams, tables, and other representations of*:

    5.4.1   Knowledge analysis representations

    5.4.2   Knowledge coding representations

    5.4.3   System diagrams

6   User documentation is critical for the successful implementation of your system. Make sure that it includes the following:

6.1   *Title sheet*:
    Copyright notice
    Notices for associated/bundled products
    System requirements
    Date and version of product and manual

6.2   *Copyright and disclaimer information*

6.3   *What is the product*?
    Why was it built?
    What can it and cannot do?
    Who would want it?

6.4   *How to install* the product

6.5   *Getting started* instructions for new users

6.6   *Sample session(s)*

6.7   *Special features* that are available in the product

6.8   *In case of difficulty*, what to do and who to contact

6.9   *Command summary* for quick reference

6.10   *Reference card* for quick reference

SUMMARY

Quality assurance is key to the success of your project. Properly managed, it can help to prevent problems before they occur and catch those that slip through the cracks before the system reaches the user. In a knowledge system, QA is particularly critical because the requirements continue to evolve until the project is complete.

The QA techniques that have been found most useful in knowledge systems include:

1. Walkthroughs — Review sessions that cover all project products including documentation, code, diagrams, etc.
2. Prototyping — Develop a model of the system so that users, developers, knowledge engineers, and experts can all explore its operation.
3. Documentation — Develop the user manual up front. This forces you to express the functionality and operation of the system in detail. It can be used to ensure that the system meets the specifications.
4. Tests and test plans — Make sure that system testing, integration testing, and unit testing are completed thoroughly

The tighter your quality assurance procedures are, the better the chances are that the system you deliver will meet the users' hopes and expectations. Plan them from the beginning and stick to them.

14

Maintenance

Software maintenance is a critical function within any organization that develops software. Seldom is software used once and discarded, and it is **not** likely that software **never** needs to change as an environment changes. Maintenance involves not only correcting errors but making the system more effective for the user.

Maintenance must not be ignored. Software maintenance accounts for 60–70% of each software dollar allocated, because over the life cycle of the project, maintenance consumes more time, money, and resources than any other aspect of the project.[1]

Software maintenance is the process of modifying existing operational software while leaving its primary functions intact. According to Barry Boehm this includes:

- Redesign and development, which consist of less than 50% new code
- Design and development of smaller interfacing packages, which requires less than 20% redesign of existing software
- Modification of code, documentation, or database structure

---

1 McCall, James A., Mary A. Herndon, Wilma M. Osborne, *Software Maintenance Management*. U.S. Department of Commerce, October 1985, NBS Special Publication 500-129.

There are several different types of maintenance. Recognizing whether or not you are performing maintenance and the type may affect how you proceed.

A software update changes functional specifications. This is not considered a maintenance activity because the changes would involve a new set of requirements, logical design, and physical design. Updates should be addressed as functional enhancements and should be developed using the knowledge systems project life cycle.

Software maintenance or repair does *not* change functional specifications. You may be required to perform corrective (20%) maintenance because actual errors occur. These repairs take place after the system is delivered. Changes in the operating environment may require adaptive (20%) maintenance. Factors external to your system, such as changes in hardware, operating system or tools may make it necessary to make modifications. On the other hand, you may want to make perfective (60%) maintenance changes to make code more easily understood. This involves updates to documentation, making code run faster, adding capabilities, and preventative work.

KNOWLEDGE SYSTEMS MAINTENANCE

Maintenance of knowledge systems has not been well explored because only a few published systems have reached the maintenance phase. One of the most well known of these is XCON by Digital Equipment Corporation (DEC).[2] There is currently an effort underway to assess its maintainability after a rewrite. In seven years it has grew from 700 rules to over 6200 in order to continue to meet Digital Equipment's needs, with 50% of the rules in XCON changing every year. More information on assessing the maintenance of XCON and coping with the problems of a very large rule base can be found in *Assessing the Maintainability of XCON-in-RIME: Coping with the Problems of a VERY Large Rule-Base.*[3]

As a large rule base changes over time, it can lose integrity in the same fashion as conventional programs. The rules become tightly

---

2   XCON and DEC are trademarks of Digital Equipment Corporation

3   Soloway, Elliot, Judy Bachant, and Keith Jensen, *Assessing the Maintainability of XCON-in-RIME: Coping with the Problems of a VERY Large Rule-Base.* AAAI-87 Proceedings, July, 1987.

coupled and incoherent. Others may wind up as dead code or, worse, forgotten code. This is magnified by the fact that most systems are maintained by people who did not develop the system. To minimize potential problems, you should take a structured and well-documented approach to maintenance.

An integrated software maintenance strategy is recommended. It is discussed in *Software Maintenance Management*. Knowledge system **maintenance** involves many of the tasks in knowledge system **development**. You can optimize activities by utilizing reusable code modules, code libraries, and tools.[4]

MANAGING MAINTENANCE

Maintenance management begins during the design and development phases of a project. You must decide on an approach that fits your application, environment, and user needs. Do not wait for a finished system to address maintenance before you begin planning.

A recommended approach is to treat the maintenance of the knowledge base independently of the user interfaces and control programs. Keeping the three parts of the system separate has its advantages and disadvantages. One advantage of separating maintenance activities is that the knowledge will not become too closely tied to the control programs. You want to avoid a situation in which your control programs are no longer reusable and further validation and maintenance is difficult because knowledge is represented in several places. Another advantage is that it will focus your interviews, validation and testing. The people you need to interface with will differ depending on the part of the system you are maintaining. The expert(s) will be your key contact for changes to the knowledge, while the end-users will be your source of input regarding the user interfaces.

A disadvantage of separating the maintenance activities is that the system may have required the use of knowledge that is coded and used externally to the actual knowledge base. For example, an interface might operate based on some knowledge about a domain, or a control program may contain knowledge. This strategy is not recommended because knowledge changes would be hard to maintain in a

---

4   McCall, op. cit.

complex system that is not fully documented or has several people responsible for maintenance. However, it is sometimes a necessary development decision to obtain the desired results. If knowledge has been coded externally to the knowledge base, it should be well documented and clearly recognizable so that the system maintenance will be less difficult. The ideal situation would be to have programming staff maintain the interfaces and control programs and a knowledge engineering staff maintain the knowledge. These teams should not be isolated from each other, but they need not be in the same group.

Maintenance activities will be similar to those of the general project life cycle defined in Chapter 10, but the steps are performed in a shorter time frame by different people. Don't be fooled into believing that you can run a maintenance effort like a development project maintenance is a unique process.

Can Domain Experts Maintain Knowledge Systems?

As we pointed out in Chapter 1, a domain expert is not usually the person of choice for maintaining a knowledge system. Large systems involve expertise in structured design, knowledge representation, knowledge coding, quality assurance, quality control, testing and maintenance. If a domain expert is truly an "expert" in his field, he probably does not have the in-depth skills in knowledge systems development or the time to spend programming. It might be appropriate for a domain expert to perform maintenance of a system if:

* the system is relatively static
* there are no control rules or control information in the knowledge base
* the system has an intelligent editor
* the logical model is documented and understandable
* standards are not an issue
* the system is small
* the system is no larger than a conventional program built by an end-user
* the only user interface needed is provided with the shell

MANAGING THE COST OF MAINTENANCE

Many systems developed today are easier to maintain than their older counterparts. This is because structured design methodologies, high-level languages and good documentation are being encouraged in many organizations.

In large organizations, "user-funded maintenance" is an important concept that provides checks and balances for the maintenance process. This means that the users fund the maintenance performed by an information systems group. Although this approach is not always compatible with an organization, there are some advantages. Users are closer to the maintenance cost, encouraging them to prioritize maintenance activities. Enhancements for efficiency become more important than spending money for seldom-used bells and whistles. The maintenance team also operates more efficiently because the team will view the users as clients and business partners.

The maintenance phase of the project life cycle is often one of the hardest to estimate costs for. You can make this easier by breaking the maintenance into manageable units.

MAINTENANCE TECHNIQUES AND TOOLS

If maintenance is to be effective it must employ the best tools and techniques available. This includes the use of consistent techniques and procedures for reporting problems. There are a wide range of tools available for maintenance. Editors and debuggers can process code and flag obvious errors. Test code generators, application generators, report generators, and simulators provide a quick method of generating and testing your plans. There are reports that provide analysis for errors, code optimizers, and online problem reporting and control systems, all of which may be used during maintenance.

One of the most effective ways to make maintenance easier is to consider maintenance during the development process. Figure 14.1 provides a summary of the maintenance activities that might be considered throughout the development process.[5]

------

5   McCall, op. cit.

PHASE	MAINTENANCE ACTIVITIES TO CONSIDER
Identification	* identify maintainability as a primary goal of development.
Conceptualization	* identify maintenance plan and resource requirements * establish design standards and conventions * document requirements and standards
Formalization	* audit design for compliance with standards * trace requirements to design
Implementation	* establish coding standards and conventions * audit code for compliance with standards * document and comment code * develop a maintenance manual
Testing	* document all errors * maintain code and documents during error correction * transfer text cases and tools to maintenance

Figure 14-1 Maintenance considerations during development.

Incorporating maintenance activities with development will provide for a successful maintenance effort when the project is in use. Maintenance should be planned and organized.

Model Maintenance Plan

Developing a maintenance plan is another important technique for effective maintenance. The activities in the previous table will help you to create the maintenance plan for your project. A good plan facilitates the use of well-documented and agreed-upon procedures. The plan should be detailed in all aspects of the maintenance process. The content will differ for every project, yet you may find it valuable to agree on an outline structure for the plan. A sample outline is included here to illustrate the information that should be included.

Plan Outline. Descriptions — provide sufficient information about the system components to make a new maintenance person fairly comfortable. Make sure to include:

• product
• hardware
• software
• definitions/glossary

Responsibilities — Identify the types of maintenance that may be required and whose responsibility each type falls under. The following people should be aware of what will be expected of them in the future:

- management
- user
- developer
- maintainer

Procedures — Describe how system changes are to be requested and what the procedures are for reporting a problem in each of the following areas:

- system change request and problem reporting
- customer access
- configuration control
- quality assurance
- testing

Resources — Provide a list of key personnel contacts who can provide additional support and information about the following:

- hardware
- software
- personnel
- facilities
- supplies
- funding

SUMMARY

Even the best developed software will need maintenance. It is not just a necessary evil to poorly written code, it is an activity that has to be anticipated and planned for during development. A maintenance plan is essential for managing maintenance. Make sure that system documentation provides adequate information for the maintenance person, then outline responsibilities, procedures to be followed, and where additional information can be obtained. There are a variety of tools for assisting in the maintenance activities including debuggers, code generators, databases, and development tools. Choose the tools that best fit your project.

Auto Repair Demonstration
Source Code Listing

The following source code listing has been generalized so that you can implement it in the tool of your choice. If you would rather not code it all yourself, you may obtain a complete, working copy of the Auto Repair Demonstration System via the coupon offer in this book.

TOOLS NEEDED TO IMPLEMENT THE SYSTEM

Control Blackboard

You may use a tool that has a control blackboard, or you may write your own. The control blackboard must be capable of executing the control blackboard command scripts listed below and in particular, of queueing blackboard command scripts for prioritzed execution. An explanation of the actions of the control blackboard is presented in Chapter 1.

Rule-Based Knowledge System Shell

Any backward chaining system could be used. The tool must be capable of calling external data blackboards and graphic display interfaces or have them built in. The ability to forget information (as described below) is not essential, but highly desirable.

Data Blackboard

Any database method will suffice that can read and write small amounts of data to and from the shell. Many shells have built-in database methods that can be used for this purpose.

Graphic Display Interface

An interface is needed to display color ANSI text graphics and color bit mapped graphics. Some shells have this capability; otherwise, call an external display program.

SUMMARY OF SOURCE LISTING CONTENTS

Source listings for the following system modules are included:

Module name	Area of expertise
SYMPTOMS	Referrals
ENGINE	Engine and referrals
CHARGSYS	Charging system and battery
OILPUMP	Oil pump
FUELSYS	Fuel system pump
IGNITION	Ignition
STARTER	Starter motor and relay
CARBURET (stub)	Carburetor mixture
NOISES (stub)	Unusual noises

A module is defined here as a Control Blackboard Command Script, Rule Base Listing, and Pictures, if any, to be displayed. *Note:* A stub is incomplete, but partially functional.

NOTES ON THE SYNTAX OF THE SOURCE LISTING

Explanation of Control Blackboard Command Scripts

The blackboard command scripts contain low level commands to be executed by the control blackboard. The following commands will need to be translated into whatever your blackboard tool requires:

cls	clear the user's screen
echo	put following text (or blank line) on the user's screen
execute	execute a program as a child process; wait for completion
display	display a text or bit mapped image on the user's screen
do	queue commands in the control blackboard
include	synonym for "do"
pause	halt execution until user presses a key if
exist	execute statement if file is present if not
exist	execute statement if file not present
!	execute statement/program at operating system level

Explanation of Rule-Base Listings

The rule-base listings have been laundered to be as Englishlike as possible. The full text of questions and answers have been included in the IF portions of the rules, in the form

IF:
<question> ... <answer>
   and   <question> ... <answer>
etc.

Some tools allow full text to be entered in the rules while others require that you use abbreviations in the rules and expand the text in separate definitions.

The following command expressions must specifically be coded in a form that will work with the tool you choose to use:

Command expressions found in the IF portions of rules:

check data blackboard for info
— try to get the answer to the question from the data blackboard. If the answer cannot be obtained from the data blackboard, obtain it from another rule, or the user.

display the <picture file name> picture while asking <question>
— show the named picture while asking the question.

Command expressions found in the THEN or ELSE portions of rules:

assert <variable = value>
> — the word assert is used call call attention to those times when one rule is providing the answer to a question needed by another rule (chaining).

forget <item>
> — cause the inference engine to forget data about a particular rule or question.

display the <picture file name> picture
> — display a text or bit mapped graphic image on user's screen

display "<text>"
> — display the quoted text on user's screen

tell blackboard to include <module> with certainty=____
> — this must cause an "include " statement to be written to a file that can be intercepted by the control blackboard after the rule base finishes execution. Note that the sample blackboard scripts accomplish this by looking for a file called OPTIONAL.Q. The rule base would optionally write include and other commands as described below to the OPTIONAL.Q file, after sorting those commands in order of certainty.

tell blackboard to ignore <module> with certainty=____
> — this must cause a "disallow" statement to be written to a file that can be intercepted by the control blackboard after the rule base finishes execution. See the include example above. Once a disallow statement is executed, the control blackboard will ignore any any subsequent requests to include the module.

tell blackboard to stop session with certainty=____
> — this must cause a "stop" statement to to be written to a file that can be intercepted by the control blackboard after the rule base finishes execution. This statement will cause the blackboard to halt everything and return the user to the operating system. See the include example above.

post <variable> to the data blackboard
> — this must cause the inference engine to call a database access method to post the variable and its value to a shared database (data blackboard).

get <variable> from the data blackboard
> — this must cause the inference engine to call a database access method to attempt to obtain the value for the variable from a shared

database (data blackboard). If the answer is not on the blackboard, the inference engine must ask the user to answer the question.

Explanation of Pictures

Pictures are recommended for use when an illustration is a superior means of communication. The implementation details for pictures will depend on your choice of software and hardware.

Main Control Blackboard Command Script

This command script is to be the first script executed when the system is invoked.

```
cls
echo
echo      Copyrights and Credits
echo
echo Knowledge Bases, Images        Copyright 1987
echo Generic Control Blackboard Meta (Inference) Services, Inc.
echo Generic Data Blackboard
echo Image Interface
echo
pause
cls
display the WELCOME.MSG picture
pause
cls
echo
echo
echo Please stand by...
include SYMPTOMS.Q
cls
echo Thank you for using the Auto Repair demonstration. For
echo another session, type AUTO and press the RETURN key.
```

SYMPTOMS Control Blackboard Command Script

This command script is executed when the control blackboard processess the command "include symptoms.q" in the main command script.

```
execute symptoms rulebase
if exist OPTIONAL.Q
```

```
include OPTIONAL.Q
endif
```

SYMPTOMS Rule-Base Listing

System goal: Find a solution to the user's problem, or, determine a blackboard action.

Write blackboard actions, if any, to the OPTIONAL.q file, using the control blackboard syntax, before exiting.

RULE NUMBER: 1

IF:

SYMPTOMS: Would you prefer to begin with a particular subsystem or be asked all questions? ... I would like to start with a specific subsystem.

and SYMPTOMS: In which subsystem (or subsystems) are you interested? ... CARBURETOR

THEN:

tell blackboard to include CARBURET.Q with certainty=9/10

and display "IF YOU FAIL TO SOLVE YOUR PROBLEM, RUN A NEW CONSULTATION AND ASK FOR 'ALL QUESTIONS'"

RULE NUMBER: 2

IF:

SYMPTOMS: Would you prefer to begin with a particular subsystem or be asked all questions? ... I would like to start with a specific subsystem.

and SYMPTOMS: In which subsystem (or subsystems) are you interested? ... CHARGING SYSTEM

THEN:

tell blackboard to include CHARGSYS.Q with certainty=9/10

and display "IF YOU FAIL TO SOLVE YOUR PROBLEM, RUN A NEW CONSULTATION AND ASK FOR 'ALL QUESTIONS'"

RULE NUMBER: 3

IF:

SYMPTOMS: Would you prefer to begin with a particular sub-system or be asked all questions? ... I would like to start with a specific subsystem.

and SYMPTOMS: In which subsystem (or subsystems) are you interested? ... ENGINE

THEN:

tell blackboard to include ENGINE.Q with certainty=9/10

and display "IF YOU FAIL TO SOLVE YOUR PROBLEM, RUN A NEW CONSULTATION AND ASK FOR 'ALL QUESTIONS'"

RULE NUMBER: 4

IF:

SYMPTOMS: Would you prefer to begin with a particular sub-system or be asked all questions? ... I would like to start with a specific subsystem.

and SYMPTOMS: In which subsystem (or subsystems) are you interested? ... FUEL SYSTEM

THEN:

tell blackboard to include FUELSYS.Q with certainty=9/10

and display "IF YOU FAIL TO SOLVE YOUR PROBLEM, RUN A NEW CONSULTATION AND ASK FOR 'ALL QUESTIONS'"

RULE NUMBER: 5

IF:

SYMPTOMS: Would you prefer to begin with a particular sub-system or be asked all questions? ... I would like to start with a specific subsystem.

and SYMPTOMS: In which subsystem (or subsystems) are you interested? ... IGNITION

THEN:
   tell blackboard to include IGNITION.Q with certainty=9/10

and display "IF YOU FAIL TO SOLVE YOUR PROBLEM, RUN A
   NEW CONSULTATION AND ASK FOR 'ALL QUESTIONS'"

RULE NUMBER: 6

IF:
   SYMPTOMS: Would you prefer to begin with a particular subsystem or be asked all questions? ... I would like to start with a
   specific subsystem.

and SYMPTOMS: In which subsystem (or subsystems) are you interested? ... STARTER

THEN:
   tell blackboard to include STARTER.Q with certainty=9/10

and display "IF YOU FAIL TO SOLVE YOUR PROBLEM, RUN A
   NEW CONSULTATION AND ASK FOR 'ALL QUESTIONS'"

RULE NUMBER: 7

IF:
   SYMPTOMS: Would you prefer to begin with a particular subsystem or be asked all questions? ... I would like to be asked all
   questions.

and SYMPTOMS: What general symptom are you experiencing? ...
   WON'T START

and SYMPTOMS: Try starting the car. Does the starter crank normally? ... YES

THEN:
   tell blackboard to include ENGINE.Q with certainty=9/10

and post ENGINE SYMPTOM to the data blackboard

and post STARTER CRANKS to the data blackboard

RULE NUMBER: 8

IF:

SYMPTOMS: Would you prefer to begin with a particular subsystem or be asked all questions? ... I would like to be asked all
questions.

and SYMPTOMS: What general symptom are you experiencing? ...
STARTS BUT there is a PROBLEM WHEN RUNNING

THEN:

tell blackboard to include ENGINE.Q with certainty=9/10

and post ENGINE SYMPTOM to the data blackboard

RULE NUMBER: 9

IF:

SYMPTOMS: Would you prefer to begin with a particular subsystem or be asked all questions? ... I would like to be asked all
questions.

and   SYMPTOMS: What general symptom are you experiencing? ...
WARNING LIGHT or GAUGE trouble

and   SYMPTOMS: Which light or gauge trouble are you having? ...
ALTERNATOR LIGHT

THEN:

tell blackboard to include CHARGSYS.Q with certainty=8/10

RULE NUMBER: 10

IF:

SYMPTOMS: Would you prefer to begin with a particular subsystem or be asked all questions? ... I would like to be asked all
questions.

and SYMPTOMS: What general symptom are you experiencing? ...
WARNING LIGHT or GAUGE trouble

and SYMPTOMS: Which light or gauge trouble are you having? ...
OIL LIGHT or OIL GAUGE

THEN:
> tell blackboard to include ENGINE.Q with certainty=9/10

and post ENGINE SYMPTOM to the data blackboard

RULE NUMBER: 11

IF:
> SYMPTOMS: Would you prefer to begin with a particular sub-system or be asked all questions? ... I would like to be asked all questions.

and SYMPTOMS: What general symptom are you experiencing? ... WARNING LIGHT or GAUGE trouble

and SYMPTOMS: Which light or gauge trouble are you having? ... LIGHTS DON'T COME ON while starting engine (before it catches) BUT THE ENGINE STARTS

THEN:
> display "THIS INDICATES A TROUBLE IN EITHER THE LIGHTS, FUSES, OR WIRING TO SENSORS. "LOCATE AND REPAIR THE TROUBLE."

RULE NUMBER: 12

IF:
> SYMPTOMS: Would you prefer to begin with a particular sub-system or be asked all questions? ... I would like to be asked all questions.

and SYMPTOMS: What general symptom are you experiencing? ... NONE OF THE ABOVE

THEN:
> tell blackboard to restart session

and display "OTHER AUTOMOBILE TROUBLES ARE BEYOND THE SCOPE & BOUNDS OF THIS DEMONSTRATION. THIS DEMONSTRATION IS MEANT TO SHOW STRUCTURED KNOWLEDGE REPRESENTATION AND KNOWLEDGE BASE NETWORKING TECHNIQUES. USE IT WITHIN ITS LIMITATIONS."

RULE NUMBER: 13

IF:

SYMPTOMS: Would you prefer to begin with a particular sub-system or be asked all questions? ... I would like to be asked all questions.

and SYMPTOMS: What general symptom are you experiencing? ... WON'T START

and SYMPTOMS: Try starting the car. Does the starter crank normally? ... NO (STARTER cranks slowly)

and SYMPTOMS: This could be caused by either a starter problem or a charging system trouble. WHICH WOULD YOU LIKE TO TRY FIRST? ... CHARGING SYSTEM

THEN:

post starter symptoms to data blackboard

and tell blackboard to include CHARGSYS.Q with certainty=8/10

and tell blackboard to include STARTER.Q with certainty=7/10

RULE NUMBER: 14

IF:

SYMPTOMS: Would you prefer to begin with a particular sub-system or be asked all questions? ... I would like to be asked all questions.

and SYMPTOMS: What general symptom are you experiencing? ... WON'T START

and SYMPTOMS: Try starting the car. Does the starter crank normally? ... NO (STARTER makes loud grinding noises)

and SYMPTOMS: This could be caused by either a starter problem or a charging system trouble. WHICH WOULD YOU LIKE TO TRY FIRST? ... CHARGING SYSTEM

THEN:

post STARTER SYMPTOM to the data blackboard

and tell blackboard to include CHARGSYS.Q with certainty=8/10

and tell blackboard to include STARTER.Q with certainty=7/10

RULE NUMBER: 15

IF:
SYMPTOMS: Would you prefer to begin with a particular sub-system or be asked all questions? ... I would like to be asked all questions.

and SYMPTOMS: What general symptom are you experiencing? ... WON'T START

and SYMPTOMS: Try starting the car. Does the starter crank normally? ... NO (STARTER cranks slowly)

and SYMPTOMS: This could be caused by either a starter problem or a charging system trouble. WHICH WOULD YOU LIKE TO TRY FIRST? ... STARTER

THEN:
post STARTER SYMPTOM to the data blackboard

and tell blackboard to include STARTER.Q with certainty=8/10

and tell blackboard to include CHARGSYS.Q with certainty=7/10

RULE NUMBER: 16

IF:
SYMPTOMS: Would you prefer to begin with a particular sub-system or be asked all questions? ... I would like to be asked all questions.

and SYMPTOMS: What general symptom are you experiencing? ... WON'T START

and SYMPTOMS: Try starting the car. Does the starter crank normally? ... NO (STARTER makes loud grinding noises)

and SYMPTOMS: This could be caused by either a starter problem
or a charging system trouble. WHICH WOULD YOU LIKE TO
TRY FIRST? ... STARTER

THEN:
post STARTER SYMPTOM to the data blackboard

and tell blackboard to include STARTER.Q with certainty=8/10

and tell blackboard to include CHARGSYS.Q with certainty=7/10

ENGINE Control Blackboard Command Script

This command script is executed when the control blackboard processess the command "include engine.q" in the main command script.

```
!if exist OPTIONAL.Q erase OPTIONAL.Q
cls
echo
echo
echo
echo Transferring to the ENGINE Knowledge Base
echo
echo Please stand by...
echo
echo
echo execute engine rule base
if exist OPTIONAL.Q
  include OPTIONAL.Q
endif
```

ENGINE Rule-Base Listing

System goal: Find a solution to the user's problem, or, determine a
blackboard action.
  Write blackboard actions, if any, to the OPTIONAL.q file, using
the control blackboard syntax, before exiting.

RULE NUMBER: 1

IF:
(check data blackboard for info) ENGINE: What problem are
you experiencing? ... Engine will not start

and ENGINE: This problem could be caused by the ignition system or the fuel system. Is a high voltage spark getting to the spark plugs? ... HOW (do I check the spark)

THEN:
display the SPARK.TST picture

and FORGET the last question

and FORGET this rule fired

NOTE:
HUMAN FACTORS: SHOW "HOW" AND RETURN TO THE SAME QUESTION. NEXT TIME, THE USER MAY NOT NEED TO ASK "HOW."

RULE NUMBER: 2
IF: (check data blackboard for info) ENGINE: What problem are you experiencing? ... Engine will not start

and ENGINE: This problem could be caused by the ignition system or the fuel system. Is a high voltage spark getting to the spark plugs? ... YES

THEN:
tell blackboard to include FUELSYS.Q with certainty=8/10

and tell blackboard to include IGNITION.Q with certainty=7/10

and post ENGINE SYMPTOM to the data blackboard

RULE NUMBER: 3

IF:
(check data blackboard for info) ENGINE: What problem are you experiencing? ... Engine will not start

and
ENGINE: This problem could be caused by the ignition system or the fuel system. Is a high voltage spark getting to the spark plugs? ... NO

THEN:
> tell blackboard to include IGNITION.Q with certainty=9/10

and post ENGINE SYMPTOM to the data blackboard

RULE NUMBER: 4

IF: (check data blackboard for info) ENGINE: What problem are you experiencing? ... Engine misses

and ENGINE: How does the engine "miss"? ... steadily

and ENGINE: What happens if you disconnect a spark plug wire (ONE PLUG AT A TIME) and ground it while the engine is running? Replace the last wire before you try another ... There is a plug which can be disconnected without changing the engine miss.

and ENGINE: That cylinder is not firing. Can you draw a spark to any metal object in the engine compartment from the cap on the end of the spark plug wire? ... HOW

THEN:
> display the the SPARK.TST picture

and FORGET the last question

and FORGET this rule fired

NOTE:
SHOW "HOW" AND RETURN TO THE SAME QUESTION

RULE NUMBER: 5

IF:
> (check data blackboard for info) ENGINE: What problem are you experiencing? ... Engine misses

and ENGINE: How does the engine "miss"? ... steadily

and ENGINE: What happens if you disconnect a spark plug wire (ONE PLUG AT A TIME) and ground it while the engine is running? Replace the last wire before you try another ... There is a plug which can be disconnected without changing the engine miss.

and ENGINE: That cylinder is not firing. Can you draw a spark to any metal object in the engine compartment from the cap on the end of the spark plug wire? ... YES

THEN:
display "CHECK THE COMPRESSION ON THE SUSPECTED CYLINDER TO ISOLATE THE PROBLEM. GOOD LUCK!"

RULE NUMBER: 6

IF:
(check data blackboard for info) ENGINE: What problem are you experiencing? ... Engine misses

and ENGINE: How does the engine "miss"? ... steadily

and ENGINE: What happens if you disconnect a spark plug wire (ONE PLUG AT A TIME) and ground it while the engine is running? Replace the last wire before you try another. ... There is a plug which can be disconnected without changing the engine miss.

and ENGINE: That cylinder is not firing. Can you draw a spark to any metal object in the engine compartment from the cap on the end of the spark plug wire? ... NO

THEN:
display "CHECK THE DISTRIBUTOR CAP, WIRE, AND SPARK PLUG."

RULE NUMBER: 7

IF:
(check data blackboard for info) ENGINE: What problem are you experiencing? ... Engine misses

and ENGINE: How does the engine "miss"? ... steadily

and ENGINE: What happens if you disconnect a spark plug wire (ONE PLUG AT A TIME) and ground it while the engine is running? Replace the last wire before you try another. ... Disconnecting any plug has the same effect; the missing gets worse.

and ENGINE: All of your cylinders seem to be functioning so my strategy for "steady miss" is exhausted. Think again about the nature of your problem and choose the most appropriate of the following: ... Engine misses erratically at all speeds

THEN:

assert ENGINE: How does the engine "miss"? ... erratically at all speeds

NOTE:

THE USER HAS INDICATED AN ENGINE MISS. WHILE THEY MAY HAVE PICKED THE WRONG ATTRIBUTE FOR ENGINE MISS, WE CAN'T ASSUME THERE IS NO MISS AT THIS POINT. LET'S USE "NONMONOTONIC REASONING" AND ADD TO THE INFORMATION ALREADY KNOWN ABOUT THE MISSING ENGINE.

RULE NUMBER: 8

IF:

(check data blackboard for info) ENGINE: What problem are you experiencing? ... Engine misses

and ENGINE: How does the engine "miss"? ... steadily

and ENGINE: What happens if you disconnect a spark plug wire (ONE PLUG AT A TIME) and ground it while the engine is running? Replace the last wire before you try another. ... Disconnecting any plug has the same effect; the missing gets worse.

and ENGINE: All of your cylinders seem to be functioning so my strategy for "steady miss" is exhausted. Think again about the nature of your problem and choose the most appropriate of the following: ... Engine misses at idle only

THEN:

assert ENGINE: How does the engine "miss"? ... at idle only

NOTE:
THE USER HAS INDICATED AN ENGINE MISS. WHILE THEY
MAY HAVE PICKED THE WRONG ATTRIBUTE FOR ENGINE
MISS, WE CAN'T ASSUME THERE IS NO MISS AT THIS POINT.
LET'S USE "NONMONOTONIC REASONING" AND ADD TO THE
INFORMATION ALREADY KNOWN ABOUT THE MISSING EN-
GINE.

RULE NUMBER: 9

IF:

    (check data blackboard for info) ENGINE: What problem are
    you experiencing? ... Engine misses

and   ENGINE: How does the engine "miss"? ... steadily

and   ENGINE: What happens if you disconnect a spark plug wire
    (ONE PLUG AT A TIME) and ground it while the engine is
    running? Replace the last wire before you try another ... Discon-
    necting any plug has the same effect; the missing gets worse.

and   ENGINE: All of your cylinders seem to be functioning so my
    strategy for "steady miss" is exhausted. Think again about the
    nature of your problem and choose the most appropriate of the
    following: ... Engine misses at high speed only

THEN:
    assert ENGINE: How does the engine "miss"? ... at high speed only

NOTE:
THE USER HAS INDICATED AN ENGINE MISS. WHILE THEY
MAY HAVE PICKED THE WRONG ATTRIBUTE FOR ENGINE
MISS, WE CAN'T ASSUME THERE IS NO MISS AT THIS POINT.
LET'S USE "NONMONOTONIC REASONING" AND ADD TO THE
INFORMATION ALREADY KNOWN ABOUT THE MISSING EN-
GINE.

RULE NUMBER: 10

IF:

    (check data blackboard for info) ENGINE: What problem are
    you experiencing? ... Engine misses

and ENGINE: How does the engine "miss"? ... at high speed only

THEN:

tell blackboard to include FUELSYS.Q with certainty=8/10

and tell blackboard to include IGNITION.Q with certainty=7/10

and post ENGINE SYMPTOM to the data blackboard

RULE NUMBER: 11

IF:

(check data blackboard for info) ENGINE: What problem are you experiencing? ... Low performance at all speeds, poor acceleration

THEN:

tell blackboard to include IGNITION.Q with certainty=8/10

and tell blackboard to include FUELSYS.Q with certainty=7/10

and post ENGINE SYMPTOM to the data blackboard

RULE NUMBER: 12

IF:

(check data blackboard for info) ENGINE: What problem are you experiencing? ... Excessive fuel consumption

THEN:

tell blackboard to include FUELSYS.Q with certainty=7/10

and display "WE WILL EXAMINE THE FUEL SYSTEM NEXT. IF IT IS 'OK', "BE SURE TO CHECK FOR CLUTCH SLIPPAGE, BRAKE DRAG, BAD WHEEL BEARINGS, "AND PROBLEMS WITH YOUR FRONT END ALIGNMENT."

and post ENGINE SYMPTOM to the data blackboard

NOTE:
OTHER "SUBCLASS" RULE BASES WOULD NORMALLY BE FRONT-END ALIGNMENT (WHICH WOULD INCLUDE AN ADDTITIONAL SUBCLASS RULE BASE [WHEEL BEARINGS]),

CLUTCH, AND BRAKES. THEY ARE NOT INCLUDED IN THE DEMONSTRATION.

RULE NUMBER: 13

IF:

> (check data blackboard for info) ENGINE: What problem are you experiencing? ... Engine diesels (keeps running) after ignition is switched off

THEN:

> display the DEISEL.TST picture and tell blackboard to include FUELSYS.Q with certainty=8/10

and tell blackboard to include CARBURET.Q with certainty=7/10

and post ENGINE SYMPTOM to the data blackboard

RULE NUMBER: 14

IF:

> (check data blackboard for info) ENGINE: What problem are you experiencing? ... Oil Pressure Light problem

and ENGINE: Does the oil light come on when the ignition is switched on (without the engine running)? ... NO

and ENGINE: Check the alternator warning light. Does it light when the ignition is switched on (engine not running)? ... NO

THEN:

> tell blackboard to include CHARGSYS.Q with certainty=8/10

RULE NUMBER: 15

IF:

> (check data blackboard for info) ENGINE: What problem are you experiencing? ... Oil Pressure Light problem

and ENGINE: Does the oil light come on when the ignition is switched on (without the engine running)? ... NO

and ENGINE: Check the alternator warning light. Does it light
when the ignition is switched on (engine not running)? ... YES

and ENGINE: Check the oil sending unit. Is it OK? ... HOW (do I
check the sending unit)

THEN:
display the SENDUNIT.TST picture

and FORGET the last question

and FORGET this rule fired

NOTE:
SHOW "HOW" TO CHECK THE OIL SENDING UNIT AND RE-
TURN TO THIS QUESTION

RULE NUMBER: 16

IF:
(check data blackboard for info) ENGINE: What problem are
you experiencing? ... Oil Pressure Light problem

and ENGINE: Does the oil light come on when the ignition is
switched on (without the engine running)? ... NO

and ENGINE: Check the alternator warning light. Does it light
when the ignition is switched on (engine not running)? ... YES

and ENGINE: Check the oil sending unit. Is it OK? ... YES

THEN:
display "THE LAMP IS PROBABLY BURNED OUT. REPLACE
THE LAMP."

RULE NUMBER: 17

IF:
(check data blackboard for info) ENGINE: What problem are
you experiencing? ... Oil Pressure Light problem

and ENGINE: Does the oil light come on when the ignition is
switched on (without the engine running)? ... NO

and ENGINE: Check the alternator warning light. Does it light when the ignition is switched on (engine not running)? ... YES

and ENGINE: Check the oil sending unit. Is it OK? ... NO

and ENGINE: is the oil sending unit properly grounded? ... YES

THEN:
display "REPLACE THE OIL PRESSURE SENDING UNIT."

RULE NUMBER: 18

IF:
(check data blackboard for info) ENGINE: What problem are you experiencing? ... Oil Pressure Light problem

and ENGINE: Does the oil light come on when the ignition is switched on (without the engine running)? ... NO

and ENGINE: Check the alternator warning light. Does it light when the ignition is switched on (engine not running)? ... YES

and ENGINE: Check the oil sending unit. Is it OK? ... NO

and ENGINE: is the oil sending unit properly grounded? ... NO

THEN:
display "RESTORE A PROPER GROUND TO THE OIL PRESSURE SENDING UNIT."

RULE NUMBER: 19

IF:
(check data blackboard for info) ENGINE: What problem are you experiencing? ... Oil Pressure Light problem

and ENGINE: Does the oil light come on when the ignition is switched on (without the engine running)? ... YES

and ENGINE: Does the oil light flicker or stay on while the engine is running? ... IT FLICKERS or IT STAYS ON and (display the OILWARN.TST picture while asking) ENGINE: Check the oil level is it OK? ... NO, I found the problem.

THEN:

display "CONGRATULATIONS!! YOU FOUND THE PROBLEM!"

RULE NUMBER: 20

IF:

(check data blackboard for info) ENGINE: What problem are you experiencing? ... Oil Pressure Light problem

and ENGINE: Does the oil light come on when the ignition is switched on (without the engine running)? ... YES

and ENGINE: Does the oil light flicker or stay on while the engine is running? ... IT FLICKERS or IT STAYS ON

and (display the OILWARN.TST picture while asking) ENGINE: Check the oil level is it OK? ... YES

and ENGINE: Check the engine temperature. Is it normal? ... YES (It is normal)

and ENGINE: Check for a shorted oil pressure sender with an ohm-meter or other continuity tester. Is it OK? ... NO (I found it)

THEN:

display "CONGRATULATIONS!! YOU FOUND THE PROBLEM!"

RULE NUMBER: 21

IF:

(check data blackboard for info) ENGINE: What problem are you experiencing? ... Oil Pressure Light problem

and ENGINE: Does the oil light come on when the ignition is switched on (without the engine running)? ... YES

and ENGINE: Does the oil light flicker or stay on while the engine is running? ... IT FLICKERS or IT STAYS ON and (display the OILWARN.TST picture while asking) ENGINE: Check the oil level is it OK? ... YES

and ENGINE: Check the engine temperature. Is it normal? ... YES (It is normal)

and ENGINE: Check for a shorted oil pressure sender with an ohm-meter or other continuity tester. Is it OK? ... YES

and ENGINE: Listen for unusual noises. Is there any indication of bad bearings or internal trouble? ... YES

THEN:

display "DO NOT START THE ENGINE UNTIL YOU KNOW WHY THE LIGHT WENT ON AND THE PROBLEM HAS BEEN CORRECTED. (MAY REQUIRE ENGINE DISMAN-TLING)."

NOTE:
THE EXPERT DETERMINED IT WAS TIME TO QUIT WITHOUT EXTRA HELP FROM THE PROGRAM.

RULE NUMBER: 22

IF:

(check data blackboard for info) ENGINE: What problem are you experiencing? ... Oil Pressure Light problem

and ENGINE: Does the oil light come on when the ignition is switched on (without the engine running)? ... YES

and ENGINE: Does the oil light flicker or stay on while the engine is running? ... IT FLICKERS or IT STAYS ON

and (display the OILWARN.TST picture while asking) ENGINE: Check the oil level is it OK? ... YES

and ENGINE: Check the engine temperature. Is it normal? ... YES (It is normal)

and ENGINE: Check for a shorted oil pressure sender with an ohm-meter or other continuity tester. Is it OK? ... YES and ENGINE: Listen for unusual noises. Is there any indication of bad bearings or internal trouble? ... NO

THEN:

tell blackboard to include OILPUMP.Q with certainty=9/10

and display "DO NOT START THE ENGINE UNTIL YOU KNOW WHY THE LIGHT WENT ON AND THE PROBLEM HAS BEEN CORRECTED. (MAY REQUIRE ENGINE DISMAN-TLING)."

RULE NUMBER: 23

IF:

(check data blackboard for info) ENGINE: What problem are you experiencing? ... Oil Pressure Light problem

and ENGINE: Does the oil light come on when the ignition is switched on (without the engine running)? ... YES

and ENGINE: Does the oil light flicker or stay on while the engine is running? ... IT FLICKERS or IT STAYS ON

and (display the OILWARN.TST picture while asking) ENGINE: Check the oil level is it OK? ... YES

and ENGINE: Check the engine temperature. Is it normal? ... YES (It is normal)

and ENGINE: Check for a shorted oil pressure sender with an ohm-meter or other continuity tester. Is it OK? ... YES

and ENGINE: Listen for unusual noises. Is there any indication of bad bearings or internal trouble? ... NO

THEN:

tell blackboard to include OILPUMP.Q with certainty=9/10

and tell blackboard to stop session with certainty=8/10

and display "REPLACE OR REBUILD THE OIL PUMP."

NOTE:
THE EXPERT IS ASSUMING THE USER UNDERSTANDS HOW TO REPAIR THE OIL PUMP BECAUSE THE USER UNDERSTOOD HOW TO DISASSEMBLE AND TEST THE UNIT.

THE OILPUMP MODULE WILL BE EXECUTED BEFORE THE BLACKBOARD STOPS THE SESSION.

RULE NUMBER: 24

IF:

   (check data blackboard for info) ENGINE: What problem are you experiencing? ... Engine misses

and ENGINE: How does the engine "miss"? ... erratically at all speeds

THEN:

   tell blackboard to include IGNITION.Q with certainty=8/10

and tell blackboard to include FUELSYS.Q with certainty=6/10

and display "THIS PROBLEM COULD BE IN THE IGNITION SYSTEM, EXHAUST SYSTEM, OR FUEL SYSTEM. THIS DEMO DOES NOT COVER EXHAUST; WE WILL EXPLORE THE OTHER AREAS."

and post ENGINE SYMPTOM to the data blackboard

RULE NUMBER: 25

IF:

   (check data blackboard for info) ENGINE: What problem are you experiencing? ... Engine misses

and ENGINE: How does the engine "miss"? ... at idle only

and ENGINE: What happens if you disconnect a spark plug wire (ONE PLUG AT A TIME) and ground it while the engine is running? Replace the last wire before you try another ... Disconnecting any plug has the same effect; the missing gets worse.

THEN:
tell blackboard to ignore FUELSYS.Q with certainty=9/10

and tell blackboard to include IGNITION.Q with certainty=8/10

and tell blackboard to include CARBURET.Q with certainty=7/10

and display "THIS TROUBLE MIGHT ALSO BE THE EXHAUST RECIRCULATION SYSTEM (EGR). "THIS DEMO DOES NOT COVER THE EXHAUST SYSTEM; WE WILL EXPLORE THE "OTHER AREAS."

and post ENGINE SYMPTOM to the data blackboard

and post SPARK SYMPTOM to the data blackboard

RULE NUMBER: 26

IF:
(check data blackboard for info) ENGINE: What problem are you experiencing? ... Engine misses

and ENGINE: How does the engine "miss"? ... at idle only

and ENGINE: What happens if you disconnect a spark plug wire (ONE PLUG AT A TIME) and ground it while the engine is running? Replace the last wire before you try another ... There is a plug which can be disconnected without changing the engine miss.

THEN:
tell blackboard to ignore FUELSYS.Q with certainty=9/10

and tell blackboard to include IGNITION.Q with certainty=8/10

and tell blackboard to include CARBURET.Q with certainty=6/10

and display "THE PROBLEM MAY BE COMPRESSION, IGNITION, OR CARBURETION. THIS DEMO "DOES NOT COVER COMPRESSION; WE WILL EXAMINE THE OTHER AREAS."

and post ENGINE SYMPTOM to the data blackboard

and post SPARK SYMPTOM to the data blackboard

RULE NUMBER: 27

IF:

(check data blackboard for info) ENGINE: What problem are you experiencing? ... Oil Pressure Light problem

and ENGINE: Does the oil light come on when the ignition is switched on (without the engine running)? ... YES

and ENGINE: Does the oil light flicker or stay on while the engine is running? ... IT FLICKERS or IT STAYS ON

and (display the OILWARN.TST picture while asking) ENGINE: Check the oil level is it OK? ... YES

and ENGINE: Check the engine temperature. Is it normal? ... NO (It is high)

THEN:

display "CHECK THE COOLANT SYSTEM FOR ADEQUATE WATER SUPPLY & WATER PUMP OPERATION. "ALSO, BE SURE THE ENGINE IS NOT SEIZED DUE TO MECHANI-CAL FAILURE."

CHARGSYS Control Blackboard Command Script

This command script is executed when the control blackboard pro-cessess the command "include chargsys.q" in the main command script.

```
!if exist OPTIONAL.Q erase OPTIONAL.Q
cls
echo
echo
echo
echo Transferring to the CHARGSYS Knowledge Base
echo
echo Please stand by...
echo
echo
echo execute chargsys rulebase if exist OPTIONAL.Q
 include OPTIONAL.Q endif
```

CHARGSYS Rulebase Listing

System goal: Find a solution to the user's problem, or, determine a blackboard action.

Write blackboard actions, if any, to the OPTIONAL.q file, using the control blackboard syntax, before exiting.

RULE NUMBER: 1

IF:

CHARGING SYSTEM: What symptoms are evident? ... ALTER-NATOR WARNING LIGHT does not come on when ignition is turned on

and (check data blackboard for info) CHARGING SYSTEM: What happens when you try to start the car? ... The car won't start

THEN:

display "CHECK THE BATTERY AND THE IGNITION SWITCH."

RULE NUMBER: 2

IF:

CHARGING SYSTEM: What symptoms are evident? ... ALTER-NATOR WARNING LIGHT does not come on when ignition is turned on

and (check data blackboard for info) CHARGING SYSTEM: What happens when you try to start the car? ... The car starts

and CHARGING SYSTEM: Find the voltage regulator and disconnect the wire from terminal "L" (THIS IS THE LAMP WIRE). Ground the wire. Does the alternator lamp come on? ... YES

THEN:

tell blackboard to stop session with certainty=9/10

and display "EITHER THE VOLTAGE REGULATOR IS DEFEC-TIVE, OR THE ALTERNATOR IS NOT "PROPERLY GROUNDED, OR THE ALTERNATOR BRUSHES ARE NOT MAKING CONTACT."

RULE NUMBER: 3

IF:

CHARGING SYSTEM: What symptoms are evident? ... ALTER-NATOR WARNING LIGHT does not come on when ignition is turned on

and (check data blackboard for info) CHARGING SYSTEM: What happens when you try to start the car? ... The car starts

and CHARGING SYSTEM: Find the voltage regulator and disconnect the wire from terminal "L" (THIS IS THE LAMP WIRE). Ground the wire. Does the alternator lamp come on? ... NO

THEN:

tell blackboard to stop session with certainty=8/10

and display "THE ALTERNATOR LAMP BULB IS PROBABLY BURNED OUT; REPLACE IT."

RULE NUMBER: 4

IF:

CHARGING SYSTEM: What symptoms are evident? ... ALTER-NATOR LIGHT comes on and stays on

and CHARGING SYSTEM: This usually indicates that no charging is taking place. Check the fan belt tension. Is it adjusted correctly? ... NO (I found it)

THEN:

tell blackboard to stop session with certainty=8/10

and display "ADJUST THE FAN BELT AND CHECK THE WARN-ING LIGHT. IF THE PROBLEM PERSISTS, CONSULT ME AGAIN."

RULE NUMBER: 5

IF:

CHARGING SYSTEM: What symptoms are evident? ... ALTER-NATOR LIGHT comes on and stays on and CHARGING SYSTEM: This usually indicates that no charging is taking place. Check the fan belt tension. Is it adjusted correctly? ... YES

and (check data blackboard for info) CHARGING SYSTEM: Check the battery with a hydrometer. Does the battery test indicate the battery is OK? ... HOW (do I check?)

THEN:
display the HYDROMTR.TST picture

and FORGET the last question

and FORGET this rule fired

RULE NUMBER: 6

IF:
CHARGING SYSTEM: What symptoms are evident? ... ALTERNATOR LIGHT comes on and stays on

and CHARGING SYSTEM: This usually indicates that no charging is taking place. Check the fan belt tension. Is it adjusted correctly? ... YES

and (check data blackboard for info) CHARGING SYSTEM: Check the battery with a hydrometer. Does the battery test indicate the battery is OK? ... NO (I found it)

THEN:
tell blackboard to stop session with certainty=8/10

and display "CONGRATULATIONS! YOU FOUND IT!"

NOTE:
Because this rule sends a "tell blackboard to stop session" message to the control blackboard, we won't bother posting the battery condition on the data blackboard.

RULE NUMBER: 7

IF:

CHARGING SYSTEM: What symptoms are evident? ... ALTER-NATOR LIGHT comes on and stays on

and CHARGING SYSTEM: This usually indicates that no charging is taking place. Check the fan belt tension. Is it adjusted correctly? ... YES

and (check data blackboard for info) CHARGING SYSTEM: Check the battery with a hydrometer. Does the battery test indicate the battery is OK? ... YES

and CHARGING SYSTEM: Check all electrical connections in the charging system. Do they appear to be OK? ... YES

and CHARGING SYSTEM: Check the alternator. Is it working properly? ... HOW

THEN:

display the ALTERNAT.TST picture and FORGET the last question and FORGET this rule fired

RULE NUMBER: 8

IF:

CHARGING SYSTEM: What symptoms are evident? ... ALTER-NATOR LIGHT comes on and stays on

and CHARGING SYSTEM: This usually indicates that no charging is taking place. Check the fan belt tension. Is it adjusted correctly? ... YES

and (check data blackboard for info) CHARGING SYSTEM: Check the battery with a hydrometer. Does the battery test indicate the battery is OK? ... YES

and CHARGING SYSTEM: Check all electrical connections in the charging system. Do they appear to be OK? ... YES

and CHARGING SYSTEM: Check the alternator. Is it working properly? ... NO (I found it)

THEN:
   tell blackboard to stop session with certainty=9/10

and display "CONGRATULATIONS! YOU FOUND IT!"

RULE NUMBER: 9

IF:

   CHARGING SYSTEM: What symptoms are evident? ... ALTER-
   NATOR LIGHT comes on and stays on

and CHARGING SYSTEM: This usually indicates that no charging
   is taking place. Check the fan belt tension. Is it adjusted correctly? ... YES

and (check data blackboard for info) CHARGING SYSTEM: Check
   the battery with a hydrometer. Does the battery test indicate
   the battery is OK? ... YES

and CHARGING SYSTEM: Check all electrical connections in the
   charging system. Do they appear to be OK? ... YES

and CHARGING SYSTEM: Check the alternator. Is it working properly? ... YES

THEN:
   display "HAVE THE VOLTAGE REGULATOR TESTED."

RULE NUMBER: 10

IF:

   CHARGING SYSTEM: What symptoms are evident? ... ALTER-
   NATOR LIGHT flashes erratically

and CHARGING SYSTEM: This usually indicates the charging system is working intermittently. Check the fan belt tension. Is the
   belt properly adjusted? ... NO (I found it)

THEN:
   tell blackboard to stop session with certainty=8/10

and display "ADJUST THE FAN BELT AND CHECK THE WARN-ING LIGHT. IF THE PROBLEM PERSISTS, CONSULT ME AGAIN."

RULE NUMBER: 11

IF:

CHARGING SYSTEM: What symptoms are evident? ... ALTER-NATOR LIGHT flashes erratically

and CHARGING SYSTEM: This usually indicates the charging system is working intermittently. Check the fan belt tension. Is the belt properly adjusted? ... YES

and CHARGING SYSTEM: Check all electrical connections in the charging system. Do they appear to be OK? ... NO (I found it)

THEN:

tell blackboard to stop session with certainty=8/10

and display "CONGRATULATIONS! YOU FOUND IT!"

RULE NUMBER: 12

IF:

CHARGING SYSTEM: What symptoms are evident? ... ALTER-NATOR LIGHT flashes erratically

and CHARGING SYSTEM: This usually indicates the charging system is working intermittently. Check the fan belt tension. Is the belt properly adjusted? ... YES

and CHARGING SYSTEM: Check all electrical connections in the charging system. Do they appear to be OK? ... YES

THEN:

display "YOUR ALTERNATOR NEEDS TO BE CHECKED AND/OR REPAIRED."

RULE NUMBER: 13

IF:

CHARGING SYSTEM: What symptoms are evident? ... BAT-
TERY requires frequent additions of water

THEN:

tell blackboard to stop session with certainty=8/10

and display "THE ALTERNATOR IS PROBABLY OVERCHARG-
ING THE BATTERY DUE TO A VOLTAGE "REGULATOR
FAULT. HAVE THE REGULATOR TESTED BY A DEALER
OR COMPETENT ELECTRICAL SHOP."

RULE NUMBER: 14

IF:

CHARGING SYSTEM: What symptoms are evident? ... Excessive NOISE from alternator and CHARGING SYSTEM: Check
the alternator mountings and pulley. Are they OK? ... NO (I
found the trouble)

THEN:

tell blackboard to stop session with certainty=8/10

and display "TIGHTEN MOUNTINGS OR PULLEY TENSION [BE
SURE THE PULLEY IS NOT OUT OF" "ADJUSTMENT DUE
TO ALTERNATOR BEARING WEAR]."

RULE NUMBER: 15

IF:

CHARGING SYSTEM: What symptoms are evident? ... Excessive NOISE from alternator

and CHARGING SYSTEM: Check the alternator mountings and
pulley. Are they OK? ... YES

THEN:

display "THE PROBLEM MAY BE WORN ALTERNATOR
BEARINGS OR IMPROPERLY SEATED BRUSHES. REMOVE
THE ALTERNATOR FOR CLOSER INSPECTION & REPAIR."

RULE NUMBER: 16

IF:

> CHARGING SYSTEM: What symptoms are evident? ... NONE OF THE ABOVE

THEN:
> tell blackboard to ignore chargsys with certainty=9/10

and display "CHARGING SYSTEM HAS NO ANSWER FOR YOUR PROBLEM. PLEASE ASK A MORE QUALIFIED TECHNICIAN."

RULE NUMBER: 18

IF:

> CHARGING SYSTEM: What symptoms are evident? ... ALTERNATOR LIGHT comes on and stays on

and CHARGING SYSTEM: This usually indicates that no charging is taking place. Check the fan belt tension. Is it adjusted correctly? ... YES

and (check data blackboard for info) CHARGING SYSTEM: Check the battery with a hydrometer. Does the battery test indicate the battery is OK? ... YES

THEN:
> post BATTERY CONDITION to the data blackboard

CARBURET Control Blackboard Command Script

This command script is executed when the control blackboard processess the command "include carburet.q" in the main command script.

CARBURET is an example of a stubbed knowledge base module. A rule base has not yet been constructed. However, if called, CARBURET will display a picture explaining how to adjust idle mixture (IDLEMIX.TST).

```
cls
echo
echo
echo
```

```
echo CARBURETOR IDLE MIXTURE TEST
echo
echo Please test your carburetor idle mixture. It may
echo
echo be contributing to the problem you are experiencing
echo
echo
pause
display the IIDLEMIX.TST picture
echo
echo
echo
echo
echo
echo There is no other carburetor information at this time.
echo
echo
echo
echo
pause
cls
```

FUELSYS Control Blackboard Command Script

This command script is executed when the control blackboard processess the command "include fuelsys.q" in the main command script.

```
!if exist OPTIONAL.Q erase OPTIONAL.Q
cls
echo
echo
echo
echo Transferring to the FUELSYS Knowledge Base
echo
echo Please stand by...
echo
echo
echo execute FUELSYS rule base
if exist OPTIONAL.Q
  include OPTIONAL.Q endif
```

FUELSYS Rulebase Listing

System goal: Find a solution to the user's problem or determine a blackboard action.

Write blackboard actions, if any, to the OPTIONAL.q file, using the control blackboard syntax, before exiting.

RULE NUMBER: 1

IF:

(check data blackboard for info) FUELSYS: What problem are you experiencing? ... Engine will not start

and FUELSYS: Remove the air cleaner, look into the carburetor throat, and yank on the throttle linkage a few times. You should see and hear a stream of fuel as the accelerator pump discharges... I see the discharge

THEN:

display "YOU MAY HAVE A STICKING CHOKE, OR FLOODED CARBURETOR. LET THE CAR SIT A WHILE, THEN TRY AGAIN. IF THE CHOKE IS MANUAL, BE SURE TO CLOSE IT."

RULE NUMBER: 2

IF:

(check data blackboard for info) FUELSYS: What problem are you experiencing? ... Engine will not start

and FUELSYS: Remove the air cleaner, look into the carburetor throat, and yank on the throttle linkage a few times. You should see and hear a stream of fuel as the accelerator pump discharges... I do not see a discharge

and FUELSYS: Remove your gas cap for a moment to equalize gas tank pressure, then replace the cap. Try to start the car again. Does it start?... Yes

THEN:

tell blackboard to stop session with certainty=1/10

and display "YOU HAD A TEMPORARY VAPOR LOCK. REMEMBER THE TRICK; YOU MAY NEED IT AGAIN."

RULE NUMBER: 3

IF:

(check data blackboard for info) FUELSYS: What problem are you experiencing? ... Engine will not start and FUELSYS: Remove the air cleaner, look into the carburetor throat, and yank on the throttle linkage a few times. You should see and hear a stream of fuel as the accelerator pump discharges... I do not see a discharge and FUELSYS: Remove your gas cap for a moment to equalize gas tank pressure, then replace the cap. Try to start the car again. Does it start?... No

and FUELSYS: Disconnect the fuel line to the carburetor and pop the end of the hose from the fuel pump into a 1 pound coffee can (or some similar metal can). Crank the engine briefly. Was fuel pumped out of the tube? No

THEN:

tell blackboard to stop session with certainty=1/10

and display "TRY REPLACING THE FUEL FILTER. IF THE PROBLEM PERSISTS, REPLACE THE FUEL PUMP."

RULE NUMBER: 4

IF:

(check data blackboard for info) FUELSYS: What problem are you experiencing? ... Engine will not start

and FUELSYS: Remove the air cleaner, look into the carburetor throat, and yank on the throttle linkage a few times. You should see and hear a stream of fuel as the accelerator pump discharges... I do not see a discharge

and FUELSYS: Remove your gas cap for a moment to equalize gas tank pressure, then replace the cap. Try to start the car again. Does it start?... No

and FUELSYS: Disconnect the fuel line to the carburetor and pop the end of the hose from the fuel pump into a 1 pound coffee can (or some similar metal can). Crank the engine briefly. Was fuel pumped out of the tube? Yes

THEN:

display "HAVE YOUR CARBURETOR CHECKED OUT PROFESSIONALLY. ALTERNATIVELY, YOU MAY HAVE A WEAK FUEL PUMP OR AN IGNITION PROBLEM."

RULE NUMBER: 5

IF:

(check data blackboard for info) FUELSYS: What problem are you experiencing? ... Engine misses or low performance at all speeds, poor acceleration

and FUELSYS: You will need to check your carburetor's idle speed and idle mixture adjustments. Instructions for checking the idle mixture follow... proceed

THEN:

display the IDLEMIX.TST picture and display "IF CARBURETOR ADJUSTMENTS DO NOT RESOLVE YOUR PROBLEM, ASK FOR IGNITION ADVICE."

RULE NUMBER: 6

IF:

(check data blackboard for info) FUELSYS: What problem are you experiencing? ... Excessive fuel consumption

and FUELSYS: This is generally indicative of an overrich idle mixture. Instructions for checking the idle mixture follow... proceed

THEN:

display the IDLEMIX.TST picture

and display "CHECK ALSO THAT YOUR CHOKE IS FULLY OPEN WHEN THE ENGINE IS WARM."

RULE NUMBER: 7

IF:

(check data blackboard for info) FUELSYS: What problem are you experiencing? ... Engine diesels (keeps running) after ignition is turned off

and FUELSYS: This is generally indicative of an overrich idle mixture. Instructions for checking the idle mixture follow... proceed

THEN:

display the IDLEMIX.TST picture

and display "YOU MAY ALSO WANT TO CHECK YOUR IGNI-
TION TIMING AND SPARK PLUG HEAT RANGE. IF THE
CONDITION IS ACCOMPANIED BY OVERHE ATING,
CHECK YOUR COOLANT SYSTEM."

IGNITION Control Blackboard Command Script .e .m:2

This command script is executed when the control blackboard processess the command "include ignition.q" in the main command script.

```
!if exist OPTIONAL.Q erase OPTIONAL.Q
cls
echo
echo
echo
echo Transferring to the IGNITION Knowledge Base
echo
echo Please stand by...
echo
echo
echo
execute IGNITION rulebase if exist OPTIONAL.Q
  include OPTIONAL.Q endif
```

IGNITION Rule-Base Listing

System goal: Find a solution to the user's problem or determine a
blackboard action.

Write blackboard actions, if any, to the OPTIONAL.q file, using
the control blackboard syntax, before exiting.

RULE NUMBER: 1

IF:
> (check data blackboard for info) IGNITION: Does the starter
> crank the engine in a normal fashion?... NO

and (check data blackboard for info) IGNITION: Check the battery
with a hydrometer. Is the battery OK?... HOW (do I check)

THEN:
> and display the HYDROMTR.TST picture

and forget answer to the last question

and forget that this rule fired

RULE NUMBER: 2

IF:
> (check data blackboard for info) IGNITION: Does the starter crank the engine in a normal fashion?... NO

and (check data blackboard for info) IGNITION: Check the battery with a hydrometer. Is the battery OK?... YES

THEN:
> tell blackboard to include STARTER.Q with certainty=1/10

and post BATTERY SYMPTOM to the data blackboard

and display "THIS APPEARS TO BE A STARTER PROBLEM."

RULE NUMBER: 3

IF:
> (check data blackboard for info) IGNITION: Does the starter crank the engine in a normal fashion?... NO

and (check data blackboard for info) IGNITION: Check the battery with a hydrometer. Is the battery OK?... NO (I found it)

THEN:
> tell control blackboard to include CHARGSYS.Q with certainty=1/10

and post BATTERY SYMPTOM to the data blackboard

and display "THIS APPEARS TO BE A CHARGING SYSTEM PROBLEM."

RULE NUMBER: 4

IF:
> (check data blackboard for info) IGNITION: Does the starter crank the engine in a normal fashion?... YES

and IGNITION: Crank the engine over or run it while checking each spark plug very carefully. Disconnect a spark plug wire (ONE AT A TIME) while cranking the engine and see whether you can get a 1/4" to 1/2" spark to jump to ground... No spark to one plug

and (check data blackboard for info) IGNITION: Will the engine run? ... NO

THEN:

display "NO SPARK TO THE PLUG APPEARS TO BE THE LEAST OF YOUR PROBLEMS. YOU PROBABLY HAVE A FUEL PROBLEM." FOR STARTERS, REPLACE THE WIRE THAT CONNECTS THAT PLUG TO THE DISTRIBUTOR."

RULE NUMBER: 5

IF:

(check data blackboard for info) IGNITION: Does the starter crank the engine in a normal fashion?... YES

and IGNITION: Crank the engine over or run it while checking each spark plug very carefully. Disconnect a spark plug wire (ONE AT A TIME) while cranking the engine and see whether you can get a 1/4" to 1/2" spark to jump to ground... No spark to one plug

and (check data blackboard for info) IGNITION: Will the engine run? ... YES

THEN:

display "CHECK THE DISTRIBUTOR CAP AND ROTOR FOR BURNING AND OTHER DAMAGE. REPLACE THE WIRE THAT CONNECTS THAT PLUG TO THE DISTRIBUTOR."

RULE NUMBER: 6

IF:

(check data blackboard for info) IGNITION: Does the starter crank the engine in a normal fashion?... YES

and IGNITION: Crank the engine over or run it while checking each spark plug very carefully. Disconnect a spark plug wire (ONE

AT A TIME) while cranking the engine and see whether you can get a 1/4" to 1/2" spark to jump to ground... No spark to any plug

and IGNITION: Replace the "secondary wire" from the distributor to the coil and try the spark test again. Do you have sparks now?... No

and IGNITION: What kind of ignition do you have... mechanical

THEN:
    display the MECHIGN.TST picture

RULE NUMBER: 7

IF:
    (check data blackboard for info) IGNITION: Does the starter crank the engine in a normal fashion?... YES

and IGNITION: Crank the engine over or run it while checking each spark plug very carefully. Disconnect a spark plug wire (ONE AT A TIME) while cranking the engine and see whether you can get a 1/4" to 1/2" spark to jump to ground... No spark to any plug

and IGNITION: Replace the "secondary wire" from the distributor to the coil and try the spark test again. Do you have sparks now?... No

and IGNITION: What kind of ignition do you have?... Electronic (magnetic)

THEN:
    display the ELECIGN.TST picture

RULE NUMBER: 8

IF:
    (check data blackboard for info) IGNITION: Does the starter crank the engine in a normal fashion?... YES

and IGNITION: Crank the engine over or run it while checking each spark plug very carefully. Disconnect a spark plug wire (ONE

AT A TIME) while cranking the engine and see whether you can get a 1/4" to 1/2" spark to jump to ground... No spark to any plug

and IGNITION: Replace the "secondary wire" from the distributor to the coil and try the spark test again. Do you have sparks now?... Yes

THEN:
display "CONGRATULATIONS!! YOU FOUND IT!!"

RULE NUMBER: 9

IF:
(check data blackboard for info) IGNITION: Does the starter crank the engine in a normal fashion?... YES

and IGNITION: Crank the engine over or run it while checking each spark plug very carefully. Disconnect a spark plug wire (ONE AT A TIME) while cranking the engine and see whether you can get a 1/4" to 1/2" spark to jump to ground... Weak spark on one or more plugs

and IGNITION: What kind of ignition do you have?... Mechanical

THEN:
display "YOU MAY ALSO HAVE A BAD IGNITION COIL OR A FAULT IN THE PRIMARY WIRING."

and display the MECHIGN.TST picture

RULE NUMBER: 10

IF:
(check data blackboard for info) IGNITION: Does the starter crank the engine in a normal fashion?... YES

and IGNITION: Crank the engine over or run it while checking each spark plug very carefully. Disconnect a spark plug wire (ONE AT A TIME) while cranking the engine and see whether you can get a 1/4" to 1/2" spark to jump to ground... Weak spark on one or more plugs

and IGNITION: What kind of ignition do you have?... Electronic
(magnetic)

THEN:

display "YOU MAY ALSO HAVE A BAD IGNITION COIL,
FAULT IN THE PRIMARY WIRING, OR ELECTRONICS
FAILURE."

and display the ELECIGN.TST picture

RULE NUMBER: 11

IF:

(check data blackboard for info) IGNITION: Does the starter
crank the engine in a normal fashion?... YES

and IGNITION: Crank the engine over or run it while checking each
spark plug very carefully. Disconnect a spark plug wire (ONE
AT A TIME) while cranking the engine and see whether you
can get a 1/4" to 1/2" spark to jump to ground... None of the
above; all sparks seem normal

and (check data blackboard for info) IGNITION: Will the engine
run? ... NO

THEN:

display "CHECK IGNITION TIMING, CARBURETION, AND
YOUR FUEL SYSTEM."

RULE NUMBER: 12

IF:

(check data blackboard for info) IGNITION: Does the starter
crank the engine in a normal fashion?... YES

and IGNITION: Crank the engine over or run it while checking each
spark plug very carefully. Disconnect a spark plug wire (ONE
AT A TIME) while cranking the engine and see whether you
can get a 1/4" to 1/2" spark to jump to ground... None of the
above; all sparks seem normal

and (check data blackboard for info) IGNITION: Will the engine
run? ... YES

and (check data blackboard for info) IGNITION: What happens if you disconnect each spark plug (ONE AT A TIME) and ground it while the engine is running? Replace the last wire before you try another ... There is a plug that can be disconnected without changing the engine miss.

THEN:

display "THE EVIDENCE SUGGESTS YOU HAVE A MISFIRING SPARK PLUG. CLEAN & REGAP THE SUSPECTED PLUG. ALSO, CHECK THE DISTRIBUTOR CAP AND ROTOR FOR CRACKS, BURNING, OR OTHER DAMAGE."

RULE NUMBER: 13

IF:

(check data blackboard for info) IGNITION: Does the starter crank the engine in a normal fashion?... YES

and IGNITION: Crank the engine over or run it while checking each spark plug very carefully. Disconnect a spark plug wire (ONE AT A TIME) while cranking the engine and see whether you can get a 1/4" to 1/2" spark to jump to ground... None of the above; all sparks seem normal

and (check data blackboard for info) IGNITION: Will the engine run? ... YES

and (check data blackboard for info) IGNITION: What happens if you disconnect each spark plug (ONE AT A TIME) and ground it while the engine is running? Replace the last wire before you try another ... Disconnecting any plug has the same effect; the engine performance gets worse.

THEN:

display "CHECK YOUR IGNITION TIMING, CARBURETION, AND FUEL SYSTEM."

RULE NUMBER: 14

IF:

IGNITION: Will the engine run? ... YES

THEN:

assert IGNITION: Does the starter crank the engine in a normal fashion?... YES

NOTE:
THIS RULE ANSWERS A QUESTION FROM THE EVIDENCE SO THAT THE USER DOES NOT HAVE TO ANSWER AN "OBVIOUS" QUESTION.

STARTER Control Blackboard Command Script

This command script is executed when the control blackboard processess the command "include starter.q" in the main command script.

```
!if exist OPTIONAL.Q erase OPTIONAL.Q
cls
echo
echo
echo
echo Transferring to the STARTER Knowledge Base
echo
echo Please stand by...
echo
echo
echo
execute STARTER rule base if exist OPTIONAL.Q
  include OPTIONAL.Q endif
```

STARTER Rule-Base Listing

System goal: Find a solution to the user's problem or determine a blackboard action.

Write blackboard actions, if any, to the OPTIONAL.q file, using the control blackboard syntax, before exiting.

RULE NUMBER: 1

IF:

(check data blackboard for info) STARTER SYSTEM: What symptoms are evident? ... Engine cranks very slowly or engine does not crank at all and STARTER SYSTEM: Turn on the headlights and inspect them. Are they VERY dim? ... YES

and STARTER SYSTEM: Check the battery wiring for breaks, shorts, or dirty connections. Does everything appear to be OK? ... NO (I found it)

THEN:

tell blackboard to stop session with certainty=8/10 and display "CONGRATULATIONS!! YOU FOUND IT!"

RULE NUMBER: 2

IF:

(check data blackboard for info) STARTER SYSTEM: What symptoms are evident? ... Engine cranks very slowly or engine does not crank at all

and   STARTER SYSTEM: Turn on the headlights and inspect them. Are they VERY dim? ... YES

and STARTER SYSTEM: Check the battery wiring for breaks, shorts, or dirty connections. Does everything appear to be OK? ... YES

THEN:

assert STARTER SYSTEM: Turn on the headlights and inspect them. Are they VERY dim? ... NO (or only slightly dim)

NOTE:

THE EXPERT IS MAKING THE ASSUMPTION THAT THE USER INTERPRETED THE "LIGHTS DIM" QUESTION INCORRECTLY. WE CAN USE "NON-MONOTONIC REASONING" TO ADD TO THE FACTS ABOUT LIGHTS AND CONTINUE THE SESSION.

RULE NUMBER: 3

IF:

(check data blackboard for info) STARTER SYSTEM: What symptoms are evident? ... Engine cranks very slowly or Engine does not crank at all and STARTER SYSTEM: Turn on the headlights and inspect them. Are they VERY dim? ... NO (or only slightly dim)

and STARTER SYSTEM: Check the battery wiring for breaks, shorts, or dirty connections. Does everything appear to be OK? ... YES

and STARTER SYSTEM: Check the battery with a hydrometer. Is the battery OK? ... HOW (do I check?)

THEN:
display the HYDROMTR.TST picture

and forget answer to the last question

and forget that this rule fired

NOTE:
SHOW "HOW" TO PERFORM A HYDROMETER TEST AND ASK THE QUESTION AGAIN.

RULE NUMBER: 4

IF:
(check data blackboard for info) STARTER SYSTEM: What symptoms are evident? ... Engine cranks very slowly or engine does not crank at all

and STARTER SYSTEM: Turn on the headlights and inspect them. Are they VERY dim? ... NO (or only slightly dim)

and STARTER SYSTEM: Check the battery wiring for breaks, shorts, or dirty connections. Does everything appear to be OK? ... YES

and STARTER SYSTEM: Check the battery with a hydrometer. Is the battery OK? ... NO (I found it)

THEN:
tell blackboard to stop session with certainty=8/10

and display "CONGRATULATIONS!! YOU FOUND IT!"

RULE NUMBER: 5

IF:

(check data blackboard for info) STARTER SYSTEM: What symptoms are evident? ... Engine cranks very slowly or Engine does not crank at all

and STARTER SYSTEM: Turn on the headlights and inspect them. Are they VERY dim? ... NO (or only slightly dim)

and STARTER SYSTEM: Check the battery wiring for breaks, shorts, or dirty connections. Does everything appear to be OK? ... YES

and STARTER SYSTEM: Check the battery with a hydrometer. Is the battery OK? ... YES

and STARTER SYSTEM: With the headlights on, try to crank the engine. Do the lights dim drastically? ... YES

THEN:

display "THE STARTER IS PROBABLY SHORTED OR GROUNDED. HAVE IT TESTED OR INSTALL A NEW UNIT. I'M NOT ABSOLUTELY CERTAIN ABOUT THIS SO I WON'T RULE OUT ANY OTHER AREAS THAT MAY BE PENDING I NVESTIGATION."

RULE NUMBER: 6

IF:

(check data blackboard for info) STARTER SYSTEM: What symptoms are evident? ... Engine cranks very slowly or Engine does not crank at all

and STARTER SYSTEM: Turn on the headlights and inspect them. Are they VERY dim? ... NO (or only slightly dim)

and STARTER SYSTEM: Check the battery wiring for breaks, shorts, or dirty connections. Does everything appear to be OK? ... YES

and STARTER SYSTEM: Check the battery with a hydrometer. Is the battery OK? ... YES and STARTER SYSTEM: With the headlights on, try to crank the engine. Do the lights dim drastically? ... NO

and STARTER SYSTEM: The trouble may be in the starter, solenoid or wiring. Short the two large solenoid terminals together (NOT TO GROUND). Does the starter crank normally now? ... YES

THEN:
tell blackboard to stop session with certainty=8/10 and display "CHECK THE SOLENOID, AND THE WIRING FROM THE SOLENOID UP TO THE IGNITION SWITCH."

RULE NUMBER: 7

IF:
(check data blackboard for info) STARTER SYSTEM: What symptoms are evident? ... Engine cranks very slowly or engine does not crank at all

and STARTER SYSTEM: Turn on the headlights and inspect them. Are they VERY dim? ... NO (or only slightly dim)

and STARTER SYSTEM: Check the battery wiring for breaks, shorts, or dirty connections. Does everything appear to be OK? ... YES

and STARTER SYSTEM: Check the battery with a hydrometer. Is the battery OK? ... YES

and STARTER SYSTEM: With the headlights on, try to crank the engine. Do the lights dim drastically? ... NO

and STARTER SYSTEM: The trouble may be in the starter, solenoid or wiring. Short the two large solenoid terminals together (NOT TO GROUND). Does the starter crank normally now? ... NO

and STARTER SYSTEM: Inspect the brushes. Are they good? ... NO

THEN:
tell blackboard to stop session with certainty=8/10

and display "REPLACE THE BRUSHES. BE SURE TO CLEAN CARBON DEPOSITS OUT FROM BETWEEN THE COMMUTATOR SECTIONS."

RULE NUMBER: 8

IF:

(check data blackboard for info) STARTER SYSTEM: What symptoms are evident? ... Engine cranks very slowly or engine does not crank at all

and STARTER SYSTEM: Turn on the headlights and inspect them. Are they VERY dim? ... NO (or only slightly dim)

and STARTER SYSTEM: Check the battery wiring for breaks, shorts, or dirty connections. Does everything appear to be OK? ... YES

and STARTER SYSTEM: Check the battery with a hydrometer. Is the battery OK? ... YES

and STARTER SYSTEM: With the headlights on, try to crank the engine. Do the lights dim drastically? ... NO

and STARTER SYSTEM: The trouble may be in the starter, solenoid or wiring. Short the 2 large solenoid terminals together (NOT TO GROUND). Does the starter crank normally now? ... NO

and STARTER SYSTEM: Inspect the brushes. Are they good? ... YES

THEN:

display "HAVE THE STARTER TESTED OR INSTALL A REBUILT UNIT... I'M NOT ABSOLUTELY CERTAIN ABOUT THIS SO I WON'T RULE OUT ANY OTHER AREAS THAT MAY BE PENDING INVESTIGATION."

RULE NUMBER: 9

IF:

(check data blackboard for info) STARTER SYSTEM: What symptoms are evident? ... Starter turns, but does not engage with engine

and STARTER SYSTEM: Does your car have a manual transmission? ... YES

and STARTER SYSTEM: Place the car in high gear and rock the car. Then park the car normally again. Will the starter engage now? ... YES

THEN:

tell blackboard to stop session with certainty=9/10

and display "THERE IS EVIDENCE OF A PINION JAM ON THE FLYWHEEL. YOU HAVE ONLY TEMPORARILY SOLVED YOUR PROBLEM. THE STARTER MUST BE REMOVED."

RULE NUMBER: 10

IF:

(check data blackboard for info) STARTER SYSTEM: What symptoms are evident? ... Starter turns, but does not engage with engine

and STARTER SYSTEM: Does your car have a manual transmission? ... YES

and STARTER SYSTEM: Place the car in high gear and rock the car. Then park the car normally again. Will the starter engage now? ... NO

THEN:

tell blackboard to stop session with certainty=9/10

and display "THIS PROBLEM IS USUALLY CAUSED BY A STICKING SOLENOID, BUT OCCASIONALLY THE PINION MAY JAM ON THE FLYWHEEL. (IF YOU HAVE A PINION JAM, THE STARTER MUST BE REMOVED)."

RULE NUMBER: 11

IF:

(check data blackboard for info) STARTER SYSTEM: What symptoms are evident? ... Starter turns, but does not engage with engine

and STARTER SYSTEM: Does your car have a manual transmission? ... NO

THEN:

tell blackboard to stop session with certainty=9/10

and display "THIS PROBLEM IS USUALLY CAUSED BY A STICKING SOLENOID, BUT OCCASIONALLY THE PINION MAY JAM ON THE FLYWHEEL. (IF YOU HAVE A PINION JAM, THE STARTER MUST BE REMOVED)."

RULE NUMBER: 12

IF:

(check data blackboard for info) STARTER SYSTEM: What symptoms are evident? ... Loud grinding noises when starter runs

and STARTER SYSTEM: Remove the starter and examine the ring gear. Is the ring gear OK? ... NO (I found the trouble)

THEN:

tell blackboard to stop session with certainty=9/10

and display "REPLACE THE WORN OR BROKEN PARTS."

RULE NUMBER: 13

IF:

(check data blackboard for info) STARTER SYSTEM: What symptoms are evident? ... Loud grinding noises when starter runs

and STARTER SYSTEM: Remove the starter and examine the ring gear. Is the ring gear OK? ... YES

THEN:

> display "THE OVERRUNNING CLUTCH IS PROBABLY BROKEN. REPLACE STARTER WITH A REBUILT UNIT. I'M NOT ABSOLUTELY CERTAIN ABOUT THIS SO I WON'T RULE OUT ANY OTHER AREAS THAT MAY BE PENDING INVESTIGATION."

RULE NUMBER: 14

IF:

> (check data blackboard for info) STARTER SYSTEM: What symptoms are evident? ... NONE OF THE ABOVE

THEN:

> tell blackboard to ignore STARTER.Q

and display "STARTER HAS NO ANSWER FOR YOUR PROBLEM. PLEASE SEEK A MORE QUALIFIED TECHNICIAN."

> <<in real demo, this rule may have a syntax error. disallow may not specify the .Q extension for starter>>

RULE NUMBER: 15

IF:

> (check data blackboard for info) STARTER SYSTEM: What symptoms are evident? ... Engine cranks very slowly or engine does not crank at all

and STARTER SYSTEM: Turn on the headlights and inspect them. Are they VERY dim? ... NO (or only slightly dim)

and STARTER SYSTEM: Check the battery wiring for breaks, shorts, or dirty connections. Does everything appear to be OK? ... NO (I found it)

THEN:

> tell blackboard to stop session with certainty=9/10

and display "CONGRATULATIONS!! YOU FOUND IT!"

NOISES Control Blackboard Command Script

This command script is executed when the control blackboard processess the command "include noises.q" in the main command script.

The NOISES module is stubbed in the demonstration system. There are currently no calls to it. As an exercise, you can add rules to SYMPTOMS to access this module. Consult an auto repair book for knowledge about noises which could be used to build the rule base.

```
!if exist OPTIONAL.Q erase OPTIONAL.Q
echo
echo
echo
echo Transferring to the NOISES Knowledge Base
echo
echo Please stand by...
echo
echo
echo run IIDEMO -INOISES.MSG -K' ' -M0
echo
echo
echo
echo There is no further information on NOISES
echo
echo
echo
echo
pause
cls
```

OILPUMP Control Blackboard Command Script

This command script is executed when the control blackboard processess the command "include oilpump.q" in the main command script.

```
!if exist OPTIONAL.Q erase OPTIONAL.Q
cls
echo
echo
echo
echo Transferring to the OILPUMP Knowledge Base
echo
echo Please stand by...
echo
echo
echo
execute OILPUMP rule base
if exist OPTIONAL.Q
  include OPTIONAL.Q
endif
```

OILPUMP Rule-Base Listing

System goal: Find a solution to the user's problem or determine a blackboard action.

Write blackboard actions, if any, to the OPTIONAL.q file, using the control blackboard syntax, before exiting.

RULE NUMBER: 1

IF:

(check data blackboard for info) OILPUMP: Remove and inspect the oilpump. Are ALL parts within tolerance? ... HOW (do I check the tolerances?)

THEN:

and display the OILPUMP.TST picture

and forget answer to the last question

and forget that this rule fired

RULE NUMBER: 2

IF:

(check data blackboard for info) OILPUMP: Remove and inspect the oilpump. Are ALL parts within tolerance? ... YES

THEN:

display "OILPUMP CANNOT DETERMINE A SOLUTION TO YOUR PROBLEM. PLEASE SEEK A MORE QUALIFIED TECHNICIAN."

NOTE:

THE EXPERT IS ASSUMING THE USER UNDERSTANDS HOW TO TEST AND INSPECT THE OILPUMP BUT HAS NO FURTHER ADVICE.

RULE NUMBER: 3

IF:

(check data blackboard for info) OILPUMP: Remove and inspect the oilpump. Are ALL parts within tolerance? ... NO (I have identified a problem)

THEN:
>   tell blackboard to stop session with certainty=9/10

and display "YOU MUST REPLACE OR REBUILD THE OIL-
>   PUMP."

Illustrations displayed by the Auto Repair Demonstration System

The following files are presented as full-screen displays to the user when specifically called by rules or control blackboard commands. Displays that ask questions and expect input are bound to premises in the IF portions of rules. The online versions of these screens are displayed in full and use flashing effects where emphasis is required.

WELCOME.MSG file:

```
                Welcome to the Wonderful World of



                            AUTO REPAIR




                        A DEMONSTRATION ONLY
                  Do NOT use this program to fix
                            your car

       Copyright 1987 Meta (Inference) Services Inc.
```

HELP.MSG file:

```
WELCOME  TO  THE  AUTO  REPAIR  DEMONSTRATION
        TO  RUN  THE  DEMONSTRATION
                type  AUTO  and  press  the  RETURN  key
        TO  GET  TO  THE  HELP  UTILITY
                type  HELP  and  press  the  RETURN  key
        FOR  FURTHER  INFORMATION,  look  at:
                INTRO.MAN   - a  brief  tutorial  about  the
                              demonstration
                GCBDEMO.MAN - the  "demo"  technical
                              manual  for  Generic
                              Control  Blackboard.  You  will
                              learn  about  GCB  while
                              reading  INTRO.MAN
                TOUR.BAT    - a  demonstration  of  Image
                              Interface  and  Generic  DATA
                              Blackboard
```

ALTERNAT.TST file:

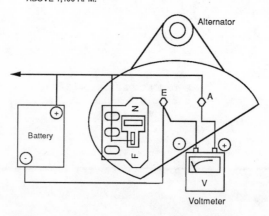

-- ALTERNATOR OUTPUT TEST --

This test requires a 30-volt voltmeter and a fully charged battery.
1. Disconnect the alternator wires. 2. Connect the voltmeter positive lead to the alternator "N" terminal. BATTERY VOLTAGE MUST BE INDICATED. 3. Set up test circuit shown below. 4. Start engine and increase the speed to 1,100 RPM. The voltmeter should read 12.5 volts or more. DO NOT RACE THE ENGINE OR RUN AT SPEEDS ABOVE 1,100 RPM.

Alternator

E

A

Battery

Z

V

Voltmeter

<<< PRESS SPACE BAR TO CONTINUE >>>

DEISEL.TST file:

```
           — ANTIDIESELING CHECKLIST —
1. Check the antidieseling solenoid (if so equipped).
2. Be sure spark plugs are the correct heat range.
3. Check for engine overheating.
4. Check valve clearance.
5. Remove and decarbonize cylinder head.

NOTE: In a complete system, each item on this checklist
      could be another "networked" rule base (object).

       * * * PRESS SPACE BAR TO CONTINUE * * *
```

ELECIGN.TST file:

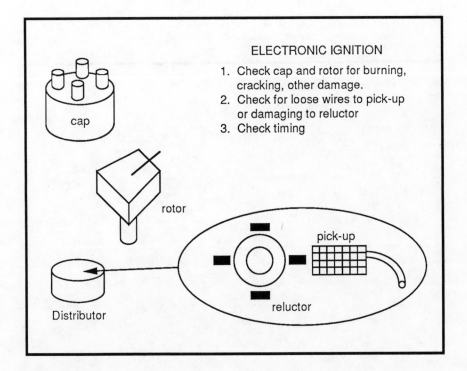

ELECTRONIC IGNITION

1. Check cap and rotor for burning, cracking, other damage.
2. Check for loose wires to pick-up or damaging to reluctor
3. Check timing

HYDROMTR.TST file:

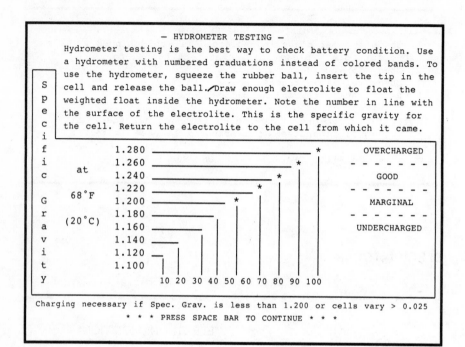

— HYDROMETER TESTING —

Hydrometer testing is the best way to check battery condition. Use a hydrometer with numbered graduations instead of colored bands. To use the hydrometer, squeeze the rubber ball, insert the tip in the cell and release the ball. Draw enough electrolite to float the weighted float inside the hydrometer. Note the number in line with the surface of the electrolite. This is the specific gravity for the cell. Return the electrolite to the cell from which it came.

```
S
p
e
c
i
f          1.280 _____ *        OVERCHARGED
i    at     1.260 _____ *         - - - - - -
c          1.240 _____ *             GOOD
           1.220 _____ *
G   68°F   1.200 _____ *                      - - - - - -
r          1.180 _____                          MARGINAL
a (20°C)   1.160 _____                            - - - - - -
v          1.140 ____                               UNDERCHARGED
i          1.120 _
t          1.100 |
y                10 20 30 40 50 60 70 80 90 100
```

Charging necessary if Spec. Grav. is less than 1.200 or cells vary > 0.025
* * * PRESS SPACE BAR TO CONTINUE * * *

IDLEMIX.TXT file:

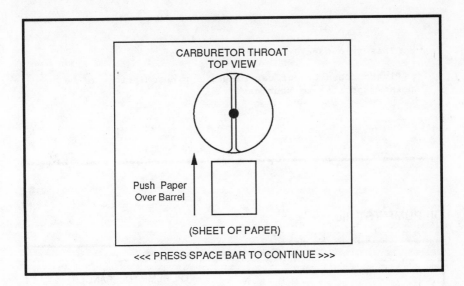

MECHIGN.TXT file:

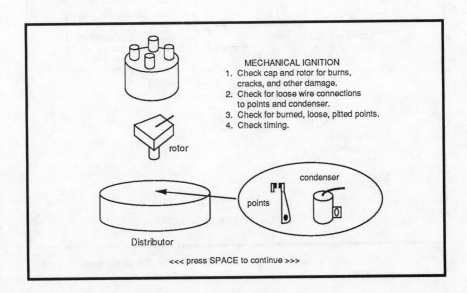

NOISES.MSG file:

"This rule base is to be implemented.

Please consult your car manual for descriptions of noises specific to your car."

OILPUMP.TST file:

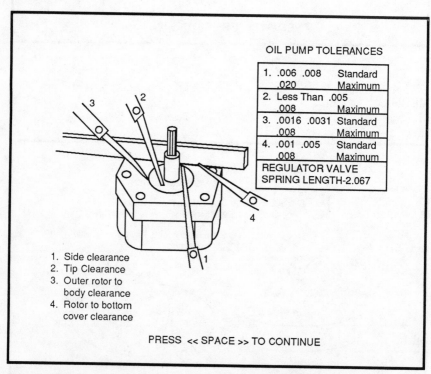

OIL PUMP TOLERANCES

1.	.006 .008	Standard	
	.020		Maximum
2.	Less Than .005		
	.008		Maximum
3.	.0016 .0031	Standard	
	.008		Maximum
4.	.001 .005	Standard	
	.008		Maximum

REGULATOR VALVE
SPRING LENGTH-2.067

1. Side clearance
2. Tip Clearance
3. Outer rotor to body clearance
4. Rotor to bottom cover clearance

PRESS << SPACE >> TO CONTINUE

From Ahlstrand, Alan, *Datsun 510, 610, 710 1968-1977 Shop Manual*. Clymer Publications, 1978. Used with permission of Clymer Publications.

OILWARN.TST file:

— OIL PRESSURE LIGHT WARNING —

STOP THE ENGINE IMMEDIATELY

Coast to a stop with the clutch disengaged (manual transmission)
or shift to neutral (automatic transmission).

This indicates LOW OIL PRESSURE or NO PRESSURE AT ALL

The cause may be merely a low oil level or an overheating engine.

ENGINE: Check the oil level. Is it OK? ...

1. YES
2. NO, (I found the trouble)

SPARK.TST file:

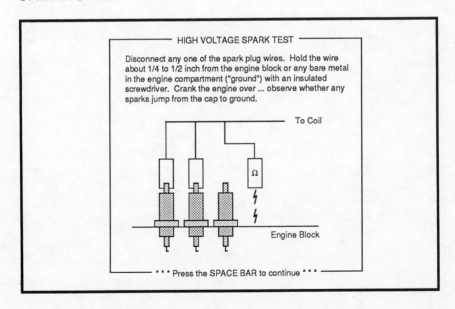

HIGH VOLTAGE SPARK TEST

Disconnect any one of the spark plug wires. Hold the wire
about 1/4 to 1/2 inch from the engine block or any bare metal
in the engine compartment ("ground") with an insulated
screwdriver. Crank the engine over ... observe whether any
sparks jump from the cap to ground.

To Coil

Ω

Engine Block

* * * Press the SPACE BAR to continue * * *

B

Resources and Other Information Sources

DEMONSTRATION DISKS ARE AVAILABLE

A companion set of disks containing working versions of the auto repair demonstration is available from:

Meta (Inference) Services, Inc.
P.O. Box 635
San Ramon, CA 94583

In the demonstration are working examples of the auto repair knowledge bases which have been referenced throughout the book. While these programs are not required to understand the material in this book, you may find a working example helpful when attempting your first knowledge-based program.

The demonstration package includes:

- Knowledge bases with internal (well remarked) documentation which describes the "inner workings" of each knowledge base
- Examples of networked knowledge bases
- Blackboard examples which pass global data between knowledge bases and dynamically queue pertinent subsystems for execution
- Static graphics displays (when appropriate) to support explanations to the user
- Tutorial manual

There is a mail-in coupon supplied with the book. If the coupon is missing, you may still obtain disks by writing to the address above.

Organizations

American Association for Artificial Intelligence (AAAI)
445 Burgess Dr.
Menlo Park, CA 94026

Institute of Electronic and Electrical Engineers (IEEE)
IEEE Computer Society
1730 Massachusetts Ave. NW
Washington, DC 20036

Association for Computing Machinery (ACM)
SIGART — Special Interest Group on Artificial Intelligence
11 West 42nd Street
3rd Floor
New York, NY 10036

SRI International, Artificial Intelligence Center
Computer Science and Technology Division
333 Ravenswood Avenue
Menlo Park, CA 94025

Artificial Intelligence Laboratory — MIT
545 Technology Square
Cambridge, MA 02138

Periodicals

Publisher	Subscription Inquiries
AI Expert Magazine Miller Howard Publications 500 Howard Street San Francisco, CA 94105	AI Expert P.O. Box 11328 Des Moines, IA 50340
AI Magazine American Association of Artificial Intelligence (AAAI) 445 Burgess Drive Menlo Park, CA 94025	
Expert Systems Learned Information (Europe) Ltd. Woodside, Hinksi Hill Oxford OX1 5AU, England	Learned Information Inc. 143 Old Marlton Pike Medford, NJ 08055
Expert System User Industrial Media Limited Blair House, High Street, Tonbridge, Kent TN9 1BQ United Kingdom phone (0732) 359990	
IEEE Expert Magazine (IEEE) IEEE Computer Society 1730 Massachusetts Ave. NW Washington, DC 20036	10662 Los Vaqueros Circle Los Alamitos, CA 90720
SIGART News (ACM) 11 West 42nd Street 3rd Floor New York, NY 10036	

Recommended Reading

Subject Cross Reference

Applications

[Ahlstrand 78] [Balram 86] [Harmon 85] [Jennings 86]

[Kahn 87] [Mantelman 86] [Newquist 87] [Schafer 87]

[Schindler 87] [Williamson 86]

Blackboard Architecture

[Girard 87-3] [Nii 87] [Reddy 81]

Human Factors

[Galitz 85]

Knowledge Acquisition and Representation

[Barr 81] [Hart 86] [Hink 87] [Langart 63]

[Lombardo 53] [Olson 87]

Overview Material

[Bobrow 86] [Girard 87-5] [Harmon 85] [Klahr 86]

[Prerau 85] [Schindler 87] [Stahi 87] [Tichy 87]

[Waterman 86] [Weiss 84] [Winston 84]

Quality Assurance and Testing

[Basili 85] [Beizer 84] [Boehm 81] [Braun 87]

[Freedman 82] [Girard 85-1] [Myers 79] [Yourdon 78]

[Weinberg 71]

Software Development Methodologies

[Boehm 81] [Connor 85] [Date 82] [Demarco 78]

[Gildersleeve 70] [Higgins 83] [McCall 85] [Page-Jones 80]

[Simon 86] [Tichy 87] [Vick 84] [Wirth 73]

[Wirth 76] [Yourdon 79]

Alphabetical Listing

[Ahlstrand 78], Ahlstrand, Alan, *Datsun 510,610,710 1968-1977 Shop Manual*. Clymer Publications, 1978. Used as a domain example in the book.

[AT&T 1], *UNIX System V Release 2 Programmer Reference Manual*. AT&T Technologies, 1984. References to the following kinds of daemons: cron, errdemon, errstop, fpudemon.

[AT&T 2], *UNIX System V Release 2 User Guide*. AT&T Technologies, 1984, Appendix F. & is a "SHELL command special character that causes processes to execute in the background" (a type of daemon).

[Balram 86], Balram, Nikhil, William P. Birmingham, Sean Brady, Robert Tremain, Daniel P. Siewiorek, *The MICON System for Single Board Computer Design*. Proceedings of the Conference on Applications of AI to Engineering Problems, 1986.

[Barr 81], Barr, A., and E. A. Feigenbaum (eds.), *The Handbook of Artificial Intelligence*, v. 1. William Kaufmann, 1981.

[Basili 85], Basili, Victor R., and Richard W. Selby, *Comparing the Effectiveness of Software Testing Strategies*. National Technical Information Service, AD-A160 136, 1985.

[Beizer 84], Beizer, Boris, *Software System Testing and Quality Assurance*. Van Nostrand Reinhold Company, 1984.

[Bobrow 86], Bobrow, Daniel G., Sanjay Mittal, and Mark J. Stefik, *Expert Systems: Perils and Promise*. Communications of the ACM, v. 29, n. 9, September, 1986.

[Boehm 81], Boehm, Barry W., *Software Engineering Economics*. Prentice-Hall, 1981.

[Braun 87], Braun, Ron, Randy Greene and John E. Girard, *Report on Software Quality Metrics work at the IEEE*. Bellcore Software Engineering Symposium, Bell Communications Research, 1987.

[Carrico 87], Carrico, Michael A., and John E. Girard, *Frame Based Programming with PC Production Rule Systems*. Pacific Bell AI Forum, Pacific Bell, 1987.

[Connor 85], Connor, Dennis, *Information Systems Specification and Design Road Map*. Prentice-Hall, 1985.

[Date 82], Date, C. J., *An Introduction to Database Systems*, 3rd ed., v. 1. Addison-Wesley, February, 1982.

[Demarco 78], DeMarco, Tom, *Structured Analysis and System Specification*. Yourdon Inc., 1978.

[Freedman 82], Freedman, Daniel R., and Gerald M. Weinberg, *Handbook of Walkthroughs, Inspections, and Technical Reviews*. Little, Brown and Company, 1982.

[Galitz 85], Galitz, Wilbert O., *Handbook of Screen Format Design*. QED Information Sciences Inc., 1985.

[Gevarter 87], Gevarter, William B., *The Nature and Evaluation of Commercial Expert Systems Building Tools*. Computer Magazine, Computer Society ot the IEEE, May 1987.

[Gildersleeve 70], Gildersleeve, Thomas R., *Decision Tables and their Practical Application in Data Processing*. Prentice-Hall, 1970.

[Girard 84], Girard, John E., *Quality Assurance Reviews and Strategies*. internal documents, Pacific Bell, June, 1984.

[Girard 85-1], Girard, John E., *Developing Company Wide Measurement Programs*. 3rd National Conference on Measuring Data Processing Quality and Productivity, Quality Assurance Institute, March, 1985.

[Girard 85-2], Girard, John E., *Strategies for Implementing AI at Pacific Bell: ICJAI-85 Report*. internal document, Pacific Bell, September, 1985.

[Girard 87-1], Girard, John E., *Evaluation of AION for the PC and VM Environments*. internal document, Pacific Bell, July, 1987.

[Girard 87-2], Girard, John E., *VP-EXPERT: The little mouse that Inferences*. AI Tech Notes, internal publication, Pacific Bell, July, 1987.

[Girard 87-3], Girard, John E. and Michael A. Carrico, *Advanced Knowledge Engineering with EXSYS*. AAAI-87, July 1987. Private conference session, EXSYS, Inc., Albuquerque, NM.

[Girard 87-4], Girard, John E., *What Is "Industrial Grade" AI*. Pacific Bell AI Forum, Pacific Bell, August, 1987.

[Girard 87-5], Girard, John E., *Strategies for Implementing Expert Systems*. PowerCAD '87, Darnell Publications, Inc., September, 1987.

[Harmon 85], Harmon, Paul and David King, *Expert Systems: AI in Business*. Wiley Press, 1985. Excellent overview; product evaluations out of date.

[Hart 86], Hart, Anna, *Knowledge Acquisition for Expert Systems.* McGraw-Hill, 1986, Interviewing and documentation techniques.

[Higgins 83], Higgins, David, *Designing Structured Programs.* Prentice-Hall, 1983.

[Hink 87], Robert F., and David L. Woods, *How Humans Process Uncertain Knowledge.* AI Magazine, V. 8, N. 3, Fall 87.

[Jennings 86], Jennings, Andrew, *INET: A System Using Simple Learning for Network Capacity Assignment.* July, 1986.

[Jones 86-1], Jones, Jennifer P. and staff, *Expert Systems Projects Group Standards Manual.* internal document, Pacific Bell, 1986.

[Jones 86-2], Jones, Jennifer P. and staff, *1987 Expert Systems Projects Group Business Plan.* internal document, Pacific Bell, 1986.

[Jones 86-3], *Strategies for Expert System Development.* internal document, Pacific Bell, February, 1986.

[Jones 86-4], *Knowledge Engineering.* internal document, Pacific Bell, February, 1986.

[Kahn 87], Kahn, Gary S., Al Kepner, and Jeff Pepper, *TEST: A model-driven Application Shell.* Carnegie Group, Inc., 1987.

[Klahr 86], Klahr, Philip and Donald Waterman, *Expert Systems — Techniques Tools and Applications.* Addison Wesley, 1986.

[Langart 63], Langart, Darrel T., *Anything you can do . . ..* Doubleday, Toronto, 1963.

[Langley 87], Langley, Pat; Herbert A. Simon; Gary L. Bradshaw; Zitkow, Jan M. — *Scientific Discovery: Computational Explorations of the Creative Process.* The MIT Press, 1987.

[Lombardo 53], Lombardo, Guy, *I'm my Own Grandpa.* Enjoy Yourself, DECCA Records DL-8136, New York, 1953

[Mantelman 86], Mantelman, Lee, *AI carves inroads: Network design, testing, and management.* Data Communications, July, 1986.

[McCall 85], McCall, James A., Mary A. Herndon, Wilma M.

Osborne, *Software Maintenance Management*. U. S. Department of Commerce, October 1985, NBS Special Publication 500-129.

[Myers 79], Myers, Glen, *The Art of Software Testing*. John Wiley and Sons, Inc., 1979.

[Newquist 87], Newquist, Harvey (III), *The Making of a Tax Expert*. AI Expert Magazine, V. 2, No. 3, Miller Freeman Publications, March 1987

[Newsweek 80], "Pet Rocks, a Tough Act to Follow," *Newsweek*. July 14, 1980, page 14.

[Nii 87], Nii, H. Penny, and Harold Brown, *Blackboard Architectures*. Tutorial HA2, AAAI-87, July, 1987.

[Olson 87], Olson, Judith Reitman, Henry H. Rueter, *Extracting expertise from experts: Methods for Knowledge Acquisition*. Expert Systems: The International Journal of Knowledge Engineering, V. 4, No. 3, Learned Information Ltd., Oxford, U.K., August 1987.

[Orr 86], *Future(s)*. Feedback '86 issue, Ken Orr & Associates, Inc., Topeka KS. Paradigm quotation by Charles Bachman, Bachman Information Systems.

[Page-Jones 80], Page-Jones, Meiler, *The Practical Guide to Structured Systems Design*. Prentice-Hall, 1980.

[Pinchot 85], Pinchot III, Gifford, *Intrapreneuring*. Harper & Row Publishers, 1985.

[Prerau 85], Prerau, David, *Selection of an Appropriate Domain*. AI Magazine, V. 6, No. 2, American Association for Artificial Intelligence, Summer, 1985. Project Feasibility Issues.

[Reddy 81], Reddy, D. R., L. D. Erman, R. D. Fennel, R. B. Neely, *The HEARSAY Speech Understanding System: An Example of the Recognition Process*. IJCAI-3, 1981.

[Schindler 87], Schindler, Paul E. Jr., *Aion is a hidden power in the Expert-Systems Field.* Information Week, CMP Publications, Issue 135, September 21, 1987.

[Scribner-Bantam 80], *Scribner-Bantam English Dictionary.* 4th printing, Bantam Books, Inc., 1980.

[Shafer 87], Don Shafer, *VP-Expert: Intelligent Front End for Spreadsheets.* Knowledge Engineering, April, 1987.

[Simon 86], Simon, Herbert A., *Whether Software Engineering Needs to be Artificially Intelligent.* IEEE Transactions of Software Engineering, v. SE-12, n. 7, July 1986.

[Soloway 87], Soloway, Elliot, Judy Bachant, and Keith Jensen, *Assessing the Maintainability of XCON-in-RIME: Coping with the Problems of a VERY large Rule-Base.* AAAI-87 Proceedings, July, 1987.

[Stahi 87], Sathi, Neena, Mark Fox, V. Baskaran, Jack Bouer, *An Artificial Intelligence Approach to the Simulation Life Cycle.* Carnegie Group Inc, 1987.

[Tichy 87], Tichy, Walter F., *What Can Software Engineers Learn from Artificial Intelligence?.* IEEE Computer, November, 1987

[Vick 84], Vick, Charles R., and C. V. Ramamoortny, *Handbook of Software Engineering.* Van Nostrand Reinhold Co. Inc., 1984.

[Waterman 86], Waterman, Don, *A Guide to Expert Systems.* Addison Wesley, 1986.

[Weinberg 71], Weinberg, Gerald M., *The Psychology of Computer Programming.* Van Nostrand Reinhold, 1971.

[Weiss 84], Weiss, Sholom M., and Casimir A. Kulikowski, *A Practical Guide to Designing Expert Systems.* Rowman And Allenheld, 1984.

[Weizenbaum 76], Weizenbaum, Joseph, *Computer Power and Human Reasoning.* W. H. Freeman and Company, 1976.

[Williamson 86], Williamson, Mickey, *Project Costing with COCOMO1*. AI Expert, November, 1986. Brief description of COCOMO1.

[Winston 84], Winston, Patrick Henry, *Artificial Intelligence*, 2nd ed. Addison-Wesley Publishing Company, July, 1984.

[Wirth 73], Wirth, N., *Systematic Programming*. Englewood Cliffs, N.J.: Prentice-Hall, 1973.

[Wirth 76], Wirth, N., *Algorithms + Data Structures = Programs*. Englewood Cliffs, N.J.: Prentice-Hall, 1976.

[Wolverton 84], Wolverton, R. W., *Software Costing*, Handbook of Software Engineering, Vick, C. R., Ramamoorthy, C. V. (eds.). Van Nostrand Reinhold Company Inc., 1984.

[Yourdon 78], Yourdon, Edward, *Structured Walkthroughs*, 2nd ed. Yourdon, Inc., 1978.

[Yourdon 79], Yourdon, Edward, *Managing the Structured Techniques*. Yourdon, Inc., 1979.

Glossary

Active Images — Interactive graphics on the user interface of a knowledge system. Typically, an active image resembles a physical device such as a switch or meter. The user can change the settings of an active image (usually with a mouse) to provide input to the system, and the system may change the settings of an active image to provide visual output to the user.

AI — *see* Artificial Intelligence

Artificial Intelligence (the study of) — 1. The discipline of creating machines that mimic human behavior or intelligence. 2. The endeavor to create machines that can sense and think.

Attribute — Data field or variable.

Backtracking — A strategy where the inference engine exhaustively pursues alternative paths to a goal by selectively "forgetting" undesirable information. Decisions are retracted until a branch point is reached that provides alternative paths to the goal, then new assertions are sought.

Backward Chaining — A common strategy inference engines use while manipulating information to locate a path to a goal. An inference engine chains backward by asking questions found in a rule or series of dependent rules which will let the inference engine reach the system goal. The system goal is reached when a rule that declares the system goal has had all of its premises (IF conditions) answered correctly.

Bequest — Data made available for other objects upon instantiation or access to a specific rule base, frame, etc. in a knowledge system. *See* Inheritance.

Bit Mapped Graphics — Pictures are constructed on a computer display screen by switching on individual "dots" or pixels. The bit mapped method allows presentation of detailed and animated illustrations.

Blackboard — The term blackboard first appeared in the HEAR-SAY project [Reddy 81] and is now considered an official area of study by the AI community. *Control Blackboard* — Global process control mechanism. The mechanism is similar to the operating system of any multiuser computer system, providing scheduling and prioritization of specific tasks within a knowledge system. The implementation of control blackboards varies widely among different shells. Control blackboards are also referred to as **meta control**. *Data Blackboard* — Global data set or global variables. The mechanism is really the same as that of a global data set available for applications to share information in any computing system, but the concept of "blackboard" is more constructive when discussing knowledge systems.

Bread and Butter — 1. The term for basic sustenance and security. 2. "Countersign" in folk superstition. (Bread & Butter **counteracts walking under a ladder.**) 3. **Signifies safety, stability, reliability, and dependability.**

Breadth-First Search — A behavior in which a knowledge system considers all information and alternatives at a given level of abstraction before selecting a "deeper" path towards a goal. In a breadth-first situation, the inference engine gathers considerable information in intermediate steps. This can be useful in a design activity where one might have to backtrack and reassess a former position.

Cause and Effect — The fundamental justification for expressing knowledge in rules. A *cause* is a distinct premise or group of premises. An *effect* is an output condition or system transformation in response to the cause.

Certainty — A mathematical property that the shell maintains in association with the system knowledge variables. When rules are used by the system, the conclusions that are reached in the THEN or ELSE clauses have their "certainty" calculated from the composite certainties of all of the variables in the IF clause. The calculation of certainty can be based on simple averaging, Bayesian probability, or other algorithms.

Certainty Factor — *See* Certainty.

Chaining — A technique used in the inference engines of rule-based knowledge systems. The inference engine will not directly ask a question of the user if the answer to a question is already known or can be obtained from a source other than the user, such as another rule. The inference engine is said to "chain together" a series of information sources.

Class — Objects that are grouped together based upon a common set of traits.

Classification — The process of grouping objects into classes.

Classification Paradigm — The process of sifting out the correct or best alternative from among several choices. The goal of classification is to identify a general pattern or trend, not to delve into details.

Confidence — *See* Certainty.

Confidence Factor — *See* Certainty.

Configuration Paradigm — *See* Design Paradigm.

Constraint — A condition which limits variations in a configuration.

Control Blackboard — *See* Blackboard.

Control Flow — Constraints provided to an inference engine which alter its fundamental search behavior.

Daemon — *See* Demon.

Data (plural of Datum) — *See* Information.

Database — A collection of related data in structures, such as tables or frames.

Data Blackboard — *See* Blackboard.

Data Structured System Design — *See* DSSD.

DBMS (Data Base Management System) — This is a trade term referring to an application development environment that integrates database functions, report generators, user data entry interfaces, audit/recovery functions, and database administration utilities.

Decision Table — A collection, in matrix or tabular form, of all conditions that are to be considered in the description of a rule together with the actions to be taken for each set of conditions.

Decision Tree — A tree where the nodes are decision points and the branches are alternative decisions. *See* Tree.

Deep Knowledge — Underlying, fundamental knowledge, as opposed to experiential, superficial knowledge. In physics, quantum mechanics could be considered deep knowledge in contrast to the more observable behavior of newtonian mechanics.

Demons — An independent process that watches and waits for a specific "state" to occur before invoking its internal function.

Depth-First Search — The default behavior of most backward chaining inference engines. Depth first refers to the fact that the inference engine is preoccupied with finding a path from the opening questions down to a goal. In a depth-first situation, the inference engine gathers as little information as necessary to find a path to a goal.

Design Paradigm — The selection of a satisfactory combination of components by arranging combinations of known components and creating new components by applying established design rules. The process is often conducted in layers or steps, starting with an abstract configuration and ending with a detailed configuration. A design system, therefore, must also contain knowledge about how to refine an intermediate design stepwise.

Diagnosis Paradigm — The process of sifting out the correct, or best, alternative from among several choices to identify a detailed cause-and-effect pattern relationship in a sea of possibilities. Because of the heavy emphasis on cause and effect, the diagnosis paradigm is easily represented as a decision tree and/or decision table.

Domain — the area of expertise of an expert. For example, the domain of an automobile mechanic is car repair.

Domain Paradigm — *See* Paradigm.

Downstream — In a project, this refers to the next phase of a project relative to the current active phase. For example, requirements definition is downstream from proposal, and logical design is downstream from requirements definition. In general, people are said to be downstream from the current phase of a project if their work will be impacted by the current phase.

DSSD™ (Data Structured System Design) — A commercial structured development methodology which focuses primarily on the identification of the data structures required in a computer system and secondarily on the events that must occur to cause the movement of data in a computer system. Data structures give rise to program modules. *See also* Object-Oriented Programming.

Expert — A person with extensive experiential and intuitive knowledge that is considered valuable.

Field — *See* Attribute.

Forward Chaining — A strategy inference engines may use forward chaining to manipulate information in a configuration problem. Initial data is applied to the rule base and rules that are eligible to be true are collected. Conflicts in recommendations made by the eligible rules are resolved by changing data. The system then looks for new eligible rules. This process continues until all conflicts are satisfactorily resolved.

Frame — A frame is a representation of an object as a data structure. Frames resemble tables in a relational database.

Frame-based Shell — A knowledge programming shell that uses frames to represent objects and their relationships. Individual frames relate to each other in a class hierarchy. Data values can be implicitly inherited by a descendant-frame from its parent-frame.

Frankenstein — In our culture, Frankenstein refers to an endeavor with a monstrous or distorted result.

Functional Decomposition — A software development philosophy focusing primarily on the functions that are performed in a computer system and secondarily on the data required to support the functions. Functions give rise to program modules. Functional decomposition has given rise to a number of structured development methodologies.

Goal — In a rule-based shell, a goal is an attribute which must be assigned a value by the inference engine through the examination of rules.

Goal-directed Behavior — An alternate term for backward chaining.

Graphics — Pictures and illustrations displayed on a computer terminal rather than text.

Heuristics — *See* Rule.

Heuristic Search — *See* Hypothesize and Test.

Hierarchical Semantic Net(work) — A semantic network where the objects and their relationships are grouped into sets or classes that are relevant to a knowledge system goal.

Hypothetical Reasoning — *See* Hypothesize and Test.

Hypothesize and Test — A kind of problem-solving strategy. A problem solution is found by searching a stored or generated set of "plausible" solutions, then selecting a "best solution" from the set.

If heuristics such as production rules are used to select the best solution, then this strategy is termed Heuristic Search.

Induction Rule Shell — One expresses knowledge to an induction rule shell in the form of a two-dimensional matrix (table) of spreadsheetlike examples. Understanding and interpretation of knowledge by the programmer is largely unnecessary. Induction-based applications tend to be less sophisticated than rule base applications because the programmer's access to the knowledge base is restricted. Induction rule shells are ideal when a set of example decisions are available, but no experts to explain the reasoning behind the decisions. The results of an induction shell analysis can be used, in turn, to develop rule systems.

Inference Engine — The part of the knowledge program that scans, selects, and applies rules and data. A specific application occurs only when a rule and its related data pertain to a system goal or subgoal.

Information — Observations obtained from investigation, study, or instruction. Information may be a collection of facts, but may not be inherently useful. *See* Knowledge.

Inheritance — An object or rule receives needed information from another object or rule in the knowledge system which already possesses the needed information. The relationship between objects that can bequest/inherit information may be predefined or dynamic. *See also* Bequest.

Interface — The connection of a computer to a peripheral or outside device. Peripherals include other computers, printers, terminals, and humans.

Knowledge — Information or data organized into useful patterns or concepts.

Knowledge Acquisition — The act of collecting information about a domain from a human expert or other source.

Knowledge-based Systems — Computer systems which contain the understanding of information in addition to providing for the algorithmic transformation of data.

Knowledge Coding — The process of converting knowledge representations into executable computer systems.

Knowledge Engineer(ing) — The process of converting the results of knowledge acquisition into knowledge representations that can be coded.

Knowledge Representation — Any of various formats used to structure human knowledge such as semantic networks, decision tables, etc.

Life Cycle — The sequence of events that must take place in order to conduct a knowledge system project.

LISP LISt Processing — A programming language developed specifically for symbolic data manipulation. LISP originally provided the necessary computer functions to stimulate research in artificial intelligence. The use of LISP is an alternative to the use of shells for knowledge systems progamming.

Mainframe Computer — A computer device wherein components of the central processing unit (central processor, arithmetic logic unit, registers, etc.) and supporting subsystems (I/O, memory, etc.) are constructed on a scale that necessitates multiple cabinets and specialized cooling systems. *See* Microcomputer, Minicomputer.

Maintenance — After delivery, providing upkeep of a product to correct defects, improve performance, or adjust it to a changing environment.

Meta Control — *See* Blackboard

Meta Knowledge — Knowledge of how and when to apply subdomain knowledge to a larger domain. (Knowledge of how to use other knowledge.)

Microcomputer — A computer device containing a central processing unit (CPU) constructed on a single microchip. *See* Mainframe Computer, Microcomputer.

Mind Mapping — A means of taking notes and encouraging "brainstorming" at a meeting of two more people. Mind mapping has a simple structure which encourages expansion of ideas and associations between different ideas expressed in the meeting, similar to a hierarchical semantic network. Mind maps are done on chalkboards or easels that are visible to everyone in the meeting. A notetaker is assigned the task of drawing the mind map. To build a mind map, the notetaker writes the goal or desired result at the middle of the board in a few words. As participants make suggestions, the notetaker writes the suggestions (again in a few words) and draws lines from the suggestions to the main topic. As people continue to make suggestions, certain ones will impact other suggestions and begin to suggest relationships. The notetaker captures new relationships by drawing lines between suggestions.

Minicomputer — A computer device wherein the central processing unit (CPU) is constructed of more than one microchip or assembly, but all CPU circuitry and supporting systems are contained in one or a few cabinets. *See* Mainframe Computer, Microcomputer.

Modular Programming — Programming techniques for developing a system or program as a collection of modules. *See* DSSD, Functional Decomposition, and Object-Oriented Programming.

Module — Convential programming: A logically separable program or subprogram in a system comprised of a number of modules. Knowledge system programming: *See* Object.

Monotonic reasoning — Values (facts) that have been determined during a session that are not subject to change.

Nonmonotonic reasoning — Values (facts) that have been determined during a session can be changed or retracted.

Navigation — The process of accessing objects in a knowledge base by charting a course based on fixed information and a dynamic (context sensitive) agenda.

NCS (Network Computing System) — An open forum originally founded by Apollo Computers which advocates vendor-independent distributed processing techniques.

Normalization — A process to classify a group of objects and remove redundant objects or data elements. Structured data is easier to maintain.

Object — A collection of information in a computer system design. An object may be a data structure, set of procedures, or combination of the two.

Object-Oriented Programming — A programming methodology based primarily on data structures (cast as "objects") and secondarily on procedures that must exist to cause communication between data structures. Procedures are "bound," or owned by objects. Objects give rise to program modules. *See* also DSSD.

Paradigm — A representation for the internal model that humans use to think about something.

PC (Personal Computer) — A trade nickname for microcomputers because of their small size and relatively low cost and the fact that single user interfaces make them attractive for individual or personal use.

Pet Rock — In 1975, Gary Dahl, a California advertising copyrighter, dreamed up the idea of packaging rocks in simple cardboard boxes with a humorous "pet rock owner's manual." In the first three months he netted $1 million. In total, he sold 1.2 million units. [Newsweek 80]

Planning Paradigm — *See* Scheduling Paradigm.

Procedural Programming — *See* Functional Decomposition.

Procedure — A set of steps to be followed to accomplish a task each time the task is to be done.

Production Rule Shell — One expresses knowledge to a production rule shell in Englishlike expressions (called heuristics or "rules of thumb"). The expert system conducts an investigation based on the content and interrelationship of the rules. The programmer of a production rule shell has analyzed and interpreted the knowledge of an expert in order to compose the set of rules, which are collectively referred to as a **rule base** or **knowledge base**.

The order of the rules in a knowledge base should not affect the operation of the program. Hence, the term "nonprocedural programming" applies. In practice, the rules must be scanned (and applied) in some order, due to the serial architecture of most computers. Production rule shells are intuitive for most people. They are ideal when there are experts available and/or when the expert's strategies have already been documented on paper.

PROLOG (PROgramming in LOGic) — A nonprocedural language for expressing data relationships and relating facts to data relationships. The use of PROLOG is an alternative to the use of shells for knowledge systems programming.

QA — *See* Quality Assurance.

Quality Assurance — A planned procedure to provide adequate supervision and confidence to assure that a project conforms to requirements.

Rule — The expression of information in a cause-effect format, i.e., IF (premise) THEN (conclusion) ELSE (conclusion). Rules may contain precise knowledge, or they may be opinions or educated guesses. Rules have been used frequently through history to preserve unwritten knowledge and are often called "rules of thumb." An example of a rule of thumb is, "If your feet are cold, then put on your hat." The implicit knowledge here is that if you are outside on a cold day and your feet are cold, you are probably losing heat through your head and neck. Sometimes rules may use words or phrases other than IF and THEN. Proverbs are an example of rules in an alternative form. For example, consider the saying, "The early bird catches the worm." This can be translated to IF you are alert and prompt, THEN you will have the best opportunity.

Rule-Based Shell — *See* Production Rule Shell.

Rules of Thumb — *See* Rule.

Scheduling Paradigm — Scheduling and planning generally involve a network of many other paradigms. The final result desired in these circumstances is not the "one" right plan or schedule, but one which accomodates all constraints stipulated by the user and is "good enough" to satisfy the user.

Schema — An information or data model. *See* Database, Semantic Network, Tree, Decision Table.

Search — Any of the various techniques used by an inference engine to obtain information in pursuit of a goal.

Semantic Net(work) — A data model consisting of objects, data, people, or any "things" (often called nodes) that are interconnected by lines (links). The links must be labeled with their explicit semantic meaning, such as "is a," "belongs to," "is one of," etc.

Shallow Knowledge — Experiential knowledge, the causal nature of which is readily observable.

Shell — A tool for building knowledge systems. Shells provide preconstructed essential utilities such as inference engines, user interfaces, and report generators, allowing the developer to concentrate on the programming of the knowledge component. Early shells, such as EMYCIN, began as research projects (MYCIN) and had their knowledge component removed in order to create a general purpose tool. Currently shells are developed directly as productivity tools. *See* 5GL.

Skill Acquisition — Learning or skill refinement. A program's ability to improve its performance over time in a selected problem domain (pattern matching with threshold analysis).

Slot — A data field in a frame.

S.O.E — *See* Standard Operating Environment.

Standard Operating Environment — The official list of hardware and software in use by an organization, data processing standard methods and procedures, and data processing policy and planning documents.

Structured Development Methodology — A comprehensive plan for developing structured programs and systems, including methods and procedures for quality assurance, programming, testing, documentation, etc.

Structured Programming — Any programming technique or methodology which advocates top-down design and implementation, strict use of structured programming constructs including modular programming, and a formal project life cycle.

Table — *See* Frame.

Tangle — A Semantic Network diagram which becomes so complex that several lines must cross over each other in order to fully define relationships between objects in the network.

Tangled Semantic Net(work) — A semantic network which has grown complex. It may contain excess objects and relationships not relevant to the application and has not been organized into class groupings.

Testing — The process of examining documents or executing programs with the intent of finding errors.

Tree — A hierarchical structure of information consisting of nodes connected by branches. There is a unique node called the root that is not subsidiary to any other node. *See* Decision Tree.

Uncertainty — *See* Confidence Factor.

Unit — *See* Frame.

Upstream — In a project, this refers to the prior phase of a project relative to the current active phase. For example, proposal is upstream from requirements definition, and requirements definition is upstream from logical design. In general, people are said to be upstream from the current phase of a project if their work impacts the current phase.

User — The user of a computer system. A relative term: One computer may be the user of another, operators are the users of system utilities, etc.

Validation — The process of evaluating a project at the end of the development phase to ensure compliance with project requirements.

Value — Data and type of data (format)

Verification — The process of determining whether or not the products of a given phase of a project fulfill the requirements established during the previous phase.

Wooden Stake — A reference to the only way to kill a vampire. Anyone who can drive a wooden stake into a vampire is a hero, but the risks are enormous and losers face a fate worse than death.

2GL (Second-Generation Language) — Generally referred to as assembler languages. Assembler languages were the first step above direct register programming of the early computers by the manipulation of mechanical switches. The programmer is directly responsible for major computer hardware functions as well as for functions relevant to the application being programmed.

3GL (Third-Generation Language) — 3GLs include BASIC, Cobol, Pascal, and other languages that are more Englishlike than 2GLs and that must be compiled or interpreted by utilities which can communicate directly with the computer hardware. 3GLs are characterized as highly procedural: The programmer must give the computer step-by-step instructions for manipulating data but has less responsibility for details of the computer's hardware states than with 2GLs.

4GL (Fourth-Generation Language) — 4GLs include code generators such as Screen Sculptor, Gamm, and Telon; DBMS such as Informix, DB2, and Oracle; and Englishlike languages such as Natural. 4GLs have libraries of complex 3GL operations predefined, freeing the programmer from more programming details and increasing productivity. 4GLs are notably limited in their abilities by the extent and philosophy of their libraries, and custom programming still leads to "escape points" to 2GLs and 3GLs.

5GL (Fifth-Generation Language) — 5GLs include PROLOG, rule base and frame-based knowledge system shells. 5GLS depart from other languages by their nonprocedural nature. Rather than define a series of steps to be performed, the programmer defines a series of patterns of information that the 5GL is expected to recognize and manipulate.

Development Team Job Descriptions

Job descriptions for the development team will vary depending on the organization, size of the project, level of complexity of the project, and the number of people composing the team. This appendix outlines some fairly complete descriptions that you can use as is or as guidelines for creating your own. Remember it is necessary to have talents in the areas critical to implementing the project life cycle. For example responsibilities should include quality assurance, testing, structured design, etc.

The job descriptions are based on the team concept, i.e., the situation wherein you have more than one knowledge engineer. There are senior as well as associate job descriptions outlined. Sample titles for the particular job descriptions are: Project Director, Senior Knowledge Engineer, Associate Knowledge Engineer, Senior AI Systems Engineer, Associate AI Systems Engineer, Knowledge Analyst.

Job Description: PROJECT DIRECTOR

The Project Director must be able to:

- Capitalize on the talents of his staff
- Earn respect and loyalty from peers and subordinates
- Estimate project size and develop time estimates for project duration

- Use management by objectives with team members
- Utilize superior interpersonal skills
- Interact well with the "user" community
- Apply cost/benefit analysis to one's work so as to assure the best products are produced in the shortest possible time at the lowest possible cost
- Lead efforts with confidence and finesse
- Prepare and manage all budgetary information
- Keep upper management informed of project's progress
- Solve problems
- Make educated decisions on all aspects of the project
- Be point of contact for project

Knowledge Engineers

The knowledge engineers will do the majority of knowledge acquisition and structuring. However, they must be competent in other areas such as software engineering. The Senior Knowledge Engineer usually leads many of the activities, but the Associate Knowledge Engineer has some key responsibilities.

Job Description: SENIOR KNOWLEDGE ENGINEER

Knowledge Engineering: 65%

Guide and train Associate Knowledge Engineers

Lead and perform knowledge acquisition interviews

Structure knowledge without assistance

Use and apply multiple tools and practices for system development and delivery

Develop system standards and methods

Make recommendations about target dates and project size

Software Engineering: 15%

Knowledge Programming:

- Perform the following functions and teach and direct the Associate Knowledge Engineer:
  — Effectively use and understanding hardware/software resources and tools for projects
  — System maintenance when the external system environment changes
  — System enhancements which add, change, and/or delete product features
- Develop and design of generic tools for knowledge engineering

  Provide testing services as follows:

- Develop and execute test plans for deliverables

  Systems library services as follows:

- Provide input and raw code for implementation and administration of the knowledge systems library

  Provide systems integration services per project design specifications

Quality Assurance: 10%

  Participate in review of domain expert interviews, knowledge representations, rule bases, feasibility studies, and other deliverables
  Host reviews of own work on an appropriate milestone basis

Communication: 5%

  Prepare instruction manuals, illustrations, and training materials
  Prepare programmer documentation

Administration: 5%

Provide status reports and work plans for assigned projects
Participate in the development of project plans and schedules

Intragroup Interaction: (as needed)

Strive for a cohesive working relationship. This includes keeping others informed of activities, keeping up to date on other activities for which the candidate is not directly responsible, and effectively using the talents and abilities of every member of the team.

Public relations: (as needed)

- Make presentations to interested groups/potential clients
- Trials of products and services

Job Description: ASSOCIATE KNOWLEDGE ENGINEER

Knowledge Engineering: 55%

Participate/perform knowledge acquisition interviews as appropriate
Structure knowledge as directed by Senior Knowledge Engineer
Learn the appropriate use of tools and practices for system development and delivery
Assist in making recommendations about target dates and project size

Software Engineering: 10%

Knowledge programming:

- Effectively use and understand hardware/software resources and tools for projects as appropriate
- Provide maintenance, as directed, on external system environment changes

- Enhancements, as directed by Senior Knowledge Engineers or clients to add, change and/or delete product features
Provide testing services as follows:

- Execute test plans for deliverables

Provide systems library services as follows:

- Provide input and raw code for implementation and administration of the knowledge systems library

Communication: 20%

Prepare instruction manuals, illustrations, and training materials
Prepare programmer documentation

Quality Assurance: 15%

Participate in review of domain expert interviews, knowledge representations, rule bases: feasibility studies, and other deliverables
Host reviews of own work on an appropriate milestone basis

Administration: (as needed)

Provide status reports and work projections for assigned projects
Participate in the development of project plans and schedules

Intragroup Interaction: (as needed)

Strive for a cohesive working relationship. This includes keeping others informed of activities, keeping up to date on other activities for which the candidate is not directly responsible, and effectively using the talents and abilities of every member of the team

Software Engineers

Job Description: SENIOR AI SYSTEMS ENGINEER

Software Engineering: 45%

Leader of software engineering efforts as follows:

Research, evaluate, and select hardware/software resources for projects

Specify, design, and direct construction, validation, training and installation of Prototype and Delivery systems in the MS-DOS, UNIX, VMS, LISP WORKSTATION, and VM/CMS environments

Specify, design, and direct construction, validation, training, and installation of tools and utilities for internal and delivery systems in the different environments

Knowledge Engineering: 15%

Assist lead Knowledge Engineer in knowledge acquisition interviews

Define and refine domain knowledge representations along with knowledge engineer, compose frames and rule bases

Prototype applications

Develop test plans and their benchmark criteria

Resource: 20%

Provide software and hardware tools, advice, techniques, and troubleshooting

Provide the technical view in administrative assistance

Provide examples, literature, and guidance for development of technical standards

Provide examples, literature, and guidance for development of generic test/validation plan procedures and support materials

Quality Assurance: 10%

Participate in review of domain expert interviews, knowledge representations, rule bases, feasibility studies, and other deliverables
Host reviews of own work on an appropriate milestone basis

Communication: 5%

Prepare instruction manuals, illustrations, and training materials
Make presentations to interested groups/potential clients

Administration: 5%

Provide status reports and projections of assigned projects
Participate in the development of project plans

Intragroup Interaction: (as needed)

Strive for a cohesive working relationship with team members.
This includes keeping others informed of his/her activities, keeping up to date on other activities, and effectively taking advantage of the talents and abilities of every member of the team

Job Description: ASSOCIATE AI SYSTEMS ENGINEER

Software Engineering: 80%

Research, evaluate, and select hardware/software resources for projects as appropriate

Direct maintenance services
• maintenance as needed due to external system environment changes
• maintenance as needed to correct internal system defects
• enhancements as requested by clients to add, change, and/or delete product features
Provide testing services as follows:
• develop and execute test plans

- arrange for testing of products on an appropriate milestone basis

Provide systems library services as follows:

- Lead in design, implementation and administration of Knowledge Systems Library

Provide systems integration services per project design specifications, as follows:

- Develop database and sensor interfaces to knowledge-based systems
- Embed knowledge-based systems in other applications

Quality Assurance: 10%

Participate in review of domain expert interviews, knowledge representations, rule bases, feasibility studies, and other deliverables
Host reviews of own work on an appropriate milestone basis

Communication: 10%

Preparation of instruction manuals, illustrations, training materials
Make presentations to interested groups/potential clients

Knowledge engineering: (as needed)

Assist lead knowledge engineer in knowledge acquisition interviews as appropriate

Administration: (as needed)

Provide status reports, budget, and staff projections of assigned projects
Participate in the development of project plans

Intragroup Interaction: (as needed)

Strive for a cohesive working relationship with team members. This includes keeping others informed of activities, keeping up to date on other activities for which the candidate is not directly responsible, and effectively taking advantage of the talents and abilities of every member of the team.

Job Description: KNOWLEDGE ANALYST

Communication

Preparation of instruction manuals, illustrations, training materials, internal and external white papers

Knowledge/Software Engineering

Assist in evaluation and selection of hardware/software resources for projects
Assist in construction, validation, and installation of
Prototype and Delivery systems in the MS-DOS, UNIX, VMS, LISP WORKSTATION, and VM/CMS environments
Assist in construction, validation, training, and installation of tools and utilities for internal and delivery systems in the MS-DOS, UNIX, VMS, LISP WORKSTATION, and VM/CMS environments

Quality assurance

Assist in development of testing and maintenance strategies, guidelines, standards, goals
Participate in review of domain expert interviews, knowledge representations, rule bases, feasibility studies, and other deliverables
Host reviews of own work on an appropriate milestone basis

Intragroup Interaction

Keep the team informed in a timely fashion, at an appropriate level of detail, of the status of all work

Domain Experts
Normal job responsibilities 70%
Working with Knowledge Engineer 30%
End-users

The end-user involvement is project-dependent. It is best to include the users in the development as much a possible. They should review project products, especially as they relate to the interfaces, system dialog, system skill level, assumptions by the expert, and compatibility with environment. These responsibilities usually take about 5% of an end-user's time, but this will vary if you have a pool of end-users or a large project.

The end-users are a critical part of development. Unfortunately they are the most often forgotten part of development too. End-user rejection is an often cited cause for project failure. If the users do not support the effort or final system, they will not use it. Developing a great system is only successful if it is used.

F

Project Feasibility Questionnaire

This questionnaire should be used during the feasibility phase of a project to assure coverage of key critical success factors. None of the questions ever receive a "final" answer. They help you assess potential roadblocks. If you are not comfortable with a particular answer, you should either resolve your difficulty, so you can change your answer, or put the project off until a resolution is found. *Important Note:* It is **very** easy to answer some of these questions too casually (i.e., OH! Of course our expert is respected by his/her peers. Otherwise they wouldn't be an expert.) Do not take anything for granted. **Any** issues which are not addressed before you begin may lead to eventual project failure.

Notations in the left column indicate which category the question addresses.

FEASIBILITY	Does the job function or area of intelligence (DOMAIN) use knowledge, judgment, and experience?
FEASIBILITY	Would conventional programming methods be satisfactory?
FEASIBILITY	Will the completed system have a **significant** payoff? (payback vs. cost)
BOUNDING THE PROBLEM	Can the task be described sufficiently to focus on specific solutions for specific problems? (i.e. it is not necessary to filter out large numbers of exceptions and common sense issues)

BOUNDING/ SCOPE	Can the project be defined very clearly?
BOUNDING/ SCOPE	Is there a subject matter expert who is already familiar with this project?
USE OF KNOWLEDGE ENG. TOOLS APPROPRIATE?	Does this project require using the computer for something other than conventional number-crunching, pattern matching, or database manipulation?
EXPERT AVAILABILITY	Is there an expert who is **available** to work on the project?
DEPTH OF EXPERT KNOWLEDGE	Can the expert provide special insights into the problem because the expertise is built over a long period of task performance?
KNOWLEDGE ACQUISITION	Are there recognized experts who solve the problem today, **or who could be resources** for solving the problem in the future?
KNOWLEDGE ACQUISITION	Is the expert cooperative and easy to work with?
KNOWLEDGE ACQUISITION	Are other resources such as procedures, policy manuals, books, etc. available?
KNOWLEDGE ACQUISITION	If written materials are available, have the task/procedure manuals been written in IF-THEN or FLOWCHARTED format? (Any documents that have been prepared in this fashion indicate that some knowledge engineering has already been completed. This will help to shorten the development life cycle.)
KNOWLEDGE ACQUISITION REPRESENTATION	Is the expert capable of **communicating** his/her & knowledge, judgment, and experience regarding the problem area?
KNOWLEDGE ACQUISITION & REPRESENTATION	Is the expert capable of **demonstrating** the methods used to apply knowledge to the problem area?
KNOWLEDGE ACQUISITION REPRESENTATION	Is the person requesting the system able to & specify many of the system features essential to requirements definition?
KNOWLEDGE ACQUISITION & TESTING	Are there past solutions to similar problems which & could be used as examples in a written format?
REPRESENTATION COMPLEXITY	How much time does the "expert component" of an average problem solution take (in days/hours/minutes)?

REPRESENTATION DIFFICULTY	Does the domain require knowledge from a large number of areas?
KNOWLEDGE REPRESENTATION AND TESTING	Is there a requirement for real-time response from the system? (*Note*: If the answer is yes, you will need to define "real time" very rigidly. Everyone has a different internal conceptualization of what "real time" is.)
SYSTEM COMPLETENESS, COST/BENEFIT, AND TESTING	Can you identify **measurable** potential payoffs to compare with how business is conducted today?
SYSTEM COMPLETENESS, COST/BENEFIT AND TESTING	Regarding the domain or task you are assessing; how is the organization's performance measured, today?
TESTING	Are there any test cases available? (i.e., History records of past decisions which could be used to test the system)
TESTING	Would experts agree on whether the knowledge system's results are valid? (Successfully testing the system output will depend upon whether a mutually acceptable set of solutions arise from the system)
SYSTEM SIZING	How long has the expert been performing this task? (years/months)?
SYSTEM SIZING	How long (in months/years) does it take for an **average person** to become *proficient* at this task (**starting with entry-level job skills**)?
SYSTEM SIZING	How long (in months/years) does it take a person to become an *expert* at this task (starting with entry-level job skills)?
MANAGEMENT SUPPORT	Is there strong support for the project from senior management? (someone who is willing to commit resources and time to the project)
MANAGEMENT SUPPORT	Is the expert's supervisor or manager willing to commit 50% of the expert's time for the life of the project?
MANAGEMENT SUPPORT	Has a source of funding been identified?
GOAL CLARIFICATION	Give examples of goals or solutions the system will be required to find. If more than one, rank their frequency and importance.

GOAL CLARIFICATION	Is the specific task within the domain jointly agreed upon by the system developers and the domain area personnel?
GOAL CLARIFICATION	Which job function(s) do you wish to capture?
GOAL CLARIFICATION	Can you describe a scenario of how the system is expected to interact with people or other systems?
HUMAN FACTORS USER ACCEPTANCE	Does the expert have credibility and authority (with the users of his/her advice? (It is important) to note whether the expert's peers consider his/her advice valuable and whether they "ACT" the expert's advice today.)
HUMAN FACTORS USER/MGMT ACCEPTANCE	Can the system be introduced with minimal disturbance to the current method being used?
HUMAN FACTORS USER ACCEPTANCE	Is the user group cooperative, patient, and willing to be trained on the knowledge system?
HUMAN FACTORS USER ACCEPTANCE	Have potential users of the system been consulted about what features they would most like to see in the program? (This information is important to the development of the human/machine interface parts of the program.)
HUMAN FACTORS ACCEPTANCE AND ULTIMATE USE	Will the **introduction** of the system be politically sensitive or controversial?
HUMAN FACTORS ACCEPTANCE AND ULTIMATE USE	Will the **system results** be politically sensitive or controversial?
URGENCY	Is this project needed because a reliable source of human expertise (for the problem domain) will not continually be available or is scarce?
SCHEDULING AND URGENCY OF TIMELY DELIVERY	Would the project be on the critical path for any other development?
SCHEDULING AND TIMELY DELIVERY	Do you anticipate any roadblocks to implementing the system?

Index

COUPON MISSING?

You can still order the demonstration software. Send your name, address, phone, and payment to:

> M(I)S, Inc.
> Book Demonstration Software Offer
> P.O. Box 635
> San Ramon, CA 94550

PRICE: $40 + shipping ($5 U.S.; $15 Foreign)
California residents add applicable sales tax

PAYMENT: Check or money order in U.S. funds drawn on a U.S. bank
Allow 4–6 weeks for delivery

DEMONSTRATION SYSTEM SOFTWARE OFFER

Use this coupon to order a working copy of the Auto Repair
Demonstration system listed in Appendix A.
You may modify the demonstration for learning puposes,
subject to license conditions.

The demonstration includes source and runtime for two popular tools, EXSYS and VP Expert. Requirements: IBM PC or compatible, hard disk, color card, and 640K RAM.

PRICE: $40 + shipping ($5 U.S.; $15 Foreign)
California residents add applicable sales tax
PAYMENT: Check or money order in U.S. funds drawn on a U.S. bank
Allow 4–6 weeks for delivery

Name: _____   Phone: _____
Address: _____
City/State: _____   Country: _____
Postal Code/Zip Code: _____

Mail to:
> M(I)S, Inc.
> Book Demonstration Software Offer
> P.O. Box 635
> San Ramon, CA 94550